THE
ROAD YEARS

Also by Rick Mercer

Streeters

Rick Mercer Report: The Book

A Nation Worth Ranting About

Final Report

Talking to Canadians

THE
ROAD YEARS

A Memoir, Continued . . .

RICK MERCER

Doubleday Canada

Doubleday Canada and colophon are registered trademarks of Penguin Random House Canada Limited

Library and Archives Canada Cataloguing in Publication

Title: The road years / Rick Mercer.
Names: Mercer, Rick, 1969- author.
Identifiers: Canadiana (print) 20230449425 | Canadiana (ebook) 20230449441 |
ISBN 9780385688901 (hardcover) | ISBN 9780385688918 (EPUB)
Subjects: LCSH: Mercer, Rick, 1969- | LCSH: Comedians—Canada—
Biography. | LCSH: Television personalities—Canada—Biography. |
LCGFT: Autobiographies.
Classification: LCC PN2308.M46 A3 2023 | DDC 792.702/8092—dc23

Jacket design: Terri Nimmo
Jacket photograph: Kara O'Keefe

Printed in the USA

Published in Canada by Doubleday Canada,
a division of Penguin Random House Canada Limited,
and distributed in the United States by Penguin Random House LLC

www.penguinrandomhouse.ca

1st Printing

Penguin
Random House
DOUBLEDAY CANADA

For Gerald

Contents

Great colleagues and better friends. The crew of Rick Mercer Report.
*We travelled from sea to sea to sea and back again, sometimes in the same
week. From the left: associate field producer and celebrity wheel man
Michal Grajewski, camera operator and DOP Donald Spence,
me, and road director John Marshall.*

Introduction

A few years back I wrote a memoir.

It was a hell of a story—a gripping tale of how a young man overcame a privileged middle-class upbringing, only to become a national treasure by telling Americans that Canada was going to legalize insulin.

I didn't really know how to write a memoir, so I just started at the beginning. I had no memory of the day I was born, but luckily, I'd taken detailed notes. And that's the way I wrote the book. I told my story in chronological order. I continued to write like that for many months until my editor called and said, "For god's sake, stop sending pages—you've got a book."

This was good news because my fingers were very tired. But the bad news is, I wasn't finished yet. The memoir ends just as my TV show *Rick Mercer Report* is starting.

In the final pages of that book I am heading out on the road to make the first show. Well, I didn't just hit the road, I stayed there. I didn't unpack for the next fifteen years. My partner, Gerald

Lunz, and I set out to create the most unapologetically Canadian TV show ever, and it worked. We shot 255 episodes and went to every part of the country. Every week was an epic adventure, and I loved every minute of it.

That is what this book is about: the stories from the road. This time, however, it is not in chronological order. I bounce around like I bounced around the country. Every week, I bounced, talking to Canadians.

In fact, I would have called this book *Talking to Canadians*, but that title was taken—by me, last time around.

My second choice was *Long Walk to Freedom*, but it turns out that was taken as well. Gerald's suggestions were *And Then I* or just *More About Me*.

But in the end, none of those titles would be accurate. Because yes, this is a memoir, but it's really about the road. And the lucky fellow who got to travel on it for all those years.

And what a glorious road it is.

Rick Mercer
Chapel's Cove, Newfoundland and Labrador

1

Have Show, Will Travel

What does it mean to be a Canadian?

Not only is it a wildly pretentious way to start a book, it is also a question that has beguiled us since day one.

Canada has been called a lot of things. We have been called one of the world's greatest democracies. We have been called a shining beacon of hope for those fleeing tyranny. Readers of the *Toronto Star* will know us as an evil construct built on the shame that is colonialism.

And, of course, we have been called stunningly beautiful and a terrible place to winter.

We are nothing if not self-deprecating. We pride ourselves on not taking ourselves too seriously.

We are prone to bouts of jingoism. Prime Minister Jean Chrétien pounded every podium in the land and declared us the greatest nation on earth. We are capable of deep insecurity. Before becoming prime minister, Chrétien's archrival Stephen Harper once stood at a podium in Washington, DC, and said that Canada was "a northern European welfare state in the worst sense of the term."

Years later he claimed he was joking. I get that. It is a hilarious line for an American audience.

It's safe to say that when it comes to Canada, the reviews have been mixed.

Me? I like the place. More than one should probably admit.

But what does it mean to be from here or to have landed here? What does it mean to *be* Canadian?

If you put ten Canadians in a room and ask them what it means to be Canadian, in three minutes they'll start talking about how we are not like Americans. This is a uniquely Canadian trait. Most nations do not define themselves by how they are different from some other country. Talking about how we aren't like Americans is a national pastime. Nine out of ten loud, brash Canadians are quick to agree: Americans are too loud and brash.

We aren't comfortable standing in a crowd chanting, "We're number one" over and over again, but hook us up to a polygraph and ask us if we are better than anyone? Most would say yes and pass with flying colours. That's *colours* with a *U*.

We stand on guard for thee, and we stand on the world's largest pedestal.

I never gave much thought to the question "What does it mean to be Canadian?" until I was in my late teens. The government of Brian Mulroney launched a royal commission that asked that very question. We were supposed to come up with the answer.

I was a bit flummoxed. I didn't know the answer, but how is it possible that nobody else knew, either? *My god*, I thought, *doesn't this country have a research department?*

But apparently in Canada, we are so clueless as to our own identity that the prime minister had to hire an academic and journalist by the name of Keith Spicer to go around the country and ask citizens to make presentations on the future of Canada and what we stood for.

In my early comedy days, I made loads of fun of this guy. "The Spicer Commission spent millions of dollars," I declared, "they produced five phone books' worth of paper—and they still didn't answer the question." I added: "Our founding fathers would have been appalled."

This was back in the day when you could use the term "founding fathers" and not get hissed at.

For those of you with a passing memory of grade-school history, our so-called founding fathers signed Canada into existence in 1867. The location was Prince Edward Island. A bloat of prosperous men from all over British North America came together and, fortified with a ridiculous amount of liquor, they argued and drank until a country was born.

It was not an immaculate conception; it was a messy one.

Modern-day Canada prides itself on being a diverse nation, and the Fathers of Confederation were no slouches in that department. There were many shades of white and a variety of English accents. Diversity was encouraged as long as everyone was Protestant. Rumours persist that there were a few Irish Catholics in the mix. If true, they kept their lifestyle on the downlow.

The man at the centre of the founding bender was Sir John A. Macdonald. He would go on to become Canada's first and drunkest prime minister. After he was sworn in for the first time, he was asked what is the most he ever spent on a bottle of whiskey. His answer? Forty-five minutes.

But legend has it that when Sir John, or JohnJohn as he was known to friends, signed the country into existence, he eloquently defined what it meant to be a Canadian. Unfortunately, the next day, crippled from the sauce, nobody could remember what it was he said. "I remember it was jolly good," said Sir Edward Barron Chandler. "*Mais oui*," said Sir Jean-Charles Chapais. "*Magnifique!*" They then had a round of straighteners and started all over again.

The answer to what it means to be Canadian was lost to the ages.

For his part Macdonald had no recollection of signing anything important, let alone saying anything profound. In fact, he only learned he'd helped form a country when he read about it in a day-old newspaper on the train home. That's a hell of a thing to find out you've done while you're nursing a hangover. Also, he was missing a shoe.

Personally, I blame this prime ministerial blackout for the fact that, 150 years later in 2004, nobody had answered the question yet.

But as luck would have it, it was around this time that I was given the perfect chance to try.

You see, it was at this time that Gerald and I were given the keys to a glorious kingdom. And by glorious kingdom I mean we landed an eight o'clock time slot on CBC Television.

I promise, that will be the last time in this book that our public broadcaster will be called a glorious kingdom. But it's exactly how I felt when we were given this opportunity of a lifetime.

At the time I was no stranger to the CBC or its viewers. I had starred in two TV series, created the comedy special *Talking to Americans* and hosted somewhere around 1,100 Canadian award shows. I never got my docudrama *Lumber—Nature's Natural Resource* off the ground, but my track record was good. I was what TV critics often referred to as "ubiquitous."

But this was unlike any other show or gig. This was my own show. No partners; it was just Gerald and me. There was a cast of one. What a glorious opportunity to show the entire country that you were a fraud from day one.

Inside the CBC we had powerful supporters. Slawko Klymkiw, director of network programming, was running English-language TV and very much on our side. George Anthony, who was creative head of arts, music, science and variety, had long been a champion of mine. He was the guy who, many years earlier, had come to see my one-man theatre show and declared, "You belong on the CBC!" It was George who guaranteed I was in the room when *This Hour Has 22 Minutes* was created.

Having your own show is always the end goal for people in comedy. In America young comics dream of hosting *The Tonight Show*, they dream of landing a sitcom. In Canada young comics dream of going to America. I was a bit of an anomaly. I always dreamed of being on the CBC.

I won't go into how important the CBC was in my formative years and in my career. Anyone who is curious about this scintillating period of Canadian history can read my previous memoir, *Talking to Canadians*. The *Globe and Mail* has called it "A very affordable read." If you have not read it, do not fear; it's not a prerequisite.

Now you are all caught up.

Gerald sold this new show to the CBC by promising them everything and nothing. He promised them ratings and promised them gold, but wisely didn't commit to anything beyond "Rick will be on the road."

I say this as if we had some grand plan. Gerald might have but I honestly didn't know what the show was going to look like.

I was terrified and Gerald was putting on a brave face. But Gerald had great faith in not just his abilities, but mine as well. I suffered from a titch of imposter syndrome. Gerald had none.

There was a lot to do. We had to put a creative team together, we had to find a place to live in Toronto. We had to come up with a title, and we had to appear at the upfronts.

The upfronts are a series of events held by the networks each fall, in which they parade their stars and hype new programs in front of advertisers and the media. Typically, the CBC waves the flag and says they are the Canadian network where you will find Canadian stories. CTV, the country's dominant private network, does the same thing—they too declare they are the place to see Canadian stories and then bring out the stars of *The Bionic Woman* or *America's Best Pimple-Popper Canada*. The American stars ingratiate themselves with the crowd by saying things like "Wow, I've never been to Canada. You have good restaurants here. Give yourself a round of applause!"

That year at the upfronts the CBC was hyping us big-time. The network had a lot riding on us. No pressure. Meanwhile we were launching in January and I still wasn't sure what the show was going to be.

And so, when the time came, I stood on the stage and offered smoke and mirrors, lots of laughs and lots of travel. We were selling our track record. We were saying, "We have killed before; we will kill again." In fact, I only made one firm promise. I said, "The only thing we know for certain is what our theme song will be." Then I hit play on an old-fashioned boom box and Trooper's classic rock hit "Raise a Little Hell" filled the theatre. The boomers in the audience began to clap along. When in doubt, Trooper has always been my go-to.

In the end I never kept that promise. We never used "Raise a

Little Hell" as a theme song. Instead, we hired a fellow by the name of Ed Egan to compose an opening number that, in Gerald's words, "created a false sense of urgency." It was the right call. Gerald had a vision, thank god.

And really, the only promise you need to keep in our business is the one about ratings. Everything else can be forgiven.

We had a lot to celebrate on the day of the upfronts. The schedule had been released and, amazingly, we had the time slot we wanted—Monday at 8 p.m.

Gerald had lobbied hard for that slot. Lobbying for a time slot is a tricky thing. Almost everything is negotiable in show business, but you never get to negotiate your time slot. The schedule is the network's to create, and the network is loath to have any input from producers. Gerald was singularly focused on getting us Monday at eight. George, as well, delicately put the notion in Slawko's ear. Somehow they made it happen.

Monday at eight was also the original time slot for my previous show, *This Hour Has 22 Minutes*. We felt that when the network moved *22 Minutes* it was a mistake. To me it was the perfect slot for any show that traded in current events. And I wanted that piece of real estate back.

And once we had the time slot, we announced the title: *Rick Mercer's Monday Report*. We deduced that if we put the day of the week in the title, they could never move us. Monday nights would be ours forever. How clever were we?

We opened in January 2004 with a contract for twelve episodes. Right out of the gate the show was a hit. By the time we wrapped for the year, we were the biggest show on the network.

On the day we were renewed, we were also told that we were being moved to Tuesdays. *Monday Report* was moving to Tuesday. Only on the CBC could such a thing happen.

But Tuesday it was, and it worked out. It was our home for the next fourteen years. And what a ride it was. For 255 episodes I was on the road, visiting every nook and cranny the country had to offer.

Gerald always said, "This show is about celebrating the country. As long as you do that, we can run forever."

And he was right.

But from day one I had a secret agenda. To celebrate? Yes, but also to do what the Spicer Commission set out to do so many years earlier. Answer the bloody question "What does it mean to be Canadian?"

I knew the answer was on the road. It was there that all would be revealed.

2

Location, Location, Location

When we created *Monday Report* we knew the show would evolve and change over time. Hell, after year one we evolved all the way from Monday to Tuesday.

In the beginning there were many unknowns. We were opening the show with a monologue. We had no idea if that would work. It didn't. It failed because of technical reasons. By which I mean: technically, I was bad at it.

We knew there would be some sketch element in the show, but to what extent? We weren't entirely sure. Would we do sketches live? We didn't know. Would we have "special guests"? Time would tell. Would there be guest correspondents? We were committed to giving it a shot.

But none of these unknowns seemed to bother Gerald. He said all of these questions were secondary. As far as he was concerned the only elements set in stone, the only elements that mattered, were the rant—the two-minute, direct-to-camera segment I'd created for *This Hour Has 22 Minutes*—and the road. These were the pillars that would make or break us.

As far as the rant went, we knew how that worked. All we needed was a great location and a brilliant camera operator. We had both in spades.

Don Spence agreed to come on board as our cinematographer/camera operator. He would shoot the rant, he would shoot the road and he would be principal camera operator on our sketches. Don was then, as he is now, simply the best in the business.

Don was always in demand because he shot it all: the National Ballet, the Juno Awards, skating specials, sporting events, and any big, fancy live event happening anywhere in Canada. If you can think of it, Don has shot it.

Don was the go-to guy for a dozen production companies, none of whom were happy when they found out that he had signed with us full-time.

Basically, we landed Gretzky.

Although when Don took the job, he warned me that he never stuck with any show for very long. He grew bored and always needed new challenges.

He stuck with us for fifteen seasons. Apparently, he was challenged up until the end.

As far as a location for the rant was concerned, we hit the motherlode just up the street. Ten minutes from the CBC headquarters, in the Queen and Augusta area of downtown Toronto, there were a series of "artist-friendly" alleys. These were alleys where graffiti artists could create murals without fear of arrest. Always changing, always vibrant, they were the perfect rant backdrop.

Not to say there weren't challenges. The alleys are in a very busy little corner of the city. Depending on the time of day and the weather, they were home to rats, junkies, tourists and sex workers. I got along with all of them except the rats.

Also, all manner of commercial enterprises had back doors that opened into the alleys. There were always delivery trucks coming and going. God knows the number of times a rant was ruined by one of them backing up and making the dreaded *beep beep beep* sound. When bad cameramen die and go to hell, they are surrounded by trucks unapologetically backing up and making that noise.

Those alleys, and the artists that decorated them, would be very good to us over the years.

There was never a doubt that our show was based in Toronto. We celebrated that. The opening featured the Toronto skyline— beautiful footage of the CN Tower shot on a cool, clear evening. Gerald was in the chopper for the shoot, cameras rolling, as it careened over the buildings and approached the national head- quarters of the CBC. There I was, standing on the roof of the building, with the giant CBC logo over my shoulders.

We were an independent production. We didn't work for the CBC. We owned the show, and the CBC bought it. But that said, we wore the CBC logo and brand proudly on our sleeves. We were, after all, looking to create the most unapologetically Canadian show ever. We were going to celebrate everything we could about the country. And that included the network with arguably the most famous logo in Canadian history.

But despite the Toronto skyline and the Toronto alleys, we agreed the show would have a decidedly non-Toronto feel. We wanted less big city and more big country. We came to Toronto for one reason: it was easy to leave.

To direct the road segments, Gerald hired John Marshall. These two go way back. When Gerald was a bartender in Ottawa, John was the busboy. Both had moved on from the hospitality business. John was now based in Toronto and was the long-time producer and road director for *The New Music*, the ground-breaking, international hit show produced by Citytv and MuchMusic.

With Don and John, Gerald had assembled an A team. Now all we had to do was get out there.

And I stared at the map—the giant blank canvas that was the map of Canada—and began to panic. The size of the canvas was a tad overwhelming. So, are we just going to cover the *entire* country? Where does one even start?

Any time I floated any doubts, Gerald always said the same thing: "It doesn't matter where you go. Wherever you go there are people, and you will talk to them. You're good at that. That is the show."

It seemed easier said than done.

"What am I going to do? Just talk to random people on the street?"

"Yes," he said.

I said, "Where?"

He picked up an Ontario tourism guide that was hanging around the office, opened it to a random page and read aloud.

"The annual Pembroke pumpkin weigh-off in Pembroke, Ontario, is the highlight of the fall. It features a competition with Canada's largest pumpkins, often weighing in at over one thousand pounds. Participants also use chainsaws to turn the pumpkins into watercraft, and there is a celebrity pumpkin boat race."

"So it's not all political satire?" I said.

Gerald ignored me and continued reading. "There will be a measuring of the long gourds, if you are lucky. Some of the longest gourds in Canada."

"Really?" I said. "Downie, Lightfoot or Pinsent?"
There was your comedy right there.

HE WAS RIGHT OF COURSE. There were events like this happening all over Canada, non-stop and all year round. They were the opposite of pretentious, there was nothing "big city" about them, and they were just waiting for us. All ten thousand of them.

Over the next fifteen years I went to a lot of them, including, eventually, the celebrity pumpkin boat race in Pembroke. And I have to say I not only enjoyed myself, but I had the distinct pleasure of watching local member of Parliament Cheryl Gallant almost drown while paddling a poorly engineered hollowed-out pumpkin.

Notice I said "almost drown." Obviously I would not have taken any pleasure in her passing. But the irony of her sinking and screaming for help was not lost on me—or any other Newfoundlander. Gallant had recently travelled to my home province, where she'd admonished people who make their living on the Atlantic Ocean that they should take more personal responsibility for their lives. Newfoundland fishermen on the Grand Banks should not expect to be rescued by the coast guard if they get into trouble, she said. She went on to explain that people who live on the Ottawa River use pleasure craft all the time and never call the coast guard.

It's no wonder Stephen Harper went grey so soon after he was elected prime minister. Every time he turned around, one of his MPs was going out of their way to prove that his caucus was Cro-Magnon. The irony is that Harper's government had done good work rebuilding coast guard services the Liberals had cut on the East Coast. It only took one MP's condescending lecture to fishermen and -women to take a flame-thrower to his good work on the file. Stupid and talking: the winning combination.

To this day Ms. Gallant remains one of the most popular Conservative politicians in the country. A powerful voice in the party, she currently holds the record as the longest-serving and most objectionable female in the Conservative caucus.

Looking back, it is amazing to me that I ever questioned the value of visiting a pumpkin race. It made for great TV. Not because people are mad for pumpkins, but because people saw their own communities being reflected every single week. The entire country is made up of Pembrokes. Granted, not all of them have pumpkins, but they have their own reason for being. And they love to get together on occasion to celebrate why they exist.

It's what brought me to the Trappers' Festival in The Pas, Manitoba, where I learned dogsledding, chainsaw carving and moose calling.

It's what brought me to the Yukon Sourdough Rendezvous in Whitehorse, home of the chainsaw chuck, which literally involves throwing working chainsaws around in public. I never threw any power tools, but I did take a hot tub with a local cab driver named Norm and judged the hairy-legged woman contest.

I should note that eventually I went to hundreds of these events. By picking the three aforementioned festivals as examples, I don't mean to suggest that all small-town community celebrations in Canada involve chainsaws. That would be untrue. Eighty percent of them maybe do, but not all.

Over the years I have learned that though there might be hundreds of spring flings, fall fairs and winter carnivals in this country, they all bring something unique to the table.

Winter carnivals are like snowflakes—no two are alike. Some are triggered by language, others by words.

If you ever find yourself in the West Kootenay region of south-central British Columbia, for example, you should check out the Rossland Winter Carnival. It was started, if you can believe it, in 1898. It's old. Its founder was a Norwegian miner by the name of Olaus Jeldness. This is the oldest continuously running festival in the country. Two world wars couldn't stop this carnival.

And Olaus was a character. He was a hard-rock miner who chased his fortune all over the world before settling in Rossland. It was there that he tried his hand at prospecting. He is known for discovering a few relatively insignificant mineral finds, which he sold to the English for handsome sums of money. This infusion of cash allowed him to explore his true love, the relatively new practice of throwing oneself down mountains and off jumps on skis.

On the day I arrived in Rossland for the opening of the festival, it seemed like everyone was on the street. It was a real party atmosphere. Folks were very proud, and rightly so, of their town, and they were eager to show it off. At the entrance to the festival grounds there was a large snow sculpture of my head and the CBC logo. It was an incredible likeness, and if can you believe it, no yellow snow.

But the buzz on the street was all about the bobsled races.

I was there to explore and experience the festival, and so when I was asked in advance to join a bobsled team, I said yes. In fact, I had a bit of experience in this field. I had been in a bobsled before, at Calgary's Olympic Park.

Being in a bobsled is quite terrifying. Until you experience it you will never be prepared for the speed and the violent nature of the turns. It's not unlike being in a fighter jet. And just like with a jet, it's who's flying the thing that makes the difference. When I went down the track in Calgary my pilot was an elite athlete, devoted to the sport. That is the secret. Find the best, the people who know what they are doing, and put your trust in them.

It's no different than jumping out of a plane. If you have to do it, make sure you are attached to a member of the Canadian Armed Forces. That's always been my philosophy. And it had worked so far.

Rossland is a beautiful small city. Looks great on-camera. It has the vibe of a small town, but not of a ski town. There is none of the artificiality that can come with a modern resort. It has a historic city hall, a public library, a small school and a groovy downtown. It's populated with residents, not just tourists. It also has a main street that runs from the top of the city to the bottom. It's downhill all the way.

And it's a steep downhill. In the days leading up to the winter festival, the local fire department opens the hoses and drenches the street, turning it into a river, which eventually turns into a ribbon of ice. This is the bobsled run.

Volunteers line each side of the street with hay bales. This gives people a place to sit, adds a lovely hay smell to the crisp winter air and provides a barrier that will come in handy if you happen to lose control while hurtling down the road at an ungodly speed in a sled held together by duct tape, office staples and faith in a higher power.

When I signed up for bobsledding, I assumed it would be very much like Calgary. I didn't really pick up on the homemade part. Turns out the only thing homemade bobsledding has in common with Olympic bobsledding is the name. And in the case of the homemade version, the word *bobsledding* should be in quotes.

Turns out, in the world of alpine sport, homemade bobsledding is rare. Except in Rossland, where it is mainstream. The main reason it has never caught on is simple: even in this era of extreme activities, it is just a bad idea. If you want to partake in home-made bobsledding, you need to possess a terrifying lack of self-preservation. Participants must embrace the fear and accept the carnage. Both are guaranteed to make an appearance.

Obviously, I was eager to meet the athletes who would be accompanying me downhill. When I was nervous about flying in a fighter jet in Cold Lake, Alberta, all my nerves disappeared when I met my pilot, Lieutenant-Colonel Josh Kutryk. He oozed competence. One look and you knew you were in good hands. And I was. He is now an astronaut with Canada's space program.

I needed to meet my bobsled equivalent of Josh.

I asked one of the organizers who I would be racing with, and she said, "I think you're with Greg."

"What's Greg's last name?" I asked.

She looked stumped and shouted over her shoulder. "Wanda, what's Greg's last name?"

"Which Greg?" Wanda answered. "Short Greg or Reg Greg?"

"Reg Greg."

"Don't know."

"Don't know," she passed on to me.

"Short Greg's last name is Parsons," Wanda added.

I asked, "Does Reg Greg compete in bobsled a lot?"

"Oh sure. Well, as much as anyone. Once a year."

"Where would I find this Reg Greg?"

"This time of day? He'll be in his garage."

Turns out Greg's garage was not a garage where you go for an oil change or a brake job. Greg's garage was a regular garage attached to a regular house.

I shall never forget standing in Greg's driveway when the electronic garage door opener was engaged. The door lifted slowly and steadily to reveal, inside, four exquisite athletes resplendent in winter racing gear. It remined me of the famous hero shots of the Apollo astronauts before they went into space. That is, if the astronauts were middle-aged, misshapen and wearing mismatched ski gear.

This was my team. And I had to admit, they seemed like my kind of people.

"I'm Greg," said a man wearing what seemed to be a two-piece yellow après-ski suit—the kind Jackie Kennedy popularized during the Camelot era. His head protection was a white open-faced helmet with a blue racing stripe. It had a sizable chunk missing from one side.

All the guys on the team were super friendly and relatively sober. After we got to know one another there was a ceremony where I was declared an official team member—it may have involved an old ski with five shot glasses glued to the surface. If such a hazing occurred, the camera was not rolling. We were a family show.

The bobsled we were racing wasn't so much a bobsled as an old, stripped-down Ski-Doo. Imagine if a Ski-Doo caught fire and burned for an entire day. Then imagine someone painted the remaining shell with house paint and added a plywood seat just big enough for four middle-aged men. That was our ride. It was going to be tight. But the astronauts on the Apollo mission didn't complain, so neither did I.

We loaded our craft in the back of a pickup. I was informed that tradition dictated that everyone ride to the top of the hill sitting on their sled in the back of the pickup. I loved this. I grew up in a town in a time when it was normal to ride in the back of pickups. Thanks to today's hypersensitivity around safety, bombing around in the back of a pickup for fun is unheard of, unless you're in Rossland on the day of the races.

During the drive from Greg's garage to the race site, people by the side of the road cheered us on as if were conquering heroes. Either that or young soldiers going off to fight in the Great War. I was hoping for the fate of the former and not the latter.

The arrival area was a zoo. A sea of colourful characters. John, Don and I roamed around and interviewed the team members and looked at the sleds. Each team was a fashion show, each sled a triumph of engineering.

I approached the first team in the lineup. "What are you driving there?"

"A 1982 Vespa B200."

Of course, Vespas are not sleds, they are trendy European scooters, and this one had skis welded to the wheels. Never mind "unsafe at any speed," this one looked dangerous while parked.

My favourite sled, and clearly a fan favourite too, was operated by a team called Liquid Courage.

"Why the name?" I asked.

The captain replied, "That's what we got!"

Their sled featured shag carpeting and four best friends. "We built her in high school," he said. Emphasis on the "cool."

One sled not only looked like an ancient artifact, but turned out to be the real deal. Two brothers stood proudly by their antique contraption and reported that it "was built and raced by our great-grandfather seventy years ago." This is where the history of this event really came across. You could see how proud they were to be carrying on this family legacy on this storied sled.

I asked if their grandfather was a racing legend. "Nope, he just went the once, broke his leg in two places," the boy reported.

A tradition continues.

I met a team who were racing in a sled they named The Log. As their spokesperson pointed out, "It's a hollowed-out log."

There was a jerry-rigged aluminum canoe and a silver coffin with skis attached. The creativity did not disappoint.

Our sled, which was named the Eager Beaver, suddenly looked sophisticated compared with, say, The Log, and my confidence was high. Originally when Greg told me there was a "problem with the steering"—namely, "it doesn't work very well"—I was concerned. But the canoe and the log didn't seem to have any steering at all. A definite advantage on our part.

We placed the sled at the starting line, and I was strategically placed directly behind our captain. That meant I wasn't steering, nor was I required to push the sled and then jump on for the ride. I guess you could say my role was that of ballast. A role I managed to pull off with panache.

The race had one thing in common with the professional bob-sled runs I had experienced in the past. The terror level was on par—we really did go very fast. And it was surreal that a major street was a sheet of ice. I don't know our speed, but it was well past the serious-injury tipping point.

As we raced down the hill, the Eager Beaver began to vibrate harder than anything I had ever experienced. This was a kidney-banger of a ride. The entire thing was threatening to disintegrate upon re-entry to the atmosphere. I hugged Greg harder than I have ever hugged any man.

Eventually, mercifully, Greg piloted us across the finish line. Adrenalin on bust, but completely intact. I couldn't have been happier. Not by our placing—we didn't make the top three—but because we were not en route to the local hospital. This team, this band of brothers, would live to race another day. Another year. And more likely than not for the rest of their lives. Or until their wives stepped in.

As would Liquid Courage and Team Log. Once the pins are taken out of the captain's leg, that is.

We wrapped up the piece the way we wrapped many of our road adventures, with a shot we called "the bumper." We gathered a group of civilians together to proudly shout, "You're watching the *Mercer Report* on CBC."

And then, without prompting, they shouted, "Rossland!" at the top of their lungs.

I always loved these bumpers. They always made me smile. Because they were almost always infused with hometown pride.

The trip to Rossland was a good one. And I knew that viewers across the country—in the North, in the Atlantic provinces, on the Prairies, near the shores of the Great Lakes and at the hundredth meridian, where the Great Plains begin—would watch and say, "That reminds me of home."

3

Host in Peril

It was in Varney, Ontario, that I realized I was about to die.

It was a peach of a fall day. In fact, you could say it was near perfect. Except for the part where I was being violently tossed around inside of a tiny rusted-out Japanese import. I was out of control and I had no brakes. I felt like an insect trapped inside a Coke can, inside the back of a cement truck.

And the cement truck is careening off the edge off a cliff.

Varney, for those not in the know, is a lovely small town in Grey County, Ontario. The town is not without fame. In the north end, easily visible from the road, is the world's largest Adirondack chair. It's a point of great civic pride. The chair's size in relation to other large chairs around the world has been confirmed numerous times by the international body that concerns itself with such things.

The town is also known for its kind citizens, its charitable nature, and as the location of a small racetrack that draws fans from hundreds of miles around. On the day in question it crossed my mind that the town would soon be known as the place of my demise—but that would never be anything other than a quasi-interesting footnote. It will always be, first and foremost, the home of the big chair.

But it wasn't the chair that brought me to Varney. It was the track.

THE OFFER CAME IN the form of an email. It was short and to the point. "I have seen you do an awful lot of stupid things on your show," the guy wrote. "This is about as stupid as it gets."

The subject line was "The Train of Death."

Don't let the name fool you. It's far worse than it sounds. Turns out the train of death is a popular attraction at speedways all over rural Ontario. It's a real crowd-pleaser, mainly because the chances of spectacular crashes are extremely high.

Unlike most races, this is not about individual cars going as fast as possible. This is about teams of three cars going as fast as possible. Also, the teams are chained together, which pretty much assures that when one car goes, the others will follow. The goal is to encourage high-speed pileups.

It is a motor sport invented in hell.

The car at the front of each team has a bored-out V-8 motor, a roll bar and no brakes. It's basically a car that has been customized for a suicide bomber. Behind that car there is a twelve-foot (3.7 m) length of chain, to which car number two is attached. Known as the "middle car," car number two has no brakes and no engine. Behind the wheel is a young local legend with a history of concussions and a death wish. He's the one who sent me the email inviting me to participate in the race. At the rear of his car is another chain, to which is attached a third car. This car also has no engine, but it does have brakes. And really, they might as well have taken the steering wheel out when they removed the engine. It is a placebo. It is as effective as the toy steering wheel used to amuse toddlers on a stroller. This car in the rear? This was my ride.

I found myself in the situation because it turns out there is a huge appetite for seeing me in peril. Yes, people loved the small towns and the way we celebrated the country, but what the audience really enjoyed, perhaps most of all, was watching me suffer. Dangle me high, throw me in water, or better yet, do both at once and make it in February. The colder, wetter and more terrified I was, the better. It became a running joke in the office. If we found ourselves running low on ideas for the next adventure, someone would always pipe up and say, "Can we taser him?" In the back of my mind I would think, *How far are we from that becoming real?* I could picture the taser, not on a cop's holster, but in a see-through case with words emblazoned across the front: "In event of show-business emergency, break glass."

But work is work and I am certainly not complaining. And I'm not the first guy whose job involved stuff I'm not keen on. Some people are in the porta-potty business, some people went to nursing school and now face the reality of enforced double shifts on a weekly basis. I know a guy who worked in his aunt's hair salon through all of high school and university. His job? Washing the hair of elderly ladies.

Compared to those gigs, the Train of Death was a gift.

And on paper it was pretty darn good.

For the perfect *Rick Mercer Report* segment, we needed three elements. Ideally, I would travel to a beautiful and/or interesting part of the country; I would talk with clever, fun people; and there would be some element of action. Occasionally we would throw in a famous Canadian for good measure.

The Train of Death didn't have a celebrity attached, but it had a racetrack culture worth exploring, Varney was a beautiful town (let's not forget the big chair), and this shoot didn't just offer the suggestion of action, it guaranteed it. Also, it had the word *death* in the title. Wild horses couldn't have kept me away.

Within minutes of us beginning a practice lap, I was having serious buyer's remorse. The cars I was chained to kept increasing in speed. I might not have had an engine, but every part of the vehicle was shaking. Panicked, I hit the brakes. Apparently, that's the worst thing you can do. Unfortunately, nobody explained this counterintuitive fact earlier.

The car I was in was too small and too light for the brakes to have any impact on the heavier cars ahead of me. When I hit the brakes, my wheels locked up, causing my car to suddenly whip to the side. I was the wagging tail on the Train of Death. I whipped so far and so fast to the right, and then the left, that my side door slammed into the side door of car number two. I was now facing backwards.

TO BE CLEAR, this was not the first time I had faced what I believed was certain death. A brief series of odd symptoms a few years prior led doctors to believe there might be something lurking in my brain that shouldn't be there. Tests were ordered and my doctor did her level best to appear optimistic. Which is why I found myself, at three in the morning, being fed headfirst into an MRI machine at one of Toronto's fine hospitals. All I could think the entire time was *I know how this movie ends.*

After the MRI I went home and sat on the back deck of my house and watched as the sun rose. It may be cliché, but the sounds of songbirds waking up coincided with me overcoming my fear of death. I thought to myself, *If this is it, if this goes sideways, I have had a good run.* And I truly believed that. There were no regrets.

Within days I was given the results. Thankfully, there was nothing sinister hiding in my head. Of course, I was overwhelmingly relieved. And while I didn't dwell on the experience, I was glad to have had it. Nothing puts life in perspective quite like the view from inside an MRI machine.

But this was different. There was no way I was prepared to die in this car on this track.

You do not, under any circumstances, want a comedy death. A comedy death being the kind of death that, when people hear about it, they laugh.

And I could only imagine the reaction surrounding my imminent passing. Someone would say, "Did you hear Rick Mercer died?" And the person receiving the news would react the way we are all taught to react when hearing such things. "Oh my goodness, that's terrible. How did he die?"

Then the bearer of the bad news would say, "He was taking part in something called the Train of Death."

And really, how is anyone supposed to keep a straight face when dropping that little tidbit? That's a comedy death.

A few years ago, a lawyer at a fancy downtown Toronto law firm developed a party trick to impress visiting law students. Part of his job was to give the interns at his firm a tour of the offices. When they reached the impressive boardroom he would allegedly always say, "The view is spectacular and the windows are impenetrable." And then, to prove his point, he would sprint across the boardroom and throw his body at the window with all his might.

Of course, the glass would do as it was supposed to do and

remain impenetrable. Some students would scream, all would be shocked, none would be impressed.

Until, of course, the day the glass popped out of its frame like an ice cube coming out of a perfectly twisted tray.

The students who were there to witness the lawyer's last party trick claimed that he travelled an incredible distance out of the building before gravity kicked in and did the inevitable. The few young lawyers who had been raised on vintage *Looney Tunes* cartoons commented that they'd been reminded very much of Wile E. Coyote.

Luckily, neither he nor the impenetrable glass landed on a pedestrian twenty-four storeys below. And nobody threw an anvil.

The passing of this man was reported all over the world. Not because he was a good man, not because he was a good lawyer—which he most certainly might have been—but because he died a comedy death.

People shouldn't find that kind of thing funny, but they do. For example, who among us doesn't enjoy it when an exotic pet owner is mauled by his own pet?

It happens. In 2010, the chairman of the Canadian Exotic Animal Owners' Association was mauled to death by his pet tiger. The tiger he kept as a pet in much the same way some of us have chihuahuas or goldfish.

There's the test of a news anchor's professionalism: report *that* with a straight face.

And you know what they say: once a tiger gets used to the taste of a member of an exotic pet-owners' association, they never go back.

As LUCK WOULD HAVE it I was wearing a microphone in the Train of Death—something I had momentarily forgotten. It came in handy because it was recording every word coming out of my mouth. And those words were being transmitted to the head-phones worn by camera operator Don Spence.

Don knows me very well. And he knows there is no scenario where I would start swearing while he was recording. This isn't because I'm morally above such behaviour; it's just that when you have a TV show that airs in prime time at eight o' clock, swearing is not allowed.

So, when Don heard what was coming out of my mouth, he knew I was in trouble. A man of few words, he turned to John Marshall and said, "I think he's about to die." And then, being a professional, he continued to shoot video of my car careening out of control.

Johnny was holding a walkie-talkie into which he yelled, "Abort!" Immediately, some flag person on the track waved a flag that told the lead car to lay off the gas, which he did. And just like that we came to a peaceful gradual stop. It was a miracle I was dry.

And as my heart slowly returned to normal, I swore to myself, *No more "host in peril."*

The next day, I would be seeing producer Tom Stanley early in the morning.

To quote his LinkedIn profile, Tom's job was to "conceive, plan and produce weekly cross-Canada trip segments for *RMR*." He also coordinated all research, fact checking and rights clearances.

In a nutshell, it was his job to make sure I had two places to go every week. He made it happen.

And I was going to deliver some news that would make his job a lot harder. I was going tell him that the host in peril angle had become exhausted.

Unfortunately, the next day when I went into the office, I never even had a chance to say hello before Tom said, "You're going to Ottawa."

"When?" I asked.

"In a few hours. You have a shoot early tomorrow morning."

I love shooting in Ottawa. Ottawa is my town. It's where I plied my trade for almost a decade, interviewing all manner of living prime ministers and somewhat-alive cabinet ministers.

"Ottawa is great," I said. "Who am I talking to?"

"A police sergeant," he said. "He trains a SWAT team."

"That sounds pretty good," I said.

Tom carried on. "It's cool. They teach rappelling, they have a mock-up of a hostage house where they run exercises, they have a bomb disposal unit and very cool toys."

And then he added, "The cop in charge is really looking forward to meeting you."

"That's great."

"And," Tom said, "he's offered to taser you, for real."

Silence.

Tom added, "His idea, not mine."

Silence.

Then *I* said, "Tom . . . I'm not being tasered on TV."

Tom said, "I don't blame you; nobody has done it before."

Nobody had done it before. Well, that's like saying, "Do you want to be the first man on the moon or the second?"

At that point John stuck his head in the door and said, "The Train of Death footage is hysterical." He gave us a solid thumbs-up.

And sadly, that's all I needed to hear. I suddenly forgot how afraid I was in that hellscape of a racetrack and I completely forgot what I was going to say to Tom.

Train of Death was a winner and Ottawa SWAT would be too.

———

TWO HOURS LATER I was on the plane with a printout of a Wikipedia entry on my lap.

It began: "A taser is an electroshock weapon that fires two small barbed darts intended to puncture the skin and remain attached to the target . . ."

ADVICE TO THE READER. If you are ever told, "Stop or I will taser you," it's best to stop.

Our shoot with the Ottawa police was busy and jam-packed. There was no shortage of action. Just as Tom promised, there were lots of cool toys.

The shooting day had gone so well, and we had so much material that John was completely sincere when he said, "We have more than enough stuff for a piece. I'd bail on the taser if I was you." It was tempting. And I knew nobody would mind. In fact, I was the only one who was advocating for the bit. Gerald told me to pass, as did Tom. But at this point I was all in. I had interviewed lots of young police officers that day, and they all were psyched that I was going to do it. They had all done it as part of their training.

I wasn't giving in to peer pressure. I just wanted to make some great TV.

"Nope, let's do it," I said, and we went to the gym where the officer who had kindly volunteered to shoot me was setting up.

In my briefing, I learned a few salient facts: The farther apart the two small darts hit your body, the more painful the taser will be. And *everybody* falls over. That's why there were crash mats.

Legend had it that some young cop had stayed on his feet for five seconds. Hearing that, I made a simple decision: I was going to beat the record. Success at this, I was convinced, would simply come down to mind over matter. I didn't care how much it hurt, I was going to stay on my feet. It would be epic. I could do it. I was never more convinced of anything.

I stood where I was told to stand. Don started rolling. I psyched myself up. I had interviewed boxing legend George Chuvalo and he'd told me that when he was in the ring with Muhammad Ali, he told himself over and over again that he would not go down. He said to me, "No matter what happened, no matter how hard he hit me, I knew it didn't matter, because I'm not goin' down."

And he didn't go down. He lasted twelve rounds with Ali and didn't hit the mat. After the fight, Ali went to hospital and Chuvalo took his wife dancing.

I channelled the champ. I was not goin' down. I also channelled Luke Skywalker—I was summoning the force. I'm not goin' down.

And then I heard the click. The taser became engaged.

I remember distinctly the barbs piercing my skin. One tiny barb attached itself at the very base of my spine; the other one got me in the back of the neck, above my collar. *Good lord*, I thought, *could two barbs get farther apart on the human body?*

I'm not goin' down.

And then everything was just a blur.

And I broke the record. That is, if there is a record for hitting the floor the fastest and the hardest. Whatever a nanosecond is, I wasn't on my feet for one.

It was completely insane. The pain racked every part of my body. Of course it did. What was I thinking? And the pain went on forever. I tried to remain calm, told myself it would be over soon, but it wasn't. It went on and on. Clearly, there had been a mistake. I was way past seven seconds. I passed fifteen seconds, and then thirty.

The taser gun is supposed to stop automatically, but obviously it was malfunctioning. They couldn't get it to stop. Why weren't John or Don stepping forward to pull the wires out of me? How could this still be going on? Nobody has ever been tasered for this long.

And then it ended. And there was nothing. That was the weirdest thing. I stood up as easily as if I were getting off the couch. There was no pain, no residual nerves. I wasn't shaking. There was no adrenalin rush.

"How long did that fire for?" I asked.

"Seven seconds," said Don.

"Seemed longer," I said. "How's the footage?"

"Boy, you went down fast," said Don.

Now that it was over, I was oddly elated. Elated that it was over, but also that I had gone through with it. I had committed to the bit. I knew I had done something very few people would be prepared to do.

And I knew we had a really good piece of TV.

What I didn't know was that at just about the same time as I was tasered in that gym, another man was being tasered. This fellow wasn't shooting a TV show. He got off a flight at Vancouver International Airport and allegedly caused a disturbance in the baggage area. He didn't speak English, he was disoriented, nobody knew what he was saying. And he didn't know what was being said when he was told to stop.

Why nobody knows, but he was tasered. He died instantly.

This, as they say, changed everything.

Were tasers safe? Everything up to that point had indicated they were. Now, not so much.

To air the segment would have been in bad taste. This wasn't "host in peril"; this was "host with a death wish," which I was not.

We did not want to be part of the national conversation that was suddenly happening about tasers. So we decided to wait a week and see how things played out. Give the story enough time to evolve, we thought. Within a week there would be autopsy results and we figured we would find out the man had overdosed on drugs or had a bad heart, or perhaps was in anaphylactic shock from some seafood. There would be some rational reason as to why he died.

And, as predicted, after a week all was revealed. There were no drugs, no heart condition, no allergic reaction to food. He was a confused man who died from a taser.

We decided to pull the bit. The segment never aired.

I was tasered for nothing.

PEOPLE SOMETIMES ASK ME if my show was simply me working through my personal bucket list week after week. "Not at all," I say. "I was tasered on the show, and believe me, that was not on my bucket list.

"But the guy who tasered me? It was on his."

4

Harried

There is no dignity in show business. I have said this so many times it would probably be considered a Mercer-ism—if there were such a thing.

Usually, that phrase would come tumbling out of my mouth while I was half-naked by the side of the Trans-Canada Highway—changing out of my suit and into a safety harness, perhaps. Or maybe I would suggest it while preparing to be immersed in some horrible substance whipped up in the props department. "The script requires you to swim in pudding. We need to keep adding ice to keep the consistency right."

But to say there is *no* dignity in show business is probably an exaggeration. *Very little* would be more accurate.

Also, "show business" is a pretty big catch-all. There are many people in many different occupations in my racket. But what we all have in common—the actors, the singers, the dancers, the jugglers—is that we all sing for our supper.

Look at the finest theatre festivals in the world. The folks who tread the boards during *King Lear* or *Macbeth* may look like they are wrapped up in some dignified occupation, but it's a hard old life. Most stage actors must literally beg the artistic director year after year to be included in the company. You eat at their whim.

Even a symphony orchestra—and what seems classier than that?—is not as pretty as it appears. Having performed *Peter and the Wolf* with two of Canada's finest orchestras and having featured the Toronto Symphony on the show, I can tell you that their working conditions are not the most dignified. You can't have an orchestra without a brass section huffing and puffing at an ungodly pace. And when they aren't mid-huff or puff, they are busy dumping spit valves willy-nilly all over the floor of the gazillion-dollar hallowed hall they are playing in.

During an opera or a Broadway show, the music may sound heavenly from the good seats, but down in the pit (aptly named), near the brass and woodwind section, the floor is so slick it resembles the deck of a Japanese whaling vessel. And if the lead trumpet player is required to drop his instrument and pick up the flugelhorn, the surrounding musicians would, if they were allowed, don those pink plastic ponchos that tourists wear when they ride the *Maid of the Mist* underneath Niagara Falls.

But of course, I can't speak with authority about those communities. I can only speak of comedy and TV.

And the truth is, comedians may stand on a stage much like a mezzo-soprano or a Shakespearean actor does, but there is one major difference. Comedy at its heart is often about making a spectacle of oneself. And from the moment we enter school, there is an army of teachers waiting to remind us repeatedly that making a spectacle of oneself is simply not appreciated. It's just not something a lady or a gentleman does.

But people in comedy? It's what *we* do.

Even true masters of the craft, the wittiest minds and the sharpest tongues, will, if necessary, resort to crossing their eyes and running around in circles, slapping themselves on the forehead. Anything for a laugh.

Comedians would feel more at home in a Mexican wrestling match than a production of *Hamlet*.

Now, to be clear, I'm not complaining about showbiz humiliations—I'm merely stating that they exist. I accept them. It's just part of the game. And I realize that other occupations have it far worse. Imagine being a professional hockey player. Imagine playing for the Leafs. That job involves constant humiliation accented by intentional blows to the head. Show business is a Sunday walk in the park with George compared to sports.

So I am not complaining. I *am* admitting that when I am required to revisit any grand humiliations in this book, I will couch the language to keep it all very PG.

That's not a requirement; it's just an admission to myself that, as I grow older, I find myself becoming somewhat of a prude. I find myself saying things like "I don't think it's appropriate to say that on network television at eight o'clock in the evening. Young people could be watching."

To which anyone under the age of thirty-five who might be listening would answer, "What is network television?"

It is because of this newfound prudishness that I decided I could not in good conscience allow the word *hemorrhoid* to appear thirty-plus times in one chapter. And so my promise to both you the reader and to myself is that the word will appear exactly one time, as it just did, in the previous sentence. Henceforth that unfortunate medical condition will simply be referred to as Harry.

Harry is a good, solid name. There have been presidents and

business tycoons named Harry. Also, great artists. And of course, Harry sounds somewhat British, but don't read anything into that.

Harry showed up in my life on a Monday. It was alarming. He caught me completely by surprise.

I was lucky. At this point in my life, during my forty-five-odd years on earth, I had never crossed paths with a Harry. I'd never had a single reason to visit that aisle of the drugstore.

Clearly, my luck had run out.

After an alarming Google search I was off to Shoppers Drug Mart, where I filled my basket with the abandon of a man on borrowed time shopping without a budget. I was in an "I'll take two of everything" frame of mind.

At work, I did the wise thing and sought medical advice from the writers. The writers room of *RMR* was populated with the funniest people Gerald and I knew. Some of them, like Tim Steeves and Chris Finn, were stand-up comedians who had worked with us since the very early days of *22 Minutes*. Tim was universally accepted as one of Canada's sharpest and most confident comedians. Nobody wanted to follow Tim on stage. He was a destroyer of audiences, in the best sense of the term. Finn joined us after a wildly successful stint on *MAD TV* in Los Angeles and has one of the most deliciously cynical minds ever developed.

For many years, until his death from cancer, we were lucky enough to have a true legend in the room, in the person of Irwin Barker. A genius and a gentleman, George Westerholm came from the world of music and comedy and happens to be the most effortlessly cool man in Canada. And Rick Currie, the late addition, came to us after we lost Irwin. Rick is an Ottawa Valley boy who understands pure comedy like nobody else. When Rick is not writing or performing, he is helping someone move or fixing a widow's fence.

Greg Eckler rounded out the gang. His nickname was "College"—because unlike the rest of us, he had been to one. He is a student of television like nobody I have ever met and never ceases to make me laugh. Which was true of everyone in the room.

But on this day I was not searching for laughs I was seeking medical advice. What I received was far from sympathetic. My news was greeted with guffaws and horror stories. Seems that more than a few colleagues had been down this road and were more than eager to blurt out the gory details. Although none were quite as scary as the advice given to me by our show business doctor, whom I reached on the phone a few hours later.

Being a showbiz doctor must be a terribly tedious calling. They spend a big part of their days doing insurance medicals for actors and singers. And I've met more hypochondriacs in show business than I can count. I once worked with an actor who would routinely self-diagnose herself with all manner of illnesses, real and yet to be discovered. She once left a rehearsal and went to a local emergency room seeking treatment for what she insisted was a previously undiagnosed case of spina bifida.

But though I have many faults, hypochondria is not one of them. I'm a wuss but not a hypochondriac. Blessedly, the doctor was able to take my call.

FOR THE PURPOSES OF this story, I'll call my doctor "Marv," because that's his name. He is Toronto's most prominent showbiz doctor, widely respected and often mentioned in Canadian memoirs. Most recently, Academy Award winner Sarah Polley spoke of Marv in *Run Towards the Danger*, her award-winning book of personal essays, and gave him full credit for saving her life.

"Those Harrys," he said. "Awful."

He walked me through the various over-the-counter treatments (I already had a Halloween candy sack worth of those) and told me to take it easy for a few days. "Lots of cold and hot compresses," he said, "and don't do anything too active—those things can burst, and that's no fun, I tell you."

The notion was far too horrible to contemplate.

I said goodbye to Marv, promising him I would not do anything active. I would just stand very still for the next week. I would be statuesque.

At this moment, Tom knocked on my door. He was somewhat pleased with himself.

"We have a great shoot lined up," he said. "It took a long time, but your schedules have finally lined up. We have the ambassador; he's going to teach you how to play tennis."

He was referring to the United States' ambassador to Canada, David Wilkins.

We had wanted the ambassador for quite a while. He always looked good on TV and was quick with a quip. We always suggested that we do something active with our interview subjects, and he chose tennis.

Tom was thrilled. Sports diplomacy at its finest!

Tom went on to tell me that Jill, the head of wardrobe, was already shopping for my tennis whites. "It's a requirement," he said.

Surely to God I didn't have to play tennis in whites with a time bomb in my pants. Maybe we could play chess instead? I knew better than to float the idea.

Ah yes—the show must go on.

I'D ALREADY HAD CONCERNS about playing tennis with the ambassador before I was told to avoid rigorous activity. I'd never played the game before, at all. I had never even banged a ball against a brick wall with a racquet. I like to have at least a passing familiarity with the activity I am attempting. I am a below-average skater, but I can skate. So I will gladly play hockey against a professional hockey player or perform with an Olympic figure skater. In fact I've done both. I can ride a bike, so I'll play bike polo, circle a velodrome or hurtle myself down a ski hill on a mountain bike. Again, I've done them all. I'm an okay downhill skier, so I'm happy to hit any slope anytime. Point me at the slalom gates and roll the cameras.

It's always great to have some basic skill level. And I will always try my darndest to do a good job. Sometimes beginner's luck will kick in and I'll look okay. Often, my best will come across as awful. But that's the name of the game. Sometimes they aren't laughing with you, but at you.

I remember when I attempted the trendy sport of kite skiing. This is where you race on skis across beautiful snowy meadows, being pulled by a giant kite. The sport is marked by the spectacular leaps the skiers make, rising into the sky two and three storeys at a time. It is exhilarating to watch.

The day of the shoot, I tried my best, but the snowy meadow was a sheet of ice and the pretty flurries turned to freezing rain. I spent most of the day being dragged on my face across the ice. Occasionally the lines tangled and I'd come to a halt. Then the wind picked up and the kite would once again be off like a rocket. When it was over, I was literally bloody and beaten.

After the show aired, a kid emailed me and said, "Dear Rick, you are really terrible at kite skiing, even by Rick Mercer standards." I was my own low bar.

He went on to say that when someone in his gym class did something particularly humiliating, the gym teacher would yell,

"Okay, Rick Mercer, stop putting your face in front of the medicine ball."

Gym teachers are no longer allowed to ridicule students with the string of offensive terms they once had in their arsenal, so they just substitute my name instead.

So this was my initial fear about tennis. I knew playing an epic game of tennis against the American ambassador could make for good TV, but I wasn't even sure I could manage a basic volley, let alone even attempt to be quasi-competitive.

The ambassador, by the way, was in his sixties, and a passionate competitive player. In fact, he attended university on a full tennis scholarship, so I knew I would lose and lose badly. That was a given. My concern was purely aesthetic. While I never played tennis, I had watched enough of it to know that players have a certain grace. There is a beauty in the game. I had no idea how I would pull that off—I was presently walking as if I were suffering stage-three rigor mortis in my lower extremities.

But I would be representing my country. So Harry be damned, I said. Once more unto the breach.

Also, I was dying to see the house.

I have a fascination with embassies and residences. Many years earlier, in my 22 *Minutes* days, I went to Ottawa and decided on a whim to poke around the tony neighbourhood of Rockcliffe—or as it's known in Ottawa, "Embassy Row." This was a different time. We knocked on doors without calling ahead and introduced ourselves. I asked on-camera if I could taste something from the residents' country.

To a person, the people at the door were friendly and charming. If the ambassador happened to be home, they appeared unprompted and were, for the lack of a better phrase, graciously diplomatic. It was a glorious day filled with Pakistani lemonade (still the best I've ever had), Swiss chocolate, Danish herring, Norwegian smoked salmon and French pastries. The Irish ambassador poured us a Guinness, the Japanese ambassador provided us with a tea service and the Saudi ambassador threatened to cut off our hands.

In other words, they all brought their A game.

I've always thought being an ambassador would be a fantastic gig.

Canada is considered a very good placement for most of the world's diplomatic corps, and for obvious reasons. First and foremost, we are a very stable country. And let's face it, being ambassador to Canada wouldn't be the most stressful job in the world. We aren't exactly known for getting into diplomatic spats with other countries.

My guess is that the hardest thing about being an ambassador to Canada would be coming up with creative ways to pass the time. Really, imagine that you are the Belgian ambassador to Canada. How would you even spend your days? You can only go day drinking with the Dutch ambassador so many times.

Granted, some of the ambassadorships would be very taxing. Obviously, the US ambassador has a huge job. After all, our two countries exchange two billion dollars' worth of goods and services every single day. I would also assume the Chinese ambassador must be very busy. He has to oversee the massive network of spies from China that operate here. Never mind being responsible for the secret Chinese police force that terrorizes Chinese nationals living on Canadian soil.

But if I'm ever in the position to ask a prime minister for a very large favour, I would naturally ask to be ambassador to Ireland.

There is an expression in Ottawa that every member of Parliament believes they should be in cabinet and every member of cabinet thinks they should be prime minister. The exception is any member of Parliament from Newfoundland. They go to bed at night thinking they should be ambassador to Ireland.

What a job it would be, lying around the fancy house in Dublin, representing the not very pressing interests of Canada in the land of your forefathers. The spare bedroom in the house would be filled with a steady stream of relatives and old high school buddies hell-bent on having a party and finding out where their great-grandparents are buried. The best Newfoundland musicians would be at the embassy, hobnobbing with their fiddle-playing Irish counterparts. The kitchen parties would be epic.

Mother Ireland. The Emerald Isle. The Land of Saints and Scholars.

She's easy on the eyes and hard on the liver.

Of course, Ireland is not for everyone.

They say the ferocity of the lobbying that goes on by Italian Canadian politicians for the ambassadorship to Italy is unmatched. And who wouldn't want that job? My god—the food alone! Traditionally when an ex-politician gets named ambassador to Italy, the press gallery will start an internal pool to guess exactly how many pounds the servant of Canada will gain in their first six months on the job. Forty is the average.

The American ambassador to Canada, my soon-to-be tennis partner, was himself an ex-politician with a very impressive record. David Wilkins was a Republican who served twenty-three years in the South Carolina legislature; for twelve of those years he served as Speaker of the House. He was coming very near to the end of his tenure as ambassador, and his record was very good. He was even being credited at the time with helping get a deal done to end the softwood lumber dispute between Canada and the United States.

This was quite an achievement. Any armchair historian will tell you that the softwood lumber dispute began somewhere around the day that God created heaven and earth. On the seventh day, while God rested, the United States and Canada embarked on their first failed arbitration process.

A year previous, I attended an event in Toronto where Wilkins gave remarks. His honey-soaked drawl seemed incredibly down-to-earth. And his skills as a trial lawyer were obvious when he was presenting an argument. I swear, if I were in the prisoner's box and he was arguing that I go to the gallows, I might just start a slow clap to show my admiration.

I was looking forward to meeting the man.

After three days of prep, cold compresses and standing still, Don, John and I headed to Ottawa.

It was to be a fast shoot. Fly up in the morning and fly back in the late afternoon. The ambassador, of course, was on a very tight schedule, so we would go from the airport straight to the location, without stopping at a hotel room.

Rockcliffe never disappoints if you like architecture. It's an area filled with real estate porn. And the US ambassador's residence is considered by most to be the most exquisite.

We were waved through a very impressive security gate and drove up the long, winding driveway that ends in a roundabout in front of the house. As they say in the real estate business, it "shows beautifully."

As our van came to a halt on the roundabout, the front doors of the mansion opened and out walked the ambassador and his wife, Susan. It was cinematic.

I walked to the steps and said my hello. The ambassador said, "Welcome to Lornado, official residence of the US ambassador."

It was that kind of place. It had a name. Lornado. It looked like a Lornado.

I liked the couple instantly. They were incredibly hospitable. As soon as John and Don joined me on the porch, we were offered refreshments. I could listen to people offer me something cool to drink in a South Carolina accent forever. Over cool spritzers they both were effusive in their praise for the country they were proud to serve in and made kind comments about our show—which they didn't have to do. They even went so far as to speak with some authority on previous episodes they had watched. Now, whether they had watched them on the couch together on a random Tuesday night or whether an enterprising staffer had provided them with recordings didn't matter to me. I was charmed.

We were just about to start work and mic up the ambassador when we were joined by the world's oldest dog. He walked with the gait of an animal that had not chased a squirrel or a rabbit in many years. Immediately, both the ambassador and his wife fussed over this clearly beloved pet. The ambassador proudly introduced us to Speaker the dog. Speaker took one look at us and began to pee. He wore an expression of mortified incontinence.

Within seconds the ambassador and his wife were on it, cleaning up after the poor thing, comforting the dog and apologizing to us, which obviously was entirely unnecessary. This was clearly a well-loved pet, and these two were doing everything they could to make his final stretch as comfortable as possible.

"Speaker is a good dog," the ambassador told me. "One of the best. The last little while has been hard on him. It's very difficult."

An aide gently encouraged us to start work, reminding the ambassador that they had an important engagement in just a few hours. It was, he reminded them, full black tie.

Gently chastised, we got down to it. We put a microphone on the ambassador and prepared to shoot. But first, I inquired about the washroom.

The ambassador said, "Follow me," and led me upstairs. He walked down a long, dimly lit hallway that led to a sitting area where I could rest if need be or change. Off the sitting area was a small bathroom that he said was for me.

"We call this the Reagan bathroom," he told me. "It was installed prior to President Reagan's first state visit to Canada in 1981. That's why the towels are there."

He pointed to a large collection of fluffy hand towels on the sink, all emblazoned with the seal of the President of the United States. This was one classy john.

He left me alone. I shut the door and dropped trou.

One minute later I was half-naked. One bare foot was on the sink, another was on the floor. Using the provided towels, I was applying a presidential cold compress to Harry. I silently offered an apology to President Reagan and gingerly returned to work.

We started with a tour of the residence. The getting-to-know-the-ambassador part of the segment.

As we say at home, what a spot. The house itself was magnificent. A grand old Edwardian lady oozing with charm. Built by a railway tycoon, it was picked up in 1935 by the Americans, and became their official residence. Overlooking the Ottawa River, it has a giant rooftop deck and widow's walk that gives its residents the best view of the Gatineau Hills.

One doesn't compare apples and oranges, but the US ambassador's residence is so much nicer than the prime minister's residence. It makes 24 Sussex look like a tar-paper shack.

Clearly, back in the '30s the Americans thought, "Well, if we are going to get an official residence, let's do it right. Let's make sure it has a great view, but also that it's set back off the street so it can be secure in case some hooligan wants to throw a rock."

That's what they worried about back then, hooligans throwing rocks.

The Americans have maintained this official residence with such care, you'd swear they were a First World country.

Whereas Canada? In 1950 we acquired a residence that is so close to a public street that any misfit with a bum arm, standing on the yellow line, can hit the front door with a can of tuna. What was already a security concern in 1950 is an unmanageable nightmare today. The cost of refurbishing the pile is somewhat in line with what was spent on the Beijing Olympics. That said, no amount of money in the world can fix its biggest problem: its exposure to the street.

Good money after bad—a part of our Canadian heritage.

The tour was fantastic on-camera. The walls of the house were dripping with American art. The view from the roof was majestic.

I asked the ambassador if Canada was considered a hardship post. Would he not have preferred the excitement of, say, London, England? He claimed not. He said that when offered an ambassadorship he did his research and concluded he had only one choice: Canada. He said he had no interest in London. "Once I realized that you are our largest trading partner and our best friend, it was Canada or nothing for me."

I thanked him for googling us.

It being near the end of his run, he talked effusively about having visited every part of the country. I suggested he was casing the place for our fresh water.

He sounded as excited as a kid on Christmas when he told me about the day he woke up and saw that the entire Ottawa River was frozen! "Imagine that," he said. "In South Carolina, if the dog dish freezes over, you call all the kids and bring 'em outside and show them the ice, and talk to them about how cold it had to be to make that happen! Imagine, you have whole rivers doing that!"

He said it like we were the luckiest people in the world.

Looking at a pillow emblazoned with the coat of arms of his alma mater, he seamlessly told me he'd gone to university on a tennis scholarship. "I got a free ride," he said. "Wanna play?"

I said yes.

After a trip upstairs for one last hello to the presidential seal, I took off my black suit jacket and put on the tennis whites. Whites head to toe. I looked like the loneliest gay at a Miami circuit party. This was not my look. I headed back through the dark corridor, went downstairs and declared myself ready to play.

Once he got on the court, his game increased dramatically. Not his tennis game, but his chatter. This is where he is clearly the happiest. He became my instructor, teaching me a grip, teaching me how to serve. When it got windy and I commented on how it was affecting my game, he became a sports psychologist.

"No way, man. Ignore the wind. Don't let it get to you. Don't let the wind take you down. Look at me, I live in the wind. I love the wind. I *am* the wind!"

The US ambassador suddenly sounded like he was David Crosby on an acid trip circa 1969.

The game we played had stakes. If he won, he wanted the oil sands; if I won, I would get Mount Rushmore. I had dreams of adding Neil Young and turning Lincoln into Gord Downie.

We created, on the spot, a great bit of physical comedy. Because I was terrible at hitting the soft lobs he sent my way, he began to serve like a ninja. Every one of his serves hit me, and hit me hard.

Body shots were banging off my chest, my knees, my head and ankles. I didn't have a chance. I was dancing around like someone was firing at my feet with a six-shooter. Hang in there, Harry.

Mercifully, I made it through. But we weren't finished yet. I had a last-minute idea that we should roll around Ottawa and let the ambassador say goodbye to our nation's capital. He loved the idea, but noted he was going to be in a "whole heap of trouble with head office if I'm late getting home."

But he did it anyway. And we created a little goodbye montage.

Unplanned, we hit Parliament Hill, bummed a pair of hockey sticks from some kids and played street hockey with the Parliament Buildings glowing behind us. We went for poutine in the market. We shopped for Mountie postcards, and I gifted him with an Ottawa toque for those rare South Carolina nights when the dog dish freezes over. We toasted the friendship between our nations with a BeaverTail.

In conclusion I shook his hand and said, "Thank you, Ambassador, it's been a great day." He responded, "Thank you, Canada, it's been a great three years." And I believed him. A gentleman through and through.

Together we travelled back to his residence. He was in the back of our minivan, regaling us with off-camera stories that I would have killed to have on-camera. They always do that!

But when we pulled up to his house, I could tell we had created, by adding the montage, a mild domestic disturbance, or maybe a diplomatic faux pas.

His lovely wife, Susan, was on the porch, dressed to the nines. Apparently, this so-called black-tie affair wasn't fictional. The aide next to her looked frantic.

"You are *so* late," she said. "*Go go go.*"

We bade our goodbyes and he ran into the house. We apologized to the ambassador's wife and loaded ourselves back into the van. As we pulled away, Susan ducked inside—one assumes to whip her husband into shape.

Just two minutes later, at the bottom of the driveway, before we hit the gates, it dawned on me: my black suit jacket was hanging on a hook in the Ronald Reagan presidential loo.

"I have to go back," I said. "I forgot my jacket!"

Luckily, we hadn't gone through the secure gates, so we simply backed up the driveway very slowly.

When we arrived at the residence, it already looked different. The only lights were on in a different part of the mansion. And it was getting dark outside. I ran up the steps and knocked on the door, cursing the fact that they were inside, getting ready, and now I was here to disturb them again.

There was no answer.

I knocked again.

No answer.

I guess that maybe because at this point I felt like we were old, fast friends, I did what people in Newfoundland do when knocking. I reached out, opened the door, knocked again, but stuck my head inside and yelled "*Helloooo?*"

There was no answer.

The house was dark.

I was at a loss as to what to do. I knew what was happening. He was in the shower, she was elsewhere in the house, on the phone, making excuses.

I thought, *I know where my coat is. I'll just go grab it.*

Yeah, that's it, Rick. Enter the house of the US ambassador without actually being invited inside. After all, you two go back four hours now.

I slipped off my shoes and ran up the stairs towards the Reagan bathroom. At the top of the stairs, I entered the darkened hallway. But now it was a *very* dark hallway. I wasn't going to reach out for a light switch because I knew exactly where I was going. And sure enough, within a minute I was in the Reagan bathroom, rescuing my coat.

I turned around and was making my way back down the corridor, in my socks and holding my shoes, when it happened. My foot came down in a pile of what anyone who has ever known a puppy would be familiar with.

I froze.

I wiggled my toes. It was what I thought it was. And it was substantial.

Panicked, I kept the contaminated foot in place, making sure I wouldn't move it at all, and stepped one foot forward with my clean foot in order to maintain my balance.

Foot number two suffered the exact same fate. There were a minimum of two deposits and I had found both of them.

I was in trouble. Ankle deep.

I knew what I had to do. I slowly squatted and, while praying to the gods of personal balance, I gingerly, one after another, removed my socks.

I then began to creep slowly down the dark corridor, very aware that any step could prove disastrous. God knows what else might be waiting for me. I felt like a cat burglar inside the Louvre, trying to avoid secret laser beams.

Except it wasn't just a metaphor—I was literally a burglar, or could be accused of being one. Seriously, what was I thinking?

I had to get out of there.

I padded down the staircase and made it to the front door, where standing on guard was Speaker.

God, I thought, *he might have one last hunt in him.*

"There's a good boy," I said, reaching over with my one free hand and patting him on the head. "You're a good dog."

Thank god his barking days were behind him.

John later said, "I was wondering what was taking you so long, but I didn't expect to see you run out of their house barefoot with your socks and shoes in your hand. You looked like a maniac."

I had jumped in the van yelling, "Drive! Drive and don't stop!"

Which we didn't. Except for one little pit stop to rid myself of the socks. Don and John both insisted.

I wondered if forensic scientists can test for toe prints the way they test for fingerprints. Would I be arrested for tracking poo down the corridor of the ambassador from our largest trading partner? Is that how it would all come to an end?

There really is no dignity in show business.

In the days that followed there was no call from a furious ambassador, no visit from the FBI. And on the Friday night, as I watched the piece get played back to the audience, I sat and watched with the confidence of a man who no longer had to deal with Harry.

He had left town.

Good riddance. Worst uninvited guest ever.

5

Taking It on the Chin

M ichal Grajewski was a mission-critical member of the *RMR* road crew. For the majority of our fifteen seasons, he was with us every step of the way.

Mike originally came to work in the office as a production assistant.

In the world of TV and film, production assistant is your basic entry-level position. It can be as glamorous as standing at the photocopier all day, or as exciting as guarding a generator truck in twenty-below temperatures. It can be a very tough slog, but it is the proverbial foot in the door. And once you're in, there's no telling where it might lead.

For Michal, a temporary gig doing office work for a comedy show brought him a decade of adventures up and down the Trans-Canada Highway from sea to sea to sea.

A production assistant is literally a jack of all trades; they help wherever they are needed. And when Don, John and I went on a shoot that was either in or around Toronto, we would take Mike with us. He was a great help, excellent company, but most important of all, he loved being behind the wheel.

Driving was the only part of our job that we actively disliked. Neither John nor I are cut out for that. With John behind the wheel and me navigating, we never met a turnoff we didn't miss. We didn't so much spend our time exploring the country as we did getting lost in it. How many U-turns can anyone pull in one day? We probably have the record.

So we loved having Michal behind the wheel. So much so that Gerald agreed that we should expand our road crew to four. This was a big deal for us. A small crew was part of our core philosophy. But in Gerald's eyes, safety trumped ideology. And seeing as we were routinely taking long drives in snowstorms while dodging moose or deer, he felt we needed a professional.

And Michal had the qualifications. He was funny, came from a background of improv comedy and was raised in Winnipeg. Icy roads would not be a problem.

So, when I asked Mike if he would consider a new permanent position on *RMR* that involved travelling with us on all of our shoots, everywhere in Canada, I thought his head would come off. I felt like I was telling some guy that he had won the lotto.

I hadn't even got to the part about a substantial raise, and already he was fully committed.

It's one of the best calls I ever made. To this day, if I were going to rob a bank, Mike would drive the getaway car. And he would get away. The only downside would be that the entire time we were fleeing the scene of the crime, he'd be telling me everything there is to know about the make and model of the vehicle we were escaping in. Mike has PhD-level knowledge in his head about cars and he is desperate to share it. It was his cross to bear that he spent a decade with three men who didn't care about cars.

But lest I leave the impression that Mike was simply the driver, let me be clear: he was so much more than that.

Over the months and years that followed, Mike became invaluable. When drone footage became increasingly important to our show, he became a drone operator. He is one of the best in the country now. Very early on, we began to invest in GoPro cameras. The little suckers are common now; you see them on helmets everywhere in the world. But the *Rick Mercer Report* was one of the first TV shows to use them. Mike was our GoPro guy. He was also our unit photographer responsible for taking the pictures we used in our national ad campaign in the *Globe and Mail*.

He was Don's camera assistant and John's assistant director. Sometimes he did second-unit directing. And I leaned on his skills as an improviser more times than I can count.

And yes, he drove the van. Through whatever weather was thrown at him.

But before he had the chance to prove himself so capable, he needed to face the fear factor.

If you have a fear—and let's face it, we all do—you were sure to come face to face with it eventually on our show. Fear of heights? Wait five minutes and there will be heights. A fear of snakes? It's just a matter of time before Tom announces you'll be playing with a giant anaconda. Are you remotely claustrophobic? This week we are travelling 2.3 kilometres under the earth to explore a potash mine.

If you have a normal job, if you work at a bank or as a plumber, chances are you won't have to face your fears at work. If you worked on the road with us, chances were you would come face to face with whatever fear you had.

Naturally, the chance of that happening on your first day on the job would be very slim.

Unless you're Mike.

He hadn't even had a chance to wrap his head around his new job before I told him that our first shoot, the very next day, would take place in British Columbia.

"*No way,*" he said. "We're going to BC?"

It was great to see his enthusiasm. A reminder that yes, this job is amazing and how incredible that, at the drop of a hat, the job would take us to British Columbia.

"What's in British Columbia?" he asked.

"We have two shoots," I said. "Tom hasn't nailed down the second one, but for the first we are visiting a bee colony. Some lady has, like, ten thousand bees. Tom's on his way over. He'll explain it to us. I don't really know much."

Now, I knew Mike at this point. I didn't know him that well, but I had spent time with him. I like to think I'm an intuitive person. And I like to think that when a look of abject terror flashes across someone's face, if only for a second, I can pick up on it.

Is he afraid of bees? I wondered. *Or was that indigestion?*

"Oh . . . bees?" said Mike. "Cool. Bees are important. They pollinate so many fruits and vegetables. Bees are our friends. Also, they are dying. It's a crisis. That's a good idea, bees."

Every time he said the word *bees* his voice cracked like a boy soprano entering puberty.

"Do you like bees?" he asked.

"I'm mostly indifferent," I said.

And the truth was, I *was* indifferent. I had never really given bees much thought. "I don't even know if I've been stung by a bee," I said. "I must have. When I was a kid. But maybe that was a wasp."

"Oh, I have," said Mike. "When I was a kid. I was looking at one through a magnifying glass, trying to figure out how it could fly, and it got me on my lower eyelid. It just kept swelling, my entire eye—not just my eye, but half of my face. And my mother kept putting some weird poultices on it. They smelled like sour milk."

"So you're not a fan of the bees?"

"Oh, it's fine. They pollinate many fruits and vegetables."

Mike was being a complete professional. Also, he looked like he might black out.

Luckily, Tom arrived and, having caught the end of our conversation, put everyone quickly at ease.

"Don't worry," Tom said, passing me an information sheet on the shoot. "They did say there's a good chance you might get stung, Rick, just because of the sheer volume of bees, but there will be paramedics there in case anyone has an allergic reaction."

I said, "I don't think I'm allergic, but I really don't know."

Tom said, "Well, it actually doesn't matter if you've been stung by a bee before and were fine, apparently you can have an allergic reaction the second time as an adult."

"I've been stung before," said Mike. "On the eye."

Tom told me I'd be wearing a special suit when handling the bees but added that according to the bee guy, camera crews who'd shot there before had found the suits interfered with their mobility. "So," Tom said, "he suggested that everyone else should just wear long sleeves and put duct tape around your wrists and ankles to close any openings and we will be fine."

Mike bent over and began to tuck his pants into his socks.

Well, this should be interesting, I thought. Although secretly I was starting to get worried that, Mike's reaction aside, the bees might not be that interesting at all. Or interesting enough.

The place we were visiting was ostensibly a honey farm. I would be learning how bees make honey and would be helping to harvest it. Part of the hook was the news that North America's bee population was decreasing at an alarming rate. The bee farmers we were meeting were active on the file and eager to talk about bee populations.

I was sympathetic, but talk of a dying planet was a bit of a downer.

Tom did what he always did. He began to walk me through all the things that I could do on the trip. Putting smoke in a bee house to make the bees more compliant, taking the trays out of the house, gently removing the bees, scraping the honey from the tray. Tasting the honey. Et cetera.

I could see it all, but I wasn't entirely convinced. It seemed rather languid.

And then Tom said, "Now . . . there is another option, if you want to."

Tom would often do this. He would hold something back. He was like the waiter pointing out all the perfectly fine things on the menu but then adding that the chef had a special tonight.

"What's the other option?" I asked.

"Well, the guy there, the guy who you will be talking to, is a bee expert. But he's also an expert on bee beards. He said if you wanted, you could remove your protective headgear and he would attach a queen bee to your neck and release, like, a thousand male bees who, I guess, want to copulate or at least snuggle with the queen and they will attach themselves to your face. It's called a bee beard. That's the other option. If you wanted to."

So, in seven seconds we had gone from learning how honey is being made to having a thousand stinging insects on my face.

This is why Tom is so good at his job and why on occasion I wanted to kill him. Because he knew. And I knew. Now that the chef's special had been revealed, I had no choice.

I would be getting a bee beard.

This is a classic "fight or flight" scenario. The sane me, the rational me, knew full well that only an idiot would want a thousand bees on their face. Let some other guy do that, some guy who doesn't care about his face. He can do it all day if he wants. He can join a freak show and appear on a double bill with one of those guys who drives nails up his nose with a hammer.

All I want to do is travel the country, meet interesting people and figure out what it means to be Canadian. I'm not gonna just stand there while some hippie Charles Manson wannabe from British Columbia sticks a queen bee to my Adam's apple.

That was the rational me. The irrational me, the TV performer—and more importantly the TV producer—knew only one thing: that learning how honey is made is a pleasant way to kill a few minutes on national TV, but having a bee beard put on the host? That's sensational.

Every weatherman from Hibbs Hole to Hell's Gate could go on TV and show the audience how to harvest honey. That's child's play. But how many of them would be willing to go into anaphylactic shock while the cameras were rolling, just to draw attention to the plight of the bees?

None. Only an idiot would do that. And I was going to be that idiot.

And the truth is, like all Canadians, I was deeply concerned about the plight of the planet. Also, like most Canadians, I rarely did anything about it. I did turn off the light over the porch every Earth Day, and I proudly tweeted about it, but it was time to up my game. This would be my chance.

"Fine," I said. "I'll do the bee beard. I'll do it for the endangered bees."

"Excellent," said Tom. "And I'll double-check on the paramedics."

I headed home, leaving Tom to work the phones, finalizing the coming shoots, and Mike, wearing the stare of a man who is about to be sent to sea in pursuit of the famed enemy battleship the *Bismarck*.

I packed for British Columbia and, oddly, slept very well that night. The prospect of having insects on my face is not the kind of thing that keeps me awake. Heading out to a shoot that lacked excitement is what would interfere with my slumber. And from the moment Tom talked about a man attaching a queen to my neck and releasing a thousand horny male bees, I knew we would get a good piece.

And worst-case scenario? If I had a terrible reaction to stings on my face and had to be taken to hospital, we might even end up with a Canadian Screen Award.

This was the life we had chosen.

The next morning, bright and early, we convened at Pearson and set out on a four-day jaunt to British Columbia. First stop would be Langley—an easy trip, as it's essentially on the edge of Vancouver.

Right out of the gate, the shoot was off to a fantastic start because I scored upgrades for all. This was a passion of mine. I used every tool in the toolbox. I had millions of points with Air Canada because of my travel schedule and I had upgrade coupons to spare. I loved nothing more than pulling off upgrades when we had a long haul ahead of us, and BC certainly qualified.

When it came to sucking up to Air Canada staff to get upgraded, I was entirely without shame. And at this point I had personal relationships with half of the counter staff. These were the good old days when a person at the Air Canada counter could work miracles, authorizing upgrades and making changes to a flight itinerary with a few keystrokes. Today, things are much different. A team of experts with MBAs have developed a new system where front-line staff at the airline can no longer do anything of any consequence regarding your flight. The computers in front of them are just placebo terminals designed to put the customer at ease. Really, each one is a cardboard box with a battery-powered light bulb inside.

Which is why now, in a crisis, all the staff can do is direct you to the website or have you call a special number. That number connects to a single telephone booth in Mumbai with an answering machine that says, "Thank you for your patience. Your call is important to us."

But in those days, Barb or Gus or Ranjeet could, if the seats were available and you had a full-fare ticket, put you in the front of the plane.

Which is what they did on this day.

I passed Mike his business-class ticket with such pride in my accomplishment, you would swear I was the one who had discovered insulin.

I couldn't help it. I knew he was excited about this new job. But I also knew that for Mike, a seat in business class would have practical appeal well beyond the improved service and the infamous pasta. Mike is a very tall man. Much taller even than my impressive five feet, eight inches. He comes in at six foot four in sock feet. Feet that resemble pontoons more than appendages. The extra legroom would be a blessing for Mike. "Business class!" he said. "Is this for real?"

"That's the way we roll," I said, and we headed to the fancy lounge with the free snacks and newspapers.

During the flight I went over the document Tom and the research department had prepared. These documents were designed to allow me to bluff my way through any conversation with an expert. They mostly contained salient facts that I might not have picked up during my years on earth. For example, Canada produces thirty-two thousand tonnes of honey in a single year. I did not know that. Nor did I know that a full third of the honeybee population died the previous year.

This I found shocking. I had heard many times that "the bees are disappearing," but I didn't know to what extent. One-third was horrifying to me. I thought "the bees are disappearing" was just another unproven theory like "The ocean is warming," "The climate is changing" or "The iPhone might replace the BlackBerry someday."

You didn't need to be a high school graduate to realize that if a third of the bees died in the previous year, honey might soon become a distant memory.

While I familiarized and horrified myself with the world of honey, my seatmate, Mike, did what I would soon learn was his favourite thing in the world. He sat in a seat on a plane and read *Car and Driver* magazine with an intensity that might be more fitting in an operating room. I found Mike's level of concentration when reading about the new brake pads on a Volkswagen fascinating.

Over the years I would witness him do this with untold technical manuals. That's how amazing he is: he studied every manual to every piece of technical equipment we ever bought. If Don bought a new piece of equipment for his camera package, Mike would ask to borrow the manual sometime so he could read it for fun. Like a teen in the eighties negotiating some alone time with the community copy of *Playboy*.

We chatted on the plane, but what we didn't discuss were the bees. At the risk of sounding nicer than I am, I'm not one for teasing anyone else about their irrational fears or phobias. Mike didn't like bees, but I wasn't going to bug him about it.

We all have irrational fears. My brother, for example, hates heights. He is a commercial airline pilot, and he wouldn't jump out of a plane for all the money in the world. This goes way back to when we were children. The whole family would gather around, and for entertainment, we would watch my brother climb up the stepladder and try to change the light bulbs in the cathedral ceiling without passing out. These was the good old days before that kind of thing was considered child abuse. Thinking about it now, I realize our behaviour may have contributed to, or even created, this fear rather than helping him live with it.

Me? Revolving doors are my kryptonite. I'm always afraid some stranger is going to jump in with me, or that I'm going to lose an arm or a foot. I always avoid the revolving door even when there's a sign saying PLEASE USE REVOLVING DOOR. And if I see a child near a revolving door, I feel like calling social services and reporting the parents.

So the subject of bees didn't really come up on the plane.

But on the drive to the location, it couldn't be avoided. We did what we always did: create a plan that could go out the window at any time.

None of us were keen on getting stung, and Don did volunteer the opinion that I was completely insane for contemplating a bee beard, but that he was going to enjoy watching it anyway. He had shot around bees before and said, "They're impossible to avoid. Keep your mouth shut, that's all I know. My god, when there's thousands of them, they get everywhere. I remember taking the camera apart back at the hotel room, and somehow two bees had got inside my lens."

I was more concerned with the practicality of getting stung. We had another shoot immediately following this one and I didn't relish having to only show one side of my face the entire time—or perhaps not being able to swallow.

For the most part Mike was the epitome of calm. So much so, I figured I must have imagined his negative reaction the day before. He even offered some bee facts of his own. Clearly, he had done a bit of research.

The farm was on the outskirts of Langley, and so we arrived at the address pretty quickly. Or at least what we believed was the address. We'd been given classic rural Canadian directions: go down the main road and turn right where the Quintons' barn used to be. That kind of thing. We drove down a long driveway, where we assumed we would find our guests and their thriving bee farm. What we came across was a very small farmhouse and a small barn.

We got out and looked around, and all of us quickly concluded we weren't in the right place. It didn't look particularly lived in and there were no vehicles. After a few leaks in the woods, we piled back into the van. I was in the front passenger seat with Don and John in the second row. Mike was in the driver's seat. All three doors—the two front doors and the rear sliding door—slammed simultaneously. Mike's door slammed the hardest. On his fingers. Or at least I assumed the door had slammed on his fingers. I couldn't think of any other reason a man would scream the way he did. It was guttural.

And then the explanation.

"*A bee!*" he said, pointing at what seemed to be a very large fly walking along the dashboard.

And it was big—big by fly standards. But this was British Columbia. Everything was bigger out here. The trees certainly were.

But yes, it was a fly. Which flew out the window the second I lowered it.

And then there was just silence. Nobody said a word. Nobody had to. Mike might have been the new guy, but he was to be afforded the same respect that the rest of us granted each other. Namely, if someone did something embarrassing or stupid, we didn't discuss it; we did the manly thing and ignored it and moved on as if nothing happened. The mocking would come later, and only after an appropriate amount of time had passed.

Mike put the vehicle in reverse, and we headed to our destination.

Within a few minutes we arrived at the farm of Heather Higo. She introduced herself to me as the Bee Lady.

She was great. From the minute she said hello, I knew we were going to be okay. She was relaxed and I could tell instantly how passionate she was about her work. It's always a pleasure to meet people who have found their calling. So few do.

This always baffles me. How does someone develop an obscure passion and then turn it into their life's work? Are they sitting in class in grade four and the teacher talks about frogs and a light goes off?—"That's it," they declare, "I'm going to be a frog biologist if such a job exists."

I know of a coroner whose happy place is working alone at nights. Just her and a body. She thought her passion was going to be medicine, but somewhere along the line in medical school she realized she wasn't big on people—or, as she calls them, "the living." So now she does autopsies and solves murders.

The Bee Lady had certainly found her place in the world. She was at one with the bees, and there were a lot of them. In fact, as she walked up to me to introduce herself, there were six or seven bees buzzing around her hair. It looked like they were looking for a place to live.

She shook my hand, John's hand, and then Don's hand. I looked at Mike and he stepped forward, towards the lady with bees in her hair, and reached out his hand. And smiled. "I'm Michal," he said.

If he was dying inside, he didn't show it.

I should have known. Mike is an actor, and actors have a bizarre ability to forget everything once they are treading the boards.

We set up for a quick interview wearing civilian clothes, with the idea being that once we established what our day looked like, we would get dressed in bee clothes and get to work. I would be a farmer for a day.

The first question I asked was: "How many bees are there on your farm?"

I expected an answer in the hundreds or thousands, but she said, "We have 1.5 million bees on the farm. We are currently at peak population."

"One point five million? Does that include the six bees trying to find a home in your hair, or is that where they live already?"

She seemed surprised that they were there. She was that oblivious to bees.

Clearly, these were completely harmless, and civilians like us only became uncomfortable around bees because of some myths we had bought into. These were honeybees; these were our friends—our non-stinging, pacifist, pollinating friends.

I decided to go *MythBusters* right then and there. "Bees get a bum rap, don't they? People are nervous around them, but that's completely unfounded. You're around bees all day. When were you stung last?"

"Yesterday," she said pleasantly.

I was dubious. "Seriously, when were you stung last?"

"Yesterday."

I turned to her colleague Mark Winston, the Bee Dude. "When were *you* stung last?"

Turns out he had been stung that morning.

"Oh come on," I said. "What chance do I have?"

Bee Lady said, "It's something you get used to."

One hundred percent not reassuring. There is a giant difference between something awful that you get used to and experiencing something awful for the first time.

Ever watched an old-school electrician at work? They test to see if a wire is live by squeezing it between their thumb and index finger. If the wire is live, the experienced badass electrician will feel a slight tingling between their digits, nothing more. Like Bee Lady, they're "used to it." It also means the nerves in that part of their hand have been fried so many times by 120 volts of electricity that they could jab a screwdriver into the purlicue of their hand and not feel a thing. For those of you who failed anatomy in med school, the purlicue is that fleshy, goopy part of the hand where your thumb and index finger meet.

Meanwhile, if you or I were to grab a live wire like that, the blast would throw us across the room and our purlicue would ring for a week. At which point the old-school electrician would say, "You'll get used to it."

"How about we get me into that protective clothing?" I suggested.

Which we did. And while I might have cut a dashing figure, for the life of me it didn't feel very protective. It seemed to be a crinkly, paper-thin white coverall that wouldn't look out of place in a bad '70s science fiction movie. I felt like I was in a cheap Halloween costume, not the real McCoy.

Thankfully, I was given a beekeeper's hat to wear. It had a full window in the front, so I could at least see the bees coming at me. Which they did. We headed for the hives and they came looking, landing on my hat and crawling across the protective veil six inches in front of my face.

Bee Lady and Bee Dude began to teach me about harvesting honey. Before we could do anything, we had to creep up on the wooden hives and smoke the suckers. We stuffed burning burlap into what looked like a jerry-rigged bong and blew smoke into the beehives. Bee Lady told me the smoke makes the bees happy and compliant. So, not unlike grade ten.

Once the bees had their buzz on, we pulled out the trays, which were crawling with literally thousands of the critters. And then the Bee Lady told me I was ready to taste farm-fresh honey. Naturally, to do this, my hat had to be removed and I'd have to open my mouth. My first instinct was to say, "No thank you, I had a granola bar in the van on the way over," but I am a TV professional, so off came the hat and wide open went my mouth. As she shoved a stick full of honey in my mouth, I felt it was time to hit her with the tough questions I am known for.

"Is the honey actually bee poop?" I asked. Let's face it, we have all heard that before. And it makes sense. Bees, like most of the animal kingdom, have two ends. The honey must come out of one of them. Not that I would have cared—I eat oysters by the dozens.

But it turns out, no, honey is not bee poop. "Nor is it bee vomit," she volunteered.

It was a great experience. Honey straight from the bee is like fish directly from the ocean. You can't beat it. The golden elixir was more delicious than any honey I've ever had from a bottle. I highly recommend it. Afterwards we huddled for a quick production meeting.

"This has turned out to be a nice piece," I said. "They are charming. The bees are interesting. I kind of think we don't need to do the bee beard."

John, Don and even Mike looked at me like I was a four-year-old pretending I had a tummy ache. Good try, kid.

"We need the beard," said John, in his director voice.

"Definitely want to see the beard," said Don.

"Do it for the bees," said Mike. "You're my hero."

I turned to Bee Dude. "Let's do the beard."

MAKING A BEE BEARD is a straightforward process. First up, the person who is volunteering their face is an idiot. Let's establish that right out of the gate. Then, the idiot voluntarily removes any protective headgear and goes raw dog into the wind. Duct tape is wrapped around the idiot's neck to ensure that no errant bee goes exploring under his or her clothes, which apparently is something that always ends badly. Next up, cotton balls are shoved up the idiot's nose and into their ears. Once the nose is plugged, the figurative mouth breather becomes a literal mouth breather. At this point Bee Dude reminds the moron that once the bee beard begins to grow, they should be very careful about opening their mouth. Stings on the tongue or inside the mouth are particularly painful. Swallowing a bee is also ill advised, as they don't go quietly into the hole. Can't blame them, really.

How one is supposed to keep their mouth closed while their nose is plugged is not explained.

———

AT THIS POINT THE bearding commenced. Bee Dude excitedly slapped some sort of bee pheromone on my chest directly below my chin. This stuff is like catnip for bees, apparently. It was like slathering gravy on your neck before trying to outrun an angry Doberman.

And then the fun started.

The Bee Dude pulled out a tray of bees, which he laid to one side and very gently reached in and pulled out what resembled one of those large chains of office that mayors wear. An oversized necklace crawling with bees. And at the very bottom of the chain of office, instead of a gaudy medallion, there was the queen bee. But you couldn't see the queen because she was inside of a ball of undulating male bees about the size of a wrestler's fist.

As the Bee Dude approached me I was instructed to keep my arms to my sides and lean forward as if I were about to have a gold medal placed around my neck. As he placed the necklace over my head, the sound was horrifying, despite my ears being plugged. A low and steady drone. The soundtrack to a descent into insanity. This felt less like getting a gold medal and more like putting your head through a noose. No sooner did it fall into place than I felt bees crawling up my neck—searching for their queen. Each one of them enjoying how my pink, freshly shaved face felt under their six legs.

But wait, there's more.

Bee Lady then held a square piece of plywood directly in front of my chest. It was if she was preparing to give me communion. If she'd held a bucket in the same position, I would have thought she was expecting me to be sick. Nobody explained this part to me. *What's with the board in front of my face?* I wondered. I didn't have to puzzle over it for long. Bee Dude picked up the tray the queen had come from, which was still filled with thousands of bees. They were panicked and alarmed that someone had stolen their queen. He then tipped the tray over and slammed it down on the plywood, dumping the bees into a large pile inches from my face. He then ran away, watching from afar.

This from a guy who had said "No sudden moves" to me at least fifty times in the last two hours. Hey buddy, wouldn't fleeing constitute a "sudden move?"

He returned with another tray, tipped it over and slammed it down again. The bees lost it and swarmed my face, desperate to find their leader. Which they made a bee line for. (Did you see what I did there?)

I could feel bees walking all over my neck and chin and moving up to my very pursed lips. Occasionally a bee that clearly hadn't got the memo explaining how beards worked would just abandon the rest and decide to explore my forehead. Another bee attempted to pollinate—or perhaps copulate with—my eye socket. Bee Lady graciously picked these adventurers off my face and put them back with their brothers.

I had no idea how big my beard was at this point, and I looked to John to see if we would indicate that we had achieved our goal. He just mouthed the word *wow* at me.

Don took one hand from the camera and gave me the thumbs-up. Mike took a deep breath and stepped forward with his camera and began to take pictures as if I was on a red carpet. Lost in the moment, he stepped closer and closer until the lens on his camera was inches from my face. Shades of the seven-year-old Michal trying to figure out how these things fly.

If he gets stung on the eye now, I thought, *the irony will be staggering and his mother will kill me.*

In TV we sometimes like to talk about how one can "up the stakes" suddenly without any warning to the audience. Apparently, beekeepers think the same way. "I'm going to get another queen," Bee Dude said with a giddy lilt.

Before I could protest, he grabbed another tray and from it pulled out yet another chain of office. If Lucifer were elected mayor of Langley, this is what he would wear.

My limited knowledge of bees told me there is only one queen per colony and that the queens don't mix.

"Is this a good idea?" I asked, my pulse increasing. I didn't want two queens going at it on my Adam's apple.

With the second queen in place, the slamming of the tray onto plywood happened all over again.

The bipolar nature of my occupation was about to boil over. A battle of wills was being fought in my brain. The TV performer, the TV *producer*, was thinking, "This is great TV." The civilian me was thinking this was the stupidest thing I'd ever done. This was going too far.

It was taking every bit of intestinal fortitude I had not to start slapping my own face. My instinct was to kill, paw and sweep every single bee and then search out their families. *My kingdom for a can of Raid*, I thought, and I meant it. Had the can appeared I would have sprayed my head and face like it was 1987 and I was a Valley girl getting ready for a date.

While Bee Dude looked on like a proud father it dawned on me that I didn't like bees at all. Not even a little bit. And for that matter, I didn't like honey. A world without honey would be fine with me. And the dwindling bee population? Well, if science can't find a way to pollinate crops and we all die of starvation, that's fine with me too. I will graciously accept the end of civilization as long as we can stop this now.

And then I heard those three little words I had been desperate to hear for so long. "We've got it," said John.

I looked into the camera, signed off from Langley, waited a beat, and then said to Bee Dude, "Okay, that's it. Make them fly away now."

Gently he lifted the two chains of office from me, along with the queens, and returned them to their hell boxes. He gently began to sweep bees off my face with a "special tool" that looked suspiciously like a windshield scraper from Canadian Tire with the scrape-y part cut off.

He then took me by the hand and walked me as far away from the beehives as we could get, and he told me to jump up and down on the count of three.

There was a small pond in the distance. I contemplated leaving him and diving in.

He counted me down, "Three, two, one—*jump!*"

And jump I did. When my feet hit the ground, clumps of bees were forced from my face and began to swarm.

"Again," he said. "Harder!"

And I jumped.

"Again!" he yelled. "Harder! Again!"

I was jumping up and down like a sugar-dosed youngster in a bouncy castle.

Eventually he said I could stop, and the last remaining bee on my chin flew away.

I was alive, with not a single sting—a fact that both the Bee Lady and the Bee Dude attributed to either dumb luck or a miracle. Only when it was all over did she show me that she had been stung twice while stickhandling the beard.

She thanked me profusely for coming out and doing the piece and, most importantly, highlighting the precarious bee population.

I told her I was happy to do it. "Not once," I said, "did I regret coming here to help the bees."

And for that I got a hug. We all did.

That's the way we roll.

6

Rocking All Over

Who among us has not dreamed of being a rock star?

When I was a kid my favourite pastime was lip-synching Trooper songs using my Superman hairbrush as a microphone. My sisters' records were my source material, so if I tired of hard rock I would slap on some Burton Cummings and sing a rock ballad or a lullaby to weeping secretaries. And yes, I would cleverly disguise it so it'd not been heard before.

It was a guilty pleasure. But the opportunities were slim. To do it right you needed the house to yourself. That involved the whole rigamarole of pretending you were sick so you could stay home from school. Because you can't jump up and down in your tighty-whitey Y-fronts while wearing a Halloween boa if your siblings are in the house. Imagine the mortification if one were observed.

But the real rock stars? They did it in public, in front of thousands of adoring fans. Could there *be* a better job?

My first rock concert was Tom Cochrane and Red Rider, followed by April Wine. Classic Canadian rock. Straightforward macho stuff. But my first near-riot rock concert was at the age of fifteen, when I went to see Platinum Blonde at Memorial Stadium in St John's. It was a mob scene. You'd swear the Beatles had landed. Every girl on the Avalon Peninsula (and me, apparently) wanted a piece of these hyper-androgynous, skinny dudes with huge heads of bleached hair.

They were stars. They were dangerous. They wore copious amounts of blush. The lead singer was such a badass that he walked out onstage, screamed, "Hello, Newfoundland!" and proceeded to chug an entire forty-ounce (1.14-litre) bottle of our world-famous Newfoundland screech, an extremely dark and potent rum.

We went wild. We chanted, "Chug! Chug! Chug!"

Of course, now I realize it was all an act. The lead singer weighed 106 pounds. Had there been actual screech in that bottle, he'd have been legally blind halfway through it and dead by the end.

But it was so much fun. The debauchery, the bad behaviour, everything we knew about rock and roll was personified by these five guys who wore more eye shadow and lip gloss than the sauciest girls on the bus. This was theatre, and we were an appreciative audience.

They were playing into a rock and roll cliché. They were bad boys. And everyone wants to either be a bad boy or be with one.

Which is why rock and roll beckoned.

Of course, lacking any talent in that area, I never did become a rock star. But Canadian show business being a relatively small world, I've crossed paths with many of them.

And there have been some close encounters.

I once spent thirty minutes in a shower with Bruce Cockburn.

And when it comes to huge egos, bad behaviour and complete debauchery, the Canadian musicians I know fail completely.

Whoever coined the phrase "sex, drugs and rock and roll" wasn't talking about the Canadian music industry. A more apt descriptor might be "in bed by ten."

For years my friend Heidi Bonnell and I produced a yearly benefit concert in Ottawa to raise money for Fertile Futures, a charity providing fertility options for young people fighting cancer. Amazing musicians came and helped us out. Household names. People with boatloads of Junos and gold records. Gord Downie, Sarah McLachlan, Ron Sexsmith, Alan Doyle, Randy Bachman, Jim Cuddy, Serena Ryder . . . the list goes on and on.

Total narcissists. Every time you turned around, that crowd were flying to the nation's capital and raising money so young women with cancer could freeze their eggs.

I've met more musicians at benefit concerts than I can remember. The first time I met Gord Downie from the Tragically Hip was at a benefit when I was twenty years old. It was for Friends of Medicare Toronto, held in a small theatre in the basement of Hart House.

I remember seeing Gord there and thinking, *My career is just starting. I take every gig that comes along including the free ones. But why is our greatest rock star here?*

Turns out he was there because he believed in universal health care.

In my world, the comedy TV world, the phone rings regularly with people raising money for a good cause. In the music world it never stops ringing. I swear Jann Arden could do a benefit concert every night of the year. As it stands, she does a whack of them. And literally every single day, she takes time to record celebrity messages on her telephone, wishing her fans everything from a happy Hanukkah to a happy gastroplasty. All the money goes to animal charities. She's saved more donkeys and horses than I've saved Club Z points.

And that's in a regular year. When something tragic occurs—a famine, an earthquake or a deadly tsunami—a bat signal of sorts goes out and every working musician is required on deck.

Benefits happen everywhere. From the smallest pubs to the biggest rooms.

In 2005, after the tsunami in Thailand, I was asked to co-host a pair of benefit concerts in Calgary and Vancouver. When shows like this are put together at the last minute, they can be unwieldly and difficult. In a perfect world, shows on that scale would be planned and rehearsed over a period of weeks or months. In this world, in a crisis, they came together overnight.

No easy feat. Internationally famous musicians have famously hectic schedules and even more famously complicated needs and wants from a production standpoint. Getting a bunch of them on a bill on short notice requires a miracle. Or in this case, Sarah McLachlan, who was first in and was also the woman who made personal calls to her fellow musical legends. Everyone who was asked said yes and not a single stupid showbiz request was made.

I was incredibly flattered to be the co-host along with comedian Brent Butt. Another one of those "how did I get here?" situations.

To give you an idea how big the show was, Vancouver was sold out in a matter of minutes, even before the lineup was confirmed. A lineup that would go on to include Barenaked Ladies, Avril Lavigne and Sum 41. The reason for having two hosts? I was one of the faces of CBC TV and Brent, the star of the monster hit sitcom *Corner Gas*, was the face of CTV. Both networks were going to carry the concert live and simultaneously. For the CBC and CTV to air the same show at the same time was unheard of.

Thanks to a horrible natural disaster on the other side of the planet, peace in our time had broken out in the Canadian broadcasting world.

PREPARING FOR THE FIRST SHOW was a bit of a mental nightmare. The host's job is to direct traffic and keep the night moving along while full bands are brought on and off the stage. Bringing full bands on and off seamlessly is practically impossible. There's a reason why there is always a break between an opening act and the headliner in a traditional rock concert. It's not just so you can get a beer—it's so one giant, unwieldly rock band can be moved off the stage and replaced with another.

In a show like this there would be headliner after headliner. And the networks wanted non-stop entertainment, no breaks. Both Brent and I knew that when the inevitable happened— when a drummer disappeared or a microphone stopped working—we would be called upon to "stretch" in front of eighteen thousand people on two of Canada's largest networks. No pressure at all.

Meanwhile, both Brent and I were in production on our respective TV shows. We had day jobs to attend to.

A few days before the Vancouver show I got a call from Gerald. He had just spoken with the concert organizers. They wanted to add yet another show. But this one would happen first, the day before.

This made no sense to me. How could we do two shows in Vancouver in two separate venues? He said some of the acts on the Vancouver bill had agreed to come in a day early and appear. They wanted me to host. Gerald said, "Timewise we can make it happen. You'll just fly in a day early."

This all seemed a bit odd.

"Where is it?" I asked. This is always a pertinent question. You want to know the size of the venue, to give you an idea of how much money might be raised.

"It's at a guy's house in West Van," he said. "It's in his living room."

My suspicions were confirmed. I was surprised Gerald was pitching me this as a real thing.

"Oh for god's sake," I said. "I'm not playing some guy's living room." I like to think I'm down-to-earth, but this seemed a bit absurd. We were going to do a show for eighteen thousand people in Vancouver—why would we play some guy's house?

"What am I supposed to do, stand by the couch and tell jokes?"

"I think you should do it," Gerald said. "They have a good lineup."

"Really? Who said yes?"

"Barenaked Ladies, Sarah McLachlan, Chantal Kreviazuk so far."

By this time Sarah had sold over thirty million records. She was one of the biggest stars in the world.

"There's also a few surprises. Rod Stewart is flying in, and so is Robin Williams."

Suddenly my perspective changed. "I guess if Robin Williams can tell jokes standing next to a couch, so can I. After all, it is a good cause."

For the umptieth time I took Gerald's advice.

And so it came to be that the evening before playing BC Place we went to businessman Frank Giustra's house in Vancouver and put on a little show. A little show in a big house with, if memory serves me, a Renoir hanging over the fireplace. Also, it was on the water. And in the water were actual frogmen, like in a James Bond movie.

Giustra is a Canadian mining executive and founder of Lions Gate Entertainment. He is one of those very wealthy men who have decided to hedge their bets and buy their way into heaven. Either that or he's just a very generous person. He has donated literally hundreds of millions of dollars to charity over the years. And on this night, in his home, with the help of some flush friends, he was raising a couple of million dollars. The same amount of money we would make in both Calgary and Vancouver. Attention, rich people—be more like Frank.

The audience was small by concert standards but large by living room standards. My guess is around ninety. The backstage area was cramped, as you can imagine. How I ended up in a powder room talking to Rod Stewart and one of my comedy heroes, Robin Williams, I will never know. I remember looking across the small talent-holding area at Steve Page as he picked up a pair of seriously beaten boxing gloves. They were Muhammad Ali's.

The show was lovely. To see Sarah in a room that small was magic. The Barenaked Ladies were spectacular, as was Chantal.

I did some of my old stand-up material about Canada-USA relations. Ending with the joke "The thing about Canada and the United States is, we are bigger than they are, and we're on top. If we were in prison, they'd be our bitch," I heard a sound that I would have known anywhere. I looked to my left and saw Robin Williams laughing. Put that on the list of things I'll never forget. And when I did introduce Robin, the crowd predictably went crazy. You could see Giustra vacuuming the cash out of their pockets as Robin paced the stage and gave us some of his greatest hits, including my personal favourite—the Scottish golfer. Later he riffed on my bit about Canada-USA relations, saying it's true we were on top but adding, "Canada is the nicest country in the world. You're like a really nice apartment over a meth lab."

Killer joke.

And Rod Stewart? He brought an energy that would not have been out of place in Wembley Stadium. Who has Rod Stewart play in his living room?

I HAVE TO SAY IT was the greatest house party I have ever attended. I have no expectations I'll ever experience one remotely similar.

I can't speak for anyone else on the bill but I left the show on a crazy high. But there was no time to sit back and relish it. The next night we were playing BC Place.

The show turned out to be phenomenal. Robin had such a good time the night before he stuck around and made a surprise appearance, to the massive delight of fans. The air in the stadium was electric. Everyone knew how special this show was. The artists on the bill had sold over seventy million records combined. The fact that they were on the same bill was nothing short of historic. Also, Vancouver is Sarah McLachlan's town; they love her there more than the mountains they never stop talking about. This show was her baby and the audience was all in. And for those who prefer something a little harder than a classic Sarah McLachlan love ballad there was Sum 41 and Avril Lavigne. Both at the time were at the height of their staggering popularity and they took the opportunity to show everyone exactly why by taking the roof off the place.

And the moving parts? No gears were jammed and no drummers were lost. Everything went so smoothly, you would swear the transitions had been rehearsed for weeks. At no point were Brent and I asked to "stretch." Thank God. We would have gladly sold our souls to avoid such a fate. But it was not necessary. It all came together because everyone involved on the production team brought their A game.

And then it was off to Calgary to do it all over again.

It was exhausting but fun. The week allowed me to vicariously experience the life of a rock star. It didn't disappoint.

I remember walking up to the venue in Calgary because the weather was spectacular. If you believed in omens, this was a good one. It was the middle of winter, but the sun was shining and it was a balmy fifteen degrees. An Alberta Chinook. It kills the trees but it's good for the soul.

This show was even more tangly than the BC show because I was doing double duty. I still had a TV show to do that week so Don, John and I planned to wander around backstage and grab interviews with the performers. How I was going to host this live rock concert and shoot my own TV show at the same time wasn't entirely clear, but somehow we had to make it happen.

Of course, the first thing I did after entering the Saddledome was get lost. It is the story of my life, really. Eventually, deep in the bowels of the stadium, after wandering around for twenty good minutes, I came to the door with my name and Brent Butt's on it. I went inside.

Because the venue was an arena, this was not a conventional dressing room; it was a team locker room. While I was hanging my suit up on the clothing rack, I heard someone clear their throat. It seemed to come from the bathroom, so I gave a cursory "Hello?"

"In here," a voice shouted back. "Come on in."

I hesitated for a minute but then thought, *What the hell, maybe Brent needs a spotter*.

I went to the wet area of the locker room, walked past the line of toilets, through an open archway, and on the left and right were two communal showers. There were benches on either side. And it was there that I found Bruce Cockburn. Sitting on the bench. Fully dressed.

"Okay if I borrow your shower?"

Bear in mind I had never met this man.

"Of course," I said. And really, what else would one say to Bruce Cockburn in a shower?

"Good acoustics in here," he said. "Take a seat if you want."

And I sat down across from the legendary Bruce Cockburn and watched him rehearse. He is a guitar virtuoso who has played the greatest stages and theatres in the world. He's played all the big rooms, including, that day in Calgary, my designated bathroom. And that day he delivered his hits—"Lovers in a Dangerous Time," "If I Had a Rocket Launcher," "Rumours of Glory." It was one of the greatest concerts I have ever had the pleasure of attending. Besides which, when someone asks, "Have you ever seen Bruce Cockburn at Massey Hall?" I can say, "Yes, but have you ever seen him in your shower?"

No matter what happens tonight, I thought, *no matter how I do, no matter if we get a piece for the TV show or not, thirteen thousand people are going to see Bruce Cockburn play and we are going to raise a ton of money.*

After the show began, when I wasn't onstage, I was shooting for *RMR.* Everyone on the bill did a cameo. They were all happy to do so. The tsunami horror stories didn't stop coming, neither did the visuals. Everyone was just happy to be there raising money for victims.

We shot Sarah McLachlan, in jeans and a T-shirt, playing Ping-Pong with guys from the crew. And beating them. She is so beautiful and eloquent. In our interview, I offered to give fifty bucks to tsunami relief if she would touch the tip of her tongue to

Rossland, BC: We wrapped many of our road adventures with crowd scenes like this one. We called them "bumper shots." They were always infused with local pride. I loved that viewers in every part of the country would watch and say, "That reminds me of home."

Taking part in "The Train of Death." Don't let the name fool you. It's far worse than it sounds.

Getting my beard of bees on, with help from the Bee Dude, Mark Winston. I can't tell you what's worse, the feeling of all those bees crawling on your skin or the horrifying sound they make.

Sophie Grégoire made a great first impression. "Justin," I told her husband, "you married above your station."

Paul Martin was the first prime minister to show us around 24 Sussex Drive. The place was falling apart. Later we would travel to Canadian Tire to purchase plastic for the windows at the back of the house.

Sharing time on-camera with Chrétien was like being onstage with Eugene Levy or
Martin Short. He was really that good.

Stephen Harper was the strangest, most impressive prime minister I ever met. He was
very funny in person, but he went to great pains to hide it.

I've collected Canadian prime ministers over the years, but more importantly I met every member of Rush.

With Geddy Lee shooting a "Celebrity Tip" on toboggan safety. Typical rock star, he arrived early, sober, driving his own car and was incredibly polite.

Hanging in a hangar with Alex Lifeson. We went indoor sky diving. Believe it or not this is not the most absurd thing Lifeson has worn in his rock and roll career.

Waiting for my turn on the drums behind the late, great Neil Peart, one of my childhood heroes.

With some Barenaked Ladies and Bruce Cockburn backstage at a fundraiser for Tsunami Relief. The number of benefits Canadian musicians do is astounding.

When I was asked to host a show in someone's living room, it sounded a little sketchy—until I heard Sarah McLachlan was on the bill too. (Not to mention Rod Stewart and Robin Williams and Chantal Kreviazuk . . .)

I won't say I had a spiritual experience in Algonquin Park, but it was close. Even before I laid eyes on a bear, I'd had about as perfect a day as anyone could.

her nose. She tried her best; it was worth the cash. She also showed the country, without prompting, that she can cross only one eye. As I said—elegant.

I told the Barenaked Ladies I would be entering their dressing room with a camera in ten minutes and that they should just act the way they normally would backstage. When I came in with the camera rolling, they screamed, "Hey Rick! Come in!" and started to jump up and down. Which was flattering, to say the least. Also, the Barenaked Ladies were, in fact, naked. Stark naked with bags of chips and milk bottles hiding their bits. Great gag. For months after the segment aired we received mail from people complaining they had been subjected to a cavalcade of penises in prime time. I assure you, none of the Ladies' penises were seen—or indeed, harmed—during the taping of that show.

These experiences at benefit concerts large and small over the years have shown me time and time again that in this country it is the musicians who always step up when needed.

Why is that? It's my theory that no Canadian who makes a living in show business—whether they are a global superstar or eking out a living in pubs on George Street—takes it for granted. When I think of the biggest stars I've shared air with, all their egos combined wouldn't match your standard-issue junior cabinet minister in a minority government on Parliament Hill.

And when I say stars, I mean some of the biggest stars in the galaxy.

I mean the members of Rush.

At one time or another they all appeared on *RMR*.

That members of this iconic band would even agree to do it says so much about who they are. They are the opposite of flashes in the pan. They have had one of the longest, most impressive careers in popular music. The band was formed the year I was born. By the time I was five they were producing radio hits in both Canada and the United States. Three goofy Canadian kids from Toronto who'd disappointed their parents by forming a band went on to sell forty-two million records worldwide.

And their fans? I don't think the word *fans* does them justice. *Disciples* might be more apt. There are families in South America who have exactly three sons, named Geddy, Neil and Alex. After Alex is born you get the vasectomy. Why carry on when you have completed the perfect set?

Across North America, the Rush logo has been tattooed on more men of a certain age and girth than any Japanese symbol for wisdom.

Their fans love them. For them, Geddy Lee is the greatest vocalist in the world, Alex Lifeson the greatest guitarist, and drummer Neil Peart is just a god. Fans of Neil Peart have been known to cross themselves while singing his praises.

And the thing about the guys in Rush is—and everyone who has ever known them reports this—they never changed.

When we were making up the list of guests we wanted for the "Celebrity Tips" segment on the *Mercer Report*, Geddy Lee was near the top. We had him down as a long shot. But to quote the great Ontarian winemaker Wayne Gretzky, you miss 100 percent of the shots you don't take.

I tracked down a number and called. I resisted the temptation to gather the writers around and put the call on speaker so everyone could hear his voice. Honestly, at this point it was exciting just to hear a voice mail greeting that said, "Hi, this is Geddy. Leave a message."

So I did. "Would you like to do a Celebrity Tip?"

And this is the amazing thing: he called back about an hour later.

"I like those tips," he said. "What will I do?"

I thought about it. This is a man who could spend his winters in Saint-Tropez, hot-tubbing with Elton John and Liza Minnelli—but no, he's sitting here in Toronto, complaining about the snow, watching the CBC and returning his calls personally.

"You will teach Canadians how to toboggan safely," I said.

"Ha! I love it. I'm in," he said.

It was a hell of a negotiation.

Two days later, on a very cold Saturday morning, a small crew was assembled in Toronto's Riverdale Park, home to a famous toboggan hill. We were waiting for Geddy. And it was cold. I remember it as one of the coldest shoots I was ever on—and I have fifteen years of cold shoots under my belt.

In true rock and roll fashion, Geddy showed up a few minutes early, completely sober and driving his own car. He came over, shook everyone's hands, we talked about the weather, and then we got down to business.

Very quickly. He knew the script. He had come prepared.

There were plenty of kids tobogganing that morning. And Geddy and I were talking about how different kids were these days when it came to the media. When was a kid, if I saw a TV or film crew, I would be like a moth to the flame. I would have been in their face and in their way in a heartbeat. But kids today don't get worked up over such things. Geddy and I bonded like two old fellas over this "kids today" chat. He was an incredibly down-to-earth guy and loved the idea of being the face of toboggan safety.

And standing at the top of the hill in his parka and toque, he looked every bit the part of a hoser father watching over his kids and not one iota the front man of a world-famous band.

Eventually a few kids, who were probably twelve or so, came over to check out what it was that we were up to. The glamorous sight of two cameras and a director and a few grips wandering around piqued their curiosity.

I wasn't entirely surprised by this. From the very beginning of *RMR*, hungover teachers the nation over began to use segments of my show in the classroom. These kids knew who I was. They appeared happy to meet me.

One of them had a digital camera and Geddy offered to take pictures of the kids and me. The lead singer of Rush was offering to be the photographer. Clearly, the man had a monster ego.

When Geddy had finished taking the pics, I pointed to him and said to the kids, "Let's get one with this guy too." And I asked a member of our crew to take it.

The kids went along with me. I guess they decided to humour the old man.

The bit was a gas to shoot, and Geddy was a total sport, sliding down the hill and having to hoof it up again. And again. And again—these things are never simple. And he repeatedly turned down our offer to have a production assistant pull his toboggan back up the hill for him. For Geddy, it was a Canadian point of pride to walk his own toboggan to the top of the hill.

At the top of the hill he delivered his lines with a great deadpan delivery: "Remember to always keep your hands and feet in the toboggan. And then let out a scream and don't be afraid to give 'er."

And with that he would hurtle down the hill—his famous screaming vocal reverberating over the entire Don Valley.

His final line in the toboggan video became an *RMR* classic. Standing next to a metal toboggan, he said, "And remember, those of you with a metal toboggan: *never* touch it with your tongue."

And then, of course, he did just that. And the sucker froze. For real.

His final line was delivered without much help from his tongue, his ability to enunciate reduced to "I'm gepppy leee, and I luppb wintaaar."

Only in Canada.

7

The Spirit of Television

The following year Rush guitarist Alex Lifeson agreed to come on the show, not for a Celebrity Tip, but as my date.

First Geddy, now Alex? I was like a groupie working my way through the ultimate Canadian prog rock trifecta.

The "date" concept was exactly that: it was a "getting to know you" day. I would pitch it thusly: Imagine, if you will, that we both swept left and now it's time to step away from our devices and see if the chemistry is there. It's time to see if we are going to seal the deal.

Alex agreed to be my date.

We met for the first time at Billy Bishop Airport, on Toronto Island, a stone's throw from downtown Toronto. My plan for the date was pure rock and roll excess. We would charter a private plane and whisk this world-famous rock star off to an exotic destination for a glamorous, fun-filled day he would never forget.

Of course, we didn't quite have the budget for that, so instead of chartering a Learjet and flying him to St. Barths, I chartered a prop plane to take us the seventy-two kilometres to the honeymoon capital of Southern Ontario, Niagara Falls. The Canadian side, obviously.

Take it from me: when trying to impress a rock god who has seen and done it all, bring 'em to the *Ripley's Believe It or Not!* "odditorium" in Niagara Falls. They have the shoes of the world's tallest man. And you can look at them!

I met Alex in the small hangar, and we chatted for probably ten minutes before the rest of the crew arrived. He's a very pleasant guy with a ready smile. And as far as chemistry goes? It was great. I might say it was epic. We got on famously. He laughed at my jokes, asked how I was doing, asked about my feelings. If this had been a real date, I would have been thinking, *This is the one.*

But I very quickly realized Alex has chemistry with everyone. When Don showed up, he and Alex connected over live concerts Don had shot in the past. John had produced *The New Music* TV show, so they had plenty in common. They were a house on fire. And Alex also managed to have a great connection with the pilot and the woman who worked the charter desk. We were all thinking, *This is the one.*

And I could tell he was genuine. He wasn't *acting* like he was happy to be there; he *was* happy to be there. So, with microphones on, we boarded the plane like rock stars. Big ones! Like Buddy Holly or the Big Bopper big. We were headed to the Falls.

WE DID HAVE A REASON for heading to the Falls, and it wasn't just the pickled pigs' heads at Ripley's.

A new attraction had recently opened that was screaming to be promoted. I wanted to get in on the ground floor and get it on TV before it swept the nation and became an international sport.

It was indoor skydiving.

The idea sounded completely absurd to me, and to Alex as well. But as an admirer of the absurd, he agreed to give it a shot.

Indoor skydiving was launched when some entrepreneurial visionary realized that if you got an old jet engine and buried it in the floor of a building, pointed in the right direction, you might just have a world-class attraction. When fired up, the jet engine emits a huge blast of air straight up towards the ceiling; and when you jump into that stream, wearing a combination flight suit/squirrel costume, you can float. You can fly. It seems like you're skydiving.

They had staff who could float, twist, twirl and do somersaults, all while floating in the air. They didn't look comfortable up there—they looked like they were born there. It looked easy.

As we got dressed, we talked about Alex's career. The highs and lows. Because Rush were a seminal band in the late '70s, there are many photographs of them wearing some of the tightest spandex outfits ever engineered. Alex had great fun looking at the pictures I brought and a great time talking about the fashion crimes in his past.

He only became uncomfortable when I asked him what it was like not just to have made a career of playing the guitar, but to be universally recognized as one of the best players of all time. It wasn't just some kids banging their heads in their basements who said he was the best; most of his colleagues did as well.

For the first time he looked like he wanted to crawl into a hole and disappear.

This is a guy who is incredibly comfortable in his shoes. Ask him to go on an absurd adventure, he's comfortable. Ask him to do a silly slow-motion walk-on wearing a squirrel costume, he's comfortable. Discuss what it's like to be so bloody talented and universally admired, and he suddenly wants to be anywhere else on earth.

The more I talked about his abilities as a guitar player, the more eager he became to do something he didn't know how to do at all. And so, we went indoor skydiving. And we laughed more than I had laughed in a very long time.

Turns out indoor skydiving is not easy. Almost every time we threw ourselves into the jet stream, we would get shot across the room like hockey pucks in a slapshot contest. Occasionally one of us would catch the current and float all the way to the celling, where we would lose control, fall out of the stream and get spiked into the ground so hard, you'd swear we were trying to pick a fight with the floor.

Luckily there was padding. Lots of padding. In fact, every inch of the indoor skydiving chamber is padded.

As a person who has skydived before, I can report that the great thing about that pastime is the view. As you may imagine, when you're five thousand feet in the air the view is unparalleled. And when your chute opens and you're floating around up there, it's incredibly peaceful. Indoor skydiving is not that. The roar of the jet engine is the opposite of peaceful, and the view is not so much tranquil as it is reminiscent of the padded cell in *One Flew over the Cuckoo's Nest*.

After an hour of being slammed around like the bad guys in a WWE grudge match, we called it a day.

It was a great time. And we were getting gradually better, but we couldn't dilly-dally. The day wasn't over, and neither was the date. We limped to the change room to remove our squirrel suits.

A funny thing happened in the change area. A guy was there, an employee, who had arrived late. He didn't know anything about the shoot. He looked at the camera and looked at me and asked if we were local news. "No," I said, "it's a national show. It's called *Rick Mercer Report.*" There was zero reaction. Which is fine. "It's on the CBC," I said. Again, no reaction.

And then I pointed my thumb towards Alex—a winded Alex with a red face and hair going every which way—and said, "See that guy? He's in Rush."

The dude nearly fell over. His eyes bulged out, his jaw went slack, and he spoke but barely any words came out. "Geddy?"

Alex gave him the thumbs-up.

The guy had to sit down and catch his breath. I told him it was Alex Lifeson.

When you are throwing yourself into a wind chamber with a dude, it's easy to forget what it is that person does for a living. And it's easy to forget just how big they are. Rush are not just a band. They're not even an institution. They're like the Rockies. Even if you have never gone to Banff for a gawk yourself, you are well aware of just how big a deal those mountains are, not just to Canadians but to people all over the world. Although mostly Japan. In Canada there is no avoiding the Rockies. And if you grew up in this country, you didn't avoid Rush.

Alex took a selfie with the happiest, most impressed human being I have ever seen and we headed to our plane.

THE DATE WAS NOT over. We were going to fly back to the big city and end up at Alex's College Street bar, the Orbit Room, a Toronto live music institution. Although when we were walking across the tarmac towards the plane, I noticed that Alex's limp, unlike mine, had not gone away.

"Are you okay?" I asked.

"It's fine," he said.

"Are you sure?" I said. "You want to call it a day?"

"Nope, let's go to the bar."

And we did.

And he had a surprise for me. On a big TV screen, they had set up the Rush *Guitar Hero: Warriors of Rock* video game. The game allowed players not just to play along with Alex, but to play *like* him, like a guitar god. And I did—not just like a guitar god, but *with* one as well. The kid who bounced on the bed and pretended to be a rock star was in heaven. Millions of Rush fans would be in awe. They would wonder how one mortal man could be so lucky—me, obviously, not Alex.

The day ended with pints at the bar. And then Alex announced he was going to go ice his knee. I looked down. I could see from his jeans it was not the same size as the other one. Lord, it was swollen. Up until then, the only time it had come up was because of his slight limp on the tarmac.

Oh my god, I thought, *I've torn Alex Lifeson's ACL. This is how it ends. I will be killed by a Rush fan who had tickets for an upcoming tour that was cancelled because I took Alex indoor skydiving. And people will say, "Serves him right."*

We said our goodbyes. But we stayed in touch. In fact, I stayed in touch with him daily. I stayed in touch to a point where he must have wondered what was wrong with me. I'm surprised he didn't file a restraining order. I finally stopped calling when he said, "Oh, I got the all-clear on the knee. They did a scope, it's all good. The tour is still on."

Rush was intact. Finally I would get some sleep.

———

IF I THOUGHT GEDDY LEE was a long shot, I knew Neil Peart would be damn near impossible to get on the show. In fact, I would have bet money that we wouldn't.

Neil was the main lyricist for Rush. And while the band was famous for its prog rock musical ability, fans of Rush were obsessed with the lyrics. And therefore they were obsessed with Neil.

But Neil Peart was always an intensely private person. He was never comfortable with the "star" part of being a rock star. He was "the quiet one." People assumed he was the introvert in the band. And that, as the writer of those lyrics, he was the intellectual. But Neil Peart had every right to want to lead a simple or quiet life away from any media spotlight.

It's obviously not my story to tell, but it's one that is well known and one that he eventually told himself in his memoir, *Ghost Rider: Travels on the Healing Road*.

In the late '90s, arguably at the height of Rush's fame, Neil's daughter was killed in a car accident. One year later he lost his wife to cancer. He told his bandmates, "Consider me retired." Being best friends, they took him at his word and Rush closed down. Neil then got on his motorcycle and went for a drive—for two years nobody knew where he was. Friends would receive periodic postcards from South America or northern Canada. This is the only way anyone knew where the road was taking him.

Eventually he did resurface and agreed to get off the bike and get back behind the drum kit. Rush was back in business. There was a new record and a world tour. But there was a slight change. From then on there were no interviews with Neil. He no longer partook in that aspect of the rock star world. When the band rolled into Copenhagen, London or Dallas, Neil left the press to Geddy and Alex. There was going to be no opportunity for questions about his personal life or loss.

Of course, Geddy and Alex more than made up for it. They crackle in interviews. They are both gregarious and self-deprecating. And they are the oldest of friends. In interviews, Geddy is dry and Alex is giddy.

But of course, because Neil stopped doing interviews, it made him, in the eyes of Rush fans, all that more intriguing.

When I first shot with Geddy I asked him if he thought the other two would ever do the show. "Call Alex," he said. "He's goofy. He's always up for fun."

When Alex was on the show I asked him if he thought Neil ever would do it.

"You can ask him," he said. And added, "It's hard."

I interpreted that exactly the way it was intended. Alex was saying, "Don't take it personally."

But the following year, we did ask. After all, Geddy and Alex had done the show; it would be rude to avoid the drummer. To ask Neil was simply a courtesy. But we assumed it was no more than that. An invitation that would be politely turned down.

I had another reason for asking, and this was personal: *he was Neil Peart*! I harboured secret fantasies about being a drummer when I was in junior high. I took lessons. I joined the band at school and played percussion. My friend Timmy and I would sit in his room and listen to Rush records on repeat. Not for the band—back then I wasn't fussy about the band. We listened for the drumming.

Neil Peart was one of my childhood gods. And not just mine. He is universally respected as one of the greatest drummers ever.

He said yes.

We asked if Neil would give me drum lessons, and he said yes.

I don't know if I can adequately express what that was like to receive that answer. We weren't prepared, that's for sure. Sure, we have all bought a lotto ticket, but just because it's on the fridge you don't start planning how to spend the money. That would be insane.

With that yes from Neil we had just won the lotto. This man, who famously wouldn't talk to *Rolling Stone* magazine, was going to make time for us? John Marshall and I could not believe it. We went into overdrive. A drum lesson would be amazing. But where? How? What other gags? He loved motorcycles; I had a motorcycle licence.

We concocted a day with Neil where we would ride bikes—his ride being a professional road monster, mine a scooter. And his drum kit would be substantial and mine would be less so. He would be macro and I would be micro. I couldn't wait to be emasculated by this rock god.

It was suggested by his people that the drum lesson happen at Cherry Beach Sound, a studio in Toronto. Neil was working there on a project. John agreed to meet a representative of Rush there for a location scout. The studio is a storied Toronto institution, a go-to facility for national and international recording stars. It is also lit exactly like a recording studio—not exactly ideal. Think moody and subtle and not for TV. From a TV perspective, it was boring. And the drum kit that was there for our use? It was an excellent kit, but visually it was, at best, fine.

But beggars can't be choosers, so John was going through the heart-crushing motions of planning to make it work. When Neil Peart walked in.

This was unexpected. Not just for John, but for everyone at the studio. He was just popping in to pick something up. It was a fluke.

John was introduced to Neil.

"Is this going to work? For the lesson?" asked Neil, referring to the studio.

John decided to push for a plan B.

"Not really what I was hoping for," John said. And he began to explain. "Ideally, if you're going to teach Rick a lesson, it would be good if you both had kits, so you could be side by side. There's not a lot of room for that here."

Neil got it immediately.

"Right, we need a big space. And you want Rick on a small kit and me on a bigger one."

"Exactly," said John.

And then Neil turned to his guy. "Where's my touring kit—in the warehouse or in Los Angeles?"

The guy's eyebrows went up. "Um, that's in storage in Los Angeles."

"Let's bring it in," said Neil.

Well, the day had just got a lot brighter for John. Anyone who has seen footage of Neil Peart live knows his touring kits are not big, they are *huge*. They are works of art. There are more cymbals, drums and doohickeys in a Neil Peart drum kit than there are players in a symphony orchestra.

And then Neil said, "We can shoot it in the Batcave." Referring to Rush's private warehouse. Which is exactly what we did.

Weeks later, I met Neil at a nondescript urban location. I faced the camera and said, "Who among us has not considered a career as a rock star? Who among us has not sat back in awe at an awesome drum solo? Well, today I try a bit of both, as I get a lesson on drum solos from one of the greatest drummers, and one of the greatest rock stars, of them all. Please welcome, from Rush, Neil Peart."

The camera panned over to find Neil, in black leather, standing next to his beautiful large motorcycle.

He explained to me why there was a bike. That when he's not playing drums he's riding motorcycles. Neil's love of motorcycles came from a love of being on the road. In the old days, when Rush would tour, he would get the bus to stop a hundred miles (160 km) outside of a city and he'd ride a bicycle for the remainder of the trip. It awakened in him a desire to see more of Canada, the United States and elsewhere on two wheels. And for the last several tours he actually travelled by motorcycle. He slept in the tour bus, but rode his motorcycle to the next destination. In the final ten years he put two hundred thousand miles (320,000 km) on his motorcycle. The circumference of the earth is twenty-five thousand miles (40,000 km). Between epic drum solos, this man went around the earth eight times.

And then he said, "Before we play, we ride." And he threw me a helmet.

We shot a classic two-motorcycle travel scene. It was straight out of *Easy Rider*—Neil on his big, beautiful bike, me on a Vespa scooter. Let the emasculation begin!

We arrived at an unmarked warehouse on the outskirts of Toronto—unmarked, but it did have a special ramp designed so that motorcycles could drive onto the floor. Inside this building were the Rush archives and, on that day, one of the world's most famous drum kits. It was *gold*!

Welcome to the Rush Batcave.

Turns out all that gold on Neil's drums was real. It was literally a gold-plated drum kit.

My kit was also there. It was not dissimilar to the one I once owned when I fancied myself a drummer. That was back in grade eight. Compared to Neil's, mine was decidedly pre-pubescent.

But as I said, "It's not what you've got; it's how you use it." And then, as an afterthought, "But I don't know how to use it."

And then I asked Neil if he could "show us a few things."

He sat down at the kit and told me to count him in. All my life I had waited for this. I brought my sticks together and counted the master down: "One, two, three, four . . ."

And he was off. For our own viewing pleasure. We watched a Neil Peart drum solo. The kind of thing people all over the world would kill to witness in person. He was doing it for an audience of three: me, John and Don. And one Rush warehouse employee.

I glanced at John, and he glanced at me—we both knew how special this was. Neil's sticks were flying over the kit. Every drum was utilized. It was wild, yet flawless. It was uniquely Neil Peart.

He ended with a flourish. And then it was time for the lesson. This is when grade eight dreams crash into middle-age reality.

Yes, I had dreamed of this moment when I was in junior high. But that was a long time ago. And like everything else in my life in the interim, I didn't do my homework. Story of my life. I was woefully unprepared.

My actual drum instructor had been a well-known Newfoundland musician by the name of Dr. Don Wherry. He was a percussionist with the symphony orchestra. He had many students over the years, and I was not one of the best. I was not in the top ten percent, or the top fifty. I was, and this is no exaggeration, probably dead last. I loved the drums, but very quickly I knew I had no real affinity for them. And here I was, about to play drums with not just the best guy in the room, but one of the best on the planet.

But there being no dignity in show business, I began to play.

I did a little solo, and he did a larger one. I did a little more, and he did something I didn't know was humanly possible. I tried a little flourish that kind of worked and he shouted, "Beautiful!" and looked genuinely happy for me. He started giving me tips. Encouraging me. Giving me a confidence I genuinely never thought

I would muster in his presence. Never mind the gag element of the shoot, he was a good teacher.

Between breaks we talked about his start. His parents bought him drum lessons when he was thirteen. But until he showed he was serious, they would only invest in the little rubber practice pad that all students start out with. Without a drum kit he would line catalogues up on his bed and pretend they were cymbals and drums. He spent hours "beating the ink off the magazines," he said.

"What's that boy doing in his bedroom with the Sears catalogue?" I shouted. "He's been in there for hours."

"Beating the ink!" he answered.

"Is that what they're calling it now?"

We discussed his lyrics. And I touched on a sensitive subject: the drummer stereotype. To put it mildly, the drummer is usually not the songwriter in the group. Drummers are never portrayed as the intellects.

He responded by asking, "What does a drummer get on his IQ test?"

"What?" I said.

"Drool."

I delivered a rim shot.

They kept coming.

"What's a drummer use for birth control?"

"No idea."

"His personality."

Rim shot.

"What do you call a drummer with half a brain?"

"What?"

"Gifted."

Double rim shot. We were suddenly a vaudeville act.

And then it was back to the lesson. We were going to end by playing "Tom Sawyer" together. A song Geddy Lee has described as Rush's defining song of the '80s. A song that many people say defined the '80s.

Rush's fan base always skewed male—not entirely, but the percentages don't lie. And I don't believe there is a man in this country who has not at some time played the air drums to "Tom Sawyer" on a textbook, a countertop or a steering wheel. It has an insanely recognizable hook that builds to an amazing solo. You can't help but bang your head and beat the ink when this song plays.

I had listened to nothing but this song for days leading up to this shoot. If I was going to look pathetic to the legions of amateur drummers in this country who would give an arm to be in my position, I was at least going to try my very best.

We counted ourselves in and the track began to play. Geddy Lee's vocals filled the warehouse. I was keeping the beat, but Neil was on fire.

And then, suddenly, lights—actual rock and roll lights—began to flash on and off. Neil looked over at me and laughed. He looked and sounded like he was onstage in front of ten thousand screaming fans.

A good showman will always have something up his sleeve, something special for the finale. But the lights and the strobe were just the beginning. As his drumming became more and more complex, his entire drum kit began to *revolve*! I couldn't believe my eyes. It was spinning in circles. No wonder he wanted the kit brought in from Los Angeles.

I knew the end of the song was approaching, and all I wanted to do was end on the right note—hit the cymbals when the song ended. I prayed to the rock gods and they delivered. We both hit the cymbals at the right time and together.

And then, suddenly, *blam*! Explosions! Smoke and flames roared out of Neil's kit. There was pyro.

What a legend.

He leaned over and shook my hand and said, "Well done. Good lesson." Music to my ears.

I looked at the camera, nodded towards him and said, "World's greatest drummer." And I meant it.

That was in March of 2010. I never saw Neil Peart again.

I bumped into Geddy a few times in Toronto, and it seemed for a while like I was bumping into Alex every time I turned around. They really are just a couple of down-to-earth, goofy Canadians.

When the band announced in 2016 that they were taking a break from touring, it was hardly a surprise. Acts of a certain vintage are allowed to take breaks. And drumming is hard on the body.

OVER CHRISTMAS IN 2019 I received a gift from someone I had done some work for. It was unexpected and a little over-the-top. It was a bottle of vintage sherry. I felt terrible because I suspected it was expensive and I knew it would never get opened. I googled the product and what I read was far worse than I expected. Not only was it expensive, but it was described as "extremely sweet and cloying."

It dawned on me that I didn't know a single person I could regift this to. Except perhaps one: Alex Lifeson. He has a famous wine cellar and he's noted for giving vintage wines to charity. I took a picture of the bottle and texted him.

"Would you like this?" I wrote. "Honestly, I will never drink it."

He answered fairly quickly, "If it is an orphan, I shall find a good home for it."

I told him I'd drop it off in the next few days. He told me there was no hurry.

In the first week of January, I dropped the bottle off at his address. In the car on the way home, I heard that Neil Peart had died in California. Of glioblastoma.

Glioblastoma. That rare, horrible disease that has robbed so many families and robbed us of two of our greatest artists, Gord Downie and Neil Peart.

I doubt Canada will see the likes of Rush or the Tragically Hip ever again. Certainly, we will produce great bands, and we will produce great songwriters and singers. That will never stop. After all, we are the country that gave the world Joni Mitchell, Neil Young and Leonard Cohen. But will we ever produce another Rush or Hip, a band that sets up house in our collective heads like those bands did? I don't know. These are bands that are part of the psyche of Canada. And they continue to pick up new fans all the time. They will pass the test of time.

IN THE YEARS SINCE the show has wrapped, we still get email from people who watch us in reruns. Not too long ago I received a message from a man who said his son mentioned that he once saw me tobogganing in Riverdale Park. His son even had pictures somewhere on his computer and dug them out. Obviously, the kid hadn't looked at them in many years. When they both looked at the picture on the screen, they almost fell over. Not because I was there, but because standing next to his son was Geddy Lee.

The man included a picture of himself with his son. The man was about fifty-five and his son looked to be in his late twenties. The son had long hair, and in the time since I met him on the toboggan hill, his father's taste in music had clearly rubbed off. In the photo, father and son are proudly showing off their matching Rush tattoos. They got them on a road trip they took together to New Orleans in 2015. They went to see Rush.

8

Top Job, Lake Included

Prime minister of Canada. Can you imagine a better job?

I can't imagine wanting to run the affairs of any other country. We have so much going for us. And yes, while we have challenges, our problems are a walk in a national park compared to those of most countries.

When American presidents serve, they age dramatically, almost overnight. On any given day, the prime minister of Canada seems well rested.

Also, the job of prime minister of Canada comes with Harrington Lake, a stunning country estate in the Gatineau Hills in Quebec, a scant forty-five-minute drive from Parliament Hill. If you love Canada and you love a lake, this is about as good as it gets. Also, it's not just any lake; it's completely private. The only constituents nearby are loons, ducks and pike. And by loons, I mean those of the freshwater variety, not the type that make up a prime minister's voter base.

The estate has been wowing world leaders for a very long time. They simply don't make them like this anymore. If Elton John woke up tomorrow and ordered his people to go buy him the best Canadian cottage ever? Sure, he would end up with something spectacular, but not as nice as Harrington Lake.

The amazing thing is that Canadians don't really hear about Harrington. It's obviously on the public record, but prime ministers are very hush-hush about the place.

It has long been a dream of mine to spend a weekend at Harrington Lake. Ideally, there would be no prime minister present. In my dream someone just throws me the keys and tells me to make myself at home and check the date on the milk before drinking.

The only non-political staffer I know who has spent time at Harrington Lake is Jann Arden. She was there as a guest of Prime Minister Stephen Harper and his wife, Laureen. The Harpers rarely allowed Harrington Lake to be photographed because it is just too damn nice. You can't help but look like a lord of the manor with that house in the background. But once the gates are closed, it's 100 percent private. A prime minister can really let their hair down and be their true self.

For example, when Jann was there, the Harpers were serving schnapps that contained real gold flakes. They were literally drinking gold. I found this hard to believe but I googled it, and yes, it's a real thing. It's some concoction from Switzerland called Goldschläger—a schnapps flavoured with hints of honey, cinnamon and ostentation. It's the kind of aperitif a landlord would drink after a long day of evicting widows. It's not something you would see being served at the Conservative Party's annual stampede hoedown.

The Harpers worked like pit ponies to come across as a Tim Hortons–loving hockey family who wouldn't know a soup spoon from a spittoon, but at Harrington Lake they were drinking gold with Juno winners.

But it's not just the Tories who love the lake. In 2016 Justin Trudeau was the newly elected Liberal prime minister of Canada. He must have had a lot on his mind.

The CBC hired me that year to host New Year's Eve on Parliament Hill. It was set to be a big show, the kickoff for the Canada 150 celebrations marking 150 years since Confederation. Just before Christmas of that year, Johnny, Don and I travelled to Ottawa to shoot a holiday greeting with the PM that could be rolled into the live broadcast from Parliament Hill. When we arrived, a staffer greeted us and said the PM would be available shortly but was "hard at work" and needed some time.

Fair enough, I thought, *he is the prime minister. God knows what he might be dealing with.* Also, I could see into the office, and there was Trudeau, at his desk, sleeves rolled up, a look of consternation on his face. Occasionally he would put pen to paper, write something down, review it and look concerned again.

Fifteen minutes later Trudeau put the pen down and pushed his notes off to the side of his desk. Outside his office we said our hellos and agreed we would shoot the piece in another half-hour. "Feel free," he said, "to make yourself at home. You can move the desk, do whatever you need to do for the camera."

Certainly, there was a different vibe in this PMO than Stephen Harper's, where if you moved a chair, they were liable to pistol-whip you.

We moved the desk around to suit our shoot and got to work on our script. I had my notes printed out, and I did what I always do: lay the pages out side by side on a flat surface so I can run through them in my head. We also laid out fifteen recipe cards with trivia questions written on them. Part of this gag was going to involve my playing Trivial Pursuit with the PM. We needed to figure out the order of the questions.

Eventually Trudeau returned. I scooped up my notes and the now-arranged cards.

What followed was a pleasant shoot with the prime minister, in which he proved, without cheating, to be very good at Canadian Trivial Pursuit. The piece ended with him wishing the country a very happy new year. Piece of cake.

We didn't know it at the time, but he couldn't attend New Year's Eve live on the Hill because it was going to be cold and snowy and he had planned to spend the evening violating the federal Conflict of Interest Act on the Aga Khan's private island.

A few hours later, as we were driving to the airport, I pulled my script out of my briefcase and was about to put it in the van's garbage when something caught my eye. The words *Office of the Prime Minister* were at the top of a single sheet of paper. Below that was a handwritten list. Clearly, I had scooped this off the desk when I cleared it off before we shot.

Oh my god, I thought. *I've gone and purloined something from the prime minister's office.* I might have been in possession of state secrets. I might have been holding in my hands a document outlining the Trudeau government's priorities.

Well, it turns out it *did* contain priorities, but not the government's so much as his own.

It read:

HARRINGTON
Fireplace
Back Stairs
Sauna
Boats

Water's edge
Geese
Exterior
WiFi/Comms

And then, in very large, all-capital letters:

BEES!

Harrington Lake, its sauna, its boats, its geese and bees were rarely far from any prime minister's heart or mind. Politics is all about priorities.

I do not mean to suggest the job of prime minister is only desirable because of the cottage. Far from it. But sticking with a real estate theme, if countries were properties listed for sale, Canada would be about as desirable as they come.

As far as "location, location, location" goes, we cannot be beat. We have three oceans, a vast Arctic and a peaceful border with the neighbours. The neighbours did go a little cray-cray for a while, but as I write this their medication seems to be balanced.

Canada. The foundation is solid. The views are to die for.

And good-looking? I may be biased but there is insane beauty in every region.

EVEN WHEN I DON'T fancy a prime minister, I certainly have great respect for the office. That I have been able to ask every living prime minister how they felt about the job has been a singular thrill for me.

And while I have few qualifications, I am confident in my ability to determine whether or not a person has a sense of humour, whether they are truly self-deprecating or simply a two-faced monster.

I've met them all, and if there is any takeaway from this book, I can honestly say that Joe Clark, John Turner, Brian Mulroney, Kim Campbell, Jean Chrétien, Paul Martin, Stephen Harper and Justin Trudeau are all monsters. Terrible monsters.

That's my attempt at a Prince Harry–level bombshell revelation.

Truthfully, every prime minister I have met has been fascinating in their own way—they are all historic, we haven't had that many of them, and each came with their own baggage and inherent weirdness.

Politics is not an occupation for the normal person, and becoming the leader of a major political party is not something that can happen to you by accident. It takes hard work and mad skills—the exception being Justin Trudeau, who only had to remain upright. His becoming prime minister was predetermined the moment he was born on Christmas Day 1971.

In many ways Trudeau is like the Harry Potter of Canada's natural governing party. Powerful forces inside the Liberal Laurentian elite, forces we muggles could never understand, used magic and Quebec to give him the keys to the prime minister's office. No amount of blackface or condensation could stop that from happening.

But when the *Mercer Report* started in 2004, Justin Trudeau was not a political figure of any note. He was a private citizen wandering around, dropping hints that he might just have to run the country someday.

To be fair to the man, it's a big decision to embark on a meteoric rise. You must consider the impact it will have on those around you, and in Justin's case, his snowboarding time.

I had crossed paths with Justin socially over the years and had always found him nice enough. He struck me as a tad odd, but, I thought, how could he *not* be? He was as close as we have to royalty. His birth was front-page news.

As a young man visiting Jamaica, I was amazed to see that not only was Justin vacationing there at the same time I was, but that his every move was being documented in the newspapers. And Jamaica at the time was very used to A-list Hollywood stars hanging around on its beaches. Nevertheless, day after day his abs were above the fold.

My most telling interaction with Justin occurred in a bush.

It was a beautiful July night and I was in the backyard of a house in Rosedale—one of Toronto's toniest neighbourhoods.

I was not alone. The event was called "Barenaked in Rosedale," and it was a fundraiser featuring, as you may have guessed, the Barenaked Ladies.

I had been to a few fundraisers in my life, but nothing this exclusive. Walking through the backyard where the event was being held was surreal. I didn't know why I had been invited, but I was thrilled to be there. This was before I learned that at some fundraising events organizers try to paper the room—or in this case the yard—with "celebrities." And that was certainly the case on this night. Before I knew it I was standing at a small table draped in blue silk, enjoying both the company of a Grammy Award winner and my second aged Ontario cheddar tart with caramelized onions.

It was all for a good cause, of course, but I remember having no idea what the cause actually was. The backyard pool seemed to hold some clues. Inflatable lifebuoys were bobbing around in the water, and each one of them had a stick with a sign attached to it. Each sign bore a single word—*Diversity, Strength, Community,*

Teamwork, Empowerment, Hope. It was a salute to virtue signalling, and so it was no surprise that the guest speaker was celebrated private citizen Justin Trudeau.

And to his credit, Trudeau *was* a celebrity. Among the private citizens, the civilians with all the money, the ones who were expected to bid vast amounts in the silent wine auction, he was the one they wanted to meet. When he entered the garden fashionably late, the gold medallists, recording artists, Grammy and Juno Award winners, bestselling authors and certainly the TV monkeys like me paled in comparison.

He moved through the room as if he owned the place and we were his invited guests. And people were far more eager to shake his hand than anyone else's. It was a smorgasbord of selfies and infatuated ladies. *Poor fellow*, I thought. *He won't get to eat any tarts at all.*

It was a great night. The Barenaked Ladies were then—still are—hitmakers like nobody else. And that combination of Steve Page and Ed Robertson onstage together, harmonizing, is something to behold. Throw in Randy Bachman, the Philosopher Kings and Leslie Feist, and it was an astounding lineup in the most intimate of settings.

The master of ceremonies for the evening was *Canada AM* host Seamus O'Regan—and he introduced his dear friend Justin Trudeau to great applause. They hugged onstage and Seamus whispered into his ear, "These early mornings are killing me. I have to be in makeup in four hours. When can I be a cabinet minister?"

"Have patience," Trudeau responded. And then, switching sides to hug it out again, he added, "I'll be spending the winter at Whistler. I'll think about it then."

"Yes, *sensei*," Seamus responded, and then they bowed towards each another as if one of them was the Dalai Lama and the other was the host of a morning show. In that room, the gesture did not seem out of place.

It was a very good speech. Trudeau did a fine job of congratulating us all for coming, praised the organizers for their hard work and the owners of the home for the use of their garden. He mentioned that he was dedicating his life to serving Canada, and he managed to say every single word that was floating in the swimming pool at least half a dozen times.

There was certainly a buzz around him. And not only because of his celebrity-by-birth status. The political lay of the land had just changed dramatically. Paul Martin had just lost a general election, and that was decidedly not supposed to happen. Stephen Harper's Conservatives had just formed a minority government. The Liberal Party was for all intents and purposes rudderless. Martin was supposed to be around forever; now he was licking his wounds in the private sector. The Liberals were not used to being out of power, and there was a certain desperation in the air.

People were looking for a silver bullet, and in a party of tired old warhorses Justin Trudeau was certainly shiny and new. Trudeau was certainly enjoying the speculation around his future. All eyes were on him.

Much later that night, after a second encore from Barenaked Ladies and too many glasses of bubbles, I was returning from a visit to the world's nicest porta-potty (it had hardwood floors!!) when I heard a *pssst* coming from behind a tree. I looked and saw Justin Trudeau hiding behind some bushes. He waved me over, indicating that he wanted me to join him. He lifted a branch and revealed a tiny private clearing inside.

I know of only two reasons why a man might ask another man to join him in the bushes. Hopefully, this was neither of those. I discreetly wandered over and joined him in the brambles.

Turns out he was simply taking a break from selfies and wanted to make small talk. "How is the TV show doing?" he asked. "How are you?" And then he gazed directly into my eyes and asked, "Are you really happy?" This is exactly the kind of thing I have no capacity to handle. "Wow," I said. "Am I happy? That's a loaded question. I thought you called me in here to ask me to join you in serving Canada." A not-so-clever crack acknowledging all the attention he was getting.

He suddenly turned even more serious. He continued to look me directly in the eyes even more intensely. It was very unnerving. Then he placed his hand on my shoulder, squeezed it in a paternal manner and said, "No. When the time comes, if I ever have to ask you to step up and serve Canada, I will call you from my secret phone in Ottawa."

So it turns out there's a third reason a man might invite another man into the bushes: for an awkward encounter in which he reveals he is so delusional he believes he is destined to be prime minister.

But at the time, all I thought was, "Wow, this dude is nuts. And apparently, he has a Batphone."

Of course, *I* was the delusional one. Nine years later he became prime minister. And during his tenure in Ottawa, that call from the secret phone never came.

Although, just a few months after Barenaked in Rosedale, Gerald and I crossed paths with Justin again, this time fully clothed with President Clinton. It was one of the fanciest dos I have ever had the privilege of attending free of charge.

When former president Bill Clinton turned sixty, his charity, the Clinton Foundation, pulled out all the stops. I don't know if a living person had celebrated their birthday in a bigger or splashier manner. The Clinton Foundation called on Denise Donlon to produce a birthday celebration for Clinton in Toronto. It would be a fundraiser for the foundation's work in Africa, particularly pertaining to HIV and AIDS prevention and treatment.

Denise is a legendary figure in Canadian broadcasting. She was general manager of MuchMusic in its heyday, before she left to run Sony Music and then CBC Radio's English-language services. She's a business executive, author, television producer, public speaker and member of the Order of Canada. And in her youth she was tour manager for the hair-metal band Whitesnake.

She put together a mind-boggling lineup. Kevin Spacey, at the time one of Hollywood's biggest stars, was the master of ceremonies. Music was by James Taylor, Jon Bon Jovi and Sarah McLachlan. Comedy legend Billy Crystal would be appearing, and Paul Shaffer was the musical director.

We didn't plan on attending because tables started at twenty-five thousand dollars and topped out at two hundred thousand. But on the very day of the gala, Gerald got a call from Denise asking if we wanted a pair of tickets: She had two seats in the sold-out house that needed filling. It was very kind of her; she could have filled those seats with literally anyone. We were in. We donned black suits and headed on down to the Canadian Room of the Royal York Hotel to fete a former president.

I don't think I've ever seen so much money in one room. Every bigwig in the country seemed to be in attendance. Gerald was seated next to Canadian film legend Norman Jewison. I was next to former Ontario premier Mike Harris. Denise has a wicked sense of humour.

The music was incredible and the auction for charity was like nothing I had ever seen. The items on offer weren't four passes to Canada's Wonderland or dinner and some Leafs tickets. This was a whole other level. Up for grabs was a private dinner for ten with Bill Clinton at Nobu in New York—private jet included. Then there was a trip to London, England, and to Africa with the former president, also on a private jet. There were also pickup basketball games with Michael Jordan; dinner with Barbra Streisand; a hangout with Bono in Hawaii; numerous getaways to various Caribbean luxury estates; a piano that belonged to Diana Krall and Elvis Costello; and some of the best salmon fishing in the world at the Long Harbour Lodge in Newfoundland and Labrador.

In one night, in one room, they raised twenty-one million dollars for the Clinton Foundation.

Neither Gerald nor I bid on any items, but we didn't go home empty-handed. The memories were special—moments you never forget. Namely, Gerald took a leak between Jon Bon Jovi and the famous American political strategist James Carville, a.k.a. the Ragin' Cajun, and I hung out with an ex-Conservative premier.

Denise did press me into service for a little while; I was the "voice of God" on the microphone introducing Spacey and Crystal. That was more than fine with me. It brought me backstage, where I chatted with Paul Shaffer and Clarence Clemons. The famed saxophone player with Bruce Springsteen's E Street Band was there as a surprise; he would play "Happy Birthday" for Clinton.

Later, there was a small reception where we bumped into Justin, this time accompanied by his wife, Sophie Grégoire. This was the first time we'd met Sophie, and she was a treat. We were making small talk when we noticed an even smaller, perhaps even more exclusive reception happening in yet another room. A who's who of prominent Canadians—the sort of people you don't usually see lining up—were waiting their turn to get in. "What's in there?" Sophie asked.

Justin looked at their tickets and said, "That's a VIP reception with Clinton. You get your picture taken with him. We don't have that ticket."

Sophie looked at us, and then back at the line, and said, "I'm going to sneak in."

Justin looked aghast. "Sophie—you can't sneak in the line!"

"Of course I can," she said. "I used to sneak into the adult movies all the time when I was fourteen. It's easy; just look like you're supposed to be there."

And with that she wandered over and, as if by magic, seamlessly merged into the line.

Gerald said, "I like her."

I could tell that Justin was both horrified and insanely impressed. I concurred. "Justin," I said, "you married above your station."

He agreed. Sincerely.

Trudeau is the only prime minister I knew socially before he entered politics. Aside from the time in the bushes, we would on occasion cross paths on the speakers' circuit. I think once we had a beer in a hotel bar. Later on, when he began to publicly toy with the notion of running the country, both he and Sophie were guests on the show. He had not been elected yet, but he had become a legitimate public figure. They were my tour guides at the Quebec Winter Carnival, and she killed. As did he.

It was on that day that I thought for the very first time, *This guy might actually be able to beat Stephen Harper*. Which, of course, he famously did. Big time.

But by the time Trudeau took office as prime minister, I wasn't as keen to hang with PMs on TV. Times had changed. Or maybe I had. Either way, we never called the PMO looking for a date.

9

Paul's Turn

As finance minister between 1993 and 2002, Paul Martin was one of the most prominent members of Jean Chrétien's cabinet. Together, he and Chrétien achieved something that had never been done before: they convinced us that in order to right the fiscal ship, we would need to tack to the right. The belt would need to be tightened. And they admitted upfront that with the tightening, there would be suffering.

And Canadians bought into the plan. We accepted the pain. Some would say we got off on it.

Martin and Chrétien were an impressive team. But like so many great duos—Martin and Lewis, Simon and Garfunkel, Sonny and Cher—war eventually broke out.

It was a classic Shakespearean plot. Chrétien was the all-powerful king who ruled with impunity. But the forces around Martin became restless. They got the notion into their heads that it was time for the king to go. What began as a campaign of whispers eventually became all-out civil war.

In my final days at *This Hour Has 22 Minutes*, I remember being in the Air Canada lounge in Toronto when I saw not one, but two Chrétien cabinet ministers enjoying their quota of complimentary Chardonnay. Most Canadians, when confronted with the sight of cabinet ministers with a buzz on, would head the other way. I am the opposite. I go forward into the breach. I'm a front-line hero when it comes to boozy politicians.

It was an astounding interaction. After a few minutes of Hill gossip, one of the ministers—who shall remain nameless but had a face that resembled a bird—stated emphatically: "It's time for Chrétien to go. It's Paul's turn." I remember thinking, *How can she get that much lipstick on one glass?*

Her colleague, also nameless—he resembled a pug but with a thicker neck—had decided to move on from wine and was attached to the spigot of Captain Morgan.

"Paul's numbers are solid," he said. "The country wants Paul."

For those not entirely familiar with etiquette on Parliament Hill, know this: there is none. But there are a few rules. And one of them is that no cabinet minister in the history of Canada would state out loud that it was time for the boss to go, regardless of the circumstances. In Mulroney's final days, his approval rating was on par with polio and still his cabinet remained loyal.

Usually, when treason is entertained, it occurs in the quietest of ways in the most complicated of codes. It would never be said out loud, in the light of day, in the Air Canada lounge. And never in front of a comedian. I couldn't wait to call Peter Mansbridge. It was all very *Twilight Zone*-ish. What kind of lunatic cabinet ministers would take me, of all people, into their confidence on such an issue?

That's how open the rebellion was.

But what struck me as most egregious was the notion that it was "Paul's turn." Who gets such notions in their head? The

Liberal Party of Canada is one of the most successful democratic institutions in the world, not a tire swing hanging from a branch out behind the trailer. Not everyone gets a turn on it. Paul's turn? When's my turn? When's *your* turn? It doesn't work that way.

It's no wonder that Liberal lore (Chrétien's version) is that this open rebellion so enraged Madame Chrétien that it was she who decided that her husband should stick around for another term. Not to serve Canada but to frustrate Martin's open ambition. Whether this is true or not, it's a good story.

And so, Chrétien stayed. This gave Martin no choice, it was he who left and went back to Montreal. The band was forever broken up. The recently united Liberal Party was no longer. There was a serious fissure in the firmament. From that moment on, everyone toiling in the trenches of the Liberal Party had to declare whether they were a Chrétien loyalist or on Team Martin.

It's never good for the family when mommy and daddy fight.

The next few years were a time of great political upheaval in Canada. Chrétien, who had been prime minister for a decade, finally stepped down in 2003. Martin returned to the fold and won the party leadership handily, becoming prime minister. Meanwhile, the right wing finally put years of infighting and comic incompetence behind them and united under one banner. The movement's leader was Calgary-based economist Stephen Harper.

When Martin became Liberal leader and was sworn in as prime minister of Canada, he had the approval rating of a messiah. His future looked great. Accordingly, five months into his tenure he asked the Governor General to dissolve Parliament and set the table for a general election. The conventional wisdom was that Martin was unbeatable, a formidable political master, while Harper appeared at first blush to be cold, aloof and not that interested in the Canadian people—just the latest in a long line of hapless Conservative leaders who would soon disappear.

The Liberals were not worried. Pollsters predicted a bloodbath. Some went as far as to suggest that Martin would obliterate both opposition parties, putting them out of existence.

And then things went sideways. From day one of the campaign, Martin was on the defensive. Political campaigns are all about momentum. You win when you have the "big mo." Out of the gate, the Liberals were a no-go on the big mo.

Martin was simply not the candidate Canada had imagined. Whereas Chrétien could always be counted on to shoot from the hip and raise any room to the rafters, Martin's voice never rose much at all. Nor did his eyes, which were usually looking down at his notes. He lacked confidence, and some felt he lacked focus. True, the entire country perceived him to be one of the nice guys, but you know what they say about them.

A series of blunders rocked his campaign. The same people behind the Dump Chrétien movement, a gaggle of young politicos often portrayed as cocky frat boys, were in charge of a prime minister's re-election campaign. Clearly, the job was a lot harder than it looked.

When the dust settled, the Martin government was reduced to a minority. *Nobody* saw that coming. Harper had defied the odds, and was not only leader of the official Opposition, but now wielded a lot of power. Canadians had got to know him very well during the campaign, and where they once saw a cold, aloof man who didn't seem to care about Canadians, they now saw a cold, aloof man who didn't seem to care about Canadians but seemed pretty darn competent. A good-sized number of them could imagine him as prime minister.

The Liberals were on the ropes, but Martin, though wounded, was still prime minister, and I wanted him on the air. But just getting a few minutes with him wasn't enough. I wanted something that had never been done before.

On 22 *Minutes* we had scored a coup when Jean Chrétien agreed to sit down and shoot a segment with me at a Harvey's restaurant. I won't go into detail here because it's all been documented in one of my previous books. I will say, though, that regardless of what anyone thought of Chrétien as prime minister, to "work" with him was a pure pleasure, not only because of his legendary political instincts and skills but because of his comic timing. Sharing time on-camera with Chrétien was like being onstage with Eugene Levy or Martin Short. He was really that good.

But while the Chrétien piece was a hit, it also set the bar high. This time, if we were going to do a segment, we would need to trump Harvey's. No small task.

I called Scott Reid—Martin's right hand—and pitched him.

"Paul Martin is our new prime minister; we want to see him as prime minister. What better way to show the country that he's really in charge than to have him give me a tour of the prime minister's official residence?"

Not a lot was known about 24 Sussex Drive at the time. Canadians had long seen PMs walking in and out of the residence. We were used to seeing footage of Brian and Mila Mulroney with visiting dignitaries on the steps. And Canadians remembered when a disgruntled citizen broke into the house and Aline Chrétien came very close to braining him with an Inuit sculpture. But beyond that it was a bit of a mystery.

The Canadian prime minister's residence was not the White House, or even 10 Downing Street in London. It was a low-key home behind a very large gate. But no prime minister had given cameras full access, so this was our ask. We wanted to hang out with the PM, get to know him and get to know the house.

Reid said yes.

The political nerd in me was beyond excited. About Paul Martin, yes, but especially about 24 Sussex Drive, the official residence that had housed every Canadian prime minister since Louis St. Laurent. The exception being Kim Campbell, who, immediately upon becoming prime minister, called a cab to take her to the house. Unfortunately, by the time it arrived she had gone down to electoral defeat.

I don't know why historic real estate excites me, but it does. I love staying at the Château Laurier in Ottawa because it is a stone's throw from Parliament Hill. One foot inside the front door and you can hear the walls talking. A hundred and fifty years of political intrigue with MPs, rogues and senators will do that to a place.

I was excited to experience Sussex Drive for the very same reason. I wanted to gaze through the windows Pearson gazed through while pondering designs for the new Canadian flag. I wanted to stroll the grounds where Pierre Trudeau began his famous walk in the snow. I wanted to pee in the washroom that Diefenbaker, cursing his prostate, used to visit five to seven times a night.

We arrived at the house I affectionately called "the Two-Four." Before we stepped inside, John, Don and I posed for a selfie by the front door. A door that had been used by everyone from Nelson Mandela to Joni Mitchell. From Alan Eagleson to Colin Thatcher. The good, the bad and us.

We knocked and were greeted by a friendly young woman who welcomed us inside. "Paul's not here yet," she said. "You can look around; he should be here soon."

For the most part I don't care about protocol, and certainly not protocol for protocol's sake. But in all my years interacting with the people in Chrétien's office, they never referred to him by his first name. They referred to him as "the prime minister," as in "The prime minister kicked his TV in last night while watching the CBC news." They would never say, "Jean broke the TV again."

It was a little thing, but I brushed it off.

For anyone who has ever searched for an apartment to rent or a home to buy, you know the feeling of abject disappointment that can kick in the moment you step inside a residence. The listing looked good. The pictures were promising. You had high hopes. You felt it was worth a look, but now you realized immediately that you were wasting a chunk of your day.

At first glance, the Two-Four did not meet expectations.

The last people who spent any money on 24 Sussex Drive were the Mulroneys. Because this is Canada, it became a minor scandal when word got out that Mila Mulroney was "redecorating." This, even though the money spent on the refresh came not from the taxpayers but the Progressive Conservative Party. When Chrétien was elected prime minister, not only did he not redecorate, but he basically refused to let the National Capital Commission, the organization responsible for the building's upkeep, near the place.

And it showed.

In real estate circles there is an expression, "the house has good bones," meaning of course that if you can look past the outdated wallpaper and popcorn ceilings, it's a solid, well-built structure worth saving. At 24 Sussex the bones did not feel solid. If anything, they felt like they were in end-stage osteoporosis. The building might have been standing, but a strong wind could knock it over and shatter its hips like a beer bottle thrown off the CN Tower. It was suffering from benign neglect.

Upon entering, one couldn't help but notice the faded rug running up the somewhat elegant staircase. It was threadbare and its pattern was leopard skin. Something Cher would wear. Clearly, this was a relic from Mila Mulroney's redecorating binge. It looked like something out of a turn-of-the-century bordello.

The place needed more than a facelift, it needed a bypass.

In the living room we found one of Paul Martin's senior aides. A person we all knew to be one of the architects of his campaign. He was lying on the couch, typing on his BlackBerry, and greeted us as if we were old friends. We were not, but that was pleasant. Again, without being a stickler for protocol, I couldn't help wondering why he was lying on the prime minister's couch.

I swear I am not a prude; I have friends whose couches I have lain down on, but even then I take off my sneakers.

"Paul's on his way," he said. "So, what do you want to do?"

For the next fifteen minutes Don followed me around, rolling video as I went snooping. And I really did snoop. I opened cupboards, looked in drawers, checked out what books were on the end tables. Some of the footage had kind of a CSIS security camera vibe.

On-camera, the house does appear to be a bona fide mansion. The rooms are grand and sizable. And prime ministers famously get their pick of art from the Canada Council Art Bank, so the walls were dripping with impressive Canadian art, including masterpieces by the Group of Seven. A large Picasso hung in the dining room.

And you know what they say, nothing takes away the faint odour of black mould like a priceless painting.

We finished poking around just as the prime minister arrived. "Paul's here," one of his staff said, moments before he walked in the door.

"Welcome to 24 Sussex Drive," he said and shook hands with me, Don and John. "Can we get you anything?"

"Down-to-earth" is the expression that came to mind.

We sat down, and with cameras rolling, we started to chat. Seeing as everyone knew how the election had turned out, I figured I'd tackle the elephant in the room.

RICK: Hello, Prime Minister. Thank you for inviting me to your house.

PM: It's very nice to have you here.

RICK: It's a nice house.

PM: It really is.

RICK: Do you like being prime minister?

PM: I do. I really do.

RICK: So those people who ran your campaign . . . how many of them have you fired?

PM: Uh . . . none.

RICK: None?

PM: None.

RICK: They aren't running the country, are they?

Clearly, they were. Over his shoulder I could see a number of them, and they were not pleased with this line of questioning. They glanced at each other as if to say, "What's he talking about? We ran a great campaign."

Say what you want about Paul Martin, he was loyal to his people. But loyalty in politics was perhaps best summed up by US president Harry S. Truman, who said, "If you want a friend in Washington, get a dog."

All these young people who ran Martin's campaign were his friends, and he was theirs.

And then, as I am wont to do, I gave my guest the chance to say what he wanted to say. I lobbed him a softball. "Now that you are prime minister, what are you going to do?"

He got the answer out—he talked about how health care "was done"—which I interpreted as "it has been saved," as opposed to "it's dead and buried." He said young people were important, as were small cities and towns in rural Canada. He talked of a three-pronged approach.

It was the least convincing moment of our time together. The fact that he had to reach for an answer to an easy question, after a national campaign, was mind-boggling. His inability to knock a question like that out of the park had a lot to do with why he was leading a minority government. The fact that the people who ran his campaign were still in the Prime Minister's Office would ensure, I thought, that this would be his last term in office.

With the priorities of his government out of the way, it was back to the tour.

"Prime Minister, I looked around. I didn't see the pool."

"It's around the side," he said.

"Trudeau built that pool, didn't he?" I said.

"He did," the prime minister agreed.

"Do you use it?"

"Yes."

Did I sense a grimace? I could tell he was uncomfortable reminding Canadians that his house had a pool.

"Can I see it?"

There was a pause.

"Yes," he said.

And the tour continued.

We changed locations to the pool house. It was a nice pool, but hardly extravagant. When we saw it, I turned to John and said, "I should have brought my trunks."

I was silently considering how I would navigate getting into the pool in my underwear when an extraordinary thing happened. The twenty-first prime minister of Canada offered to loan me his swimming trunks.

Canada could be around another five hundred years, and I doubt that will happen again. Not every guy would give a guy in need his swim trunks. This was one laid-back dude. No wonder his staff felt comfortable lying around on his couch with their sneakers on.

I came to this house wanting to experience history, wanting to walk in the steps of prime ministers. Never did I think I would be squeezing my bare bum and no-no bits into a pair of the prime minister's shorts.

Like Pierre Trudeau before me, I dove into the pool.

Well, Trudeau dove. I did a cannonball.

For the rest of the visit, we covered topics of the day. We discussed how long a minority government could last. We covered Canada's exporting of badly needed flu vaccine to the States,

Martin's plan to reinvigorate our beef industry, and our relationship with Tony Blair, who if memory serves me was some sort of political figure in England.

We ended with a gag concerning the carving of Halloween pumpkins. And then it was time to go. On the way out the door, I offered him his trunks back. He graciously declined. "Keep them," he said. "You probably stretched the waist."

And keep them I did. For many years. They eventually left my home, fully laundered, in a bag of clothes destined for Syrian refugees.

O Canada.

Imagine having a country open its doors to you in your time of need and providing not only food and shelter, but a former prime minister's bathing suit.

It's called paying it forward.

10

Stephen Harper on the Downlow

Stephen Harper is the singularly most impressive politician I've seen in my lifetime. Not because of what he did or did not accomplish during his years in office. The impressive part is that he made it to office at all.

To be successful in politics, you need certain basic skills, the most important being the ability to talk to people. Also, it helps a heap if you like people.

A politician's journey begins on the doorstep. The ability to knock on a stranger's door and engage them in pleasant conversation is paramount. And this is not a one-time exercise. You must be able to do this over and over again, day after day, week after week.

If you ever find yourself seated next to a member of Parliament on a plane, chances are you will have a very pleasant conversation. Regardless of party, position or political persuasion, you will come away having enjoyed the company. Most MPs have this down to a science. They can feign interest in anybody, any time, on any subject. This is what they do. It is their superpower.

And the people who are good at it, the very successful politicians? They actually enjoy it.

The giants, the Jean Chrétiens, the Brian Mulroneys—they liked mixing it up with the masses, and they were equally at ease in the lunchroom of a fish plant or the boardroom of a think tank.

This does not describe Stephen Harper.

And this is not a class thing. I am not suggesting he prefers wealthy CEOs to assembly line workers. In his perfect world, he would avoid both. He would rather talk policy, quietly, with others of his kind. Preferably in a room with the blinds drawn.

The Stephen Harpers of the world are often successful, just not in politics. The fact he made it to Parliament is amazing. That he became leader of a party is astounding. That he became prime minister is another word that begins with *A*.

More than any other Canadian leader, Stephen Harper defied the odds on his way to the top. He's like that guy with no legs who conquered Everest. Sure, he proved you don't *need* legs to climb a mountain, but we all know it helps.

Most politicians try to come across as much more fun and down-to-earth than they really are. Harper is the opposite. He goes the other way. One of his speech writers reported that he would often highlight lines he thought were clever or funny. He would then tell the writer to remove them.

His image was: I don't want to be your friend; I want to be your prime minister. I am ready, willing and able to make the tough decisions. We all know the type. If he was smiling, he was probably preparing to evict someone.

For most politicians, being in front of a camera is second nature. Harper was never completely at ease in that space. Soon after he was elected in 2006, the then prime minister designate allowed reporters to tag along as he dropped his kids off at school.

The plan was to show the country he was just like any dad. Except when Harper said goodbye to his kids outside of the school there were no hugs or pats on the back. He awkwardly shook hands with both his daughter and son.

It was as emotionally charged and choreographed as an eastern European prisoner swap.

It was not his fault. He was just not cut out for that kind of photo opportunity.

Early in his tenure I had the chance to observe him outside of his natural habitat. I have to say his refusal to connect with people came very naturally to him.

It was March 2008. And it was about as far from the hallowed halls of Parliament as you can get: Yellowknife, Northwest Territories. The event was the Arctic Winter Games. Two thousand coaches, athletes and artists from as far away as Russia, Alaska, Greenland and across the Canadian North had arrived in the city for what promised to be the biggest Games yet. Which is exactly why the *Mercer Report* had landed in the sunny south of the circumpolar world. This was an event that was right up our alley. Mysterious northern sports and raw caribou awaited.

We arrived at our hotel just hours before the opening of the Games and were dragging our gear into the lobby when the manager came up to me and said hello. He was incredibly polite. He said, "Mr. Mercer, welcome to the hotel. If you need anything at all, please don't hesitate to ask."

I was blathering on about how excited we were to be there when he said, "If you have a moment, could I please introduce you to some of our staff?"

I looked over and there was a literal line of staff, perhaps five of them, dressed to the nines in various uniforms. He brought me over and introduced me to each one of them. The group was made up of representatives of the various departments, from the cleaning staff to the kitchen staff. They were all lovely.

After I'd inspected the troops, I told the manager I was a bit taken aback. In all our years on the road, I told him I'd never had a welcome quite like that. He then confessed that the prime minister was scheduled to arrive soon, that the welcoming party was for him, and that when he saw me come through the front door he decided to have a dress rehearsal.

I was the big guy's stand-in.

And at that moment, as if they were awaiting our cue, the doors to the hotel opened and RCMP officers flowed in. A minute later a motorcade pulled up to the front of the hotel. A black SUV came to a stop, the rear door was opened, and out popped the prime minister of Canada.

Harper, with an aide at his side, entered the hotel, deep in conversation. Together they marched across the room towards an open elevator. They stepped in and disappeared. The entire exercise took less than a minute. He met nobody. He made eye contact with nobody. The welcoming line awkwardly dispersed.

This is the dichotomy of Stephen Harper as prime minister. Chrétien or Mulroney would not only have taken the time to charm everyone in the welcoming line, they would have done a once-around of the lobby and then popped into the kitchen and said hello. Stephen Harper would have found that painful. It was not why he was there.

Later that evening we shot the opening ceremonies of the Games. The prime minister was front and centre. He welcomed the athletes and declared the Games open. In return he was given an over-the-top, rock star's welcome. It's not every day a prime minister travels to the North.

Once that was over, we went back to the hotel for a bite to eat. However, when we went to the small restaurant it was closed. We were about to walk away when a member of the prime minister's staff saw us and said we could grab a table inside. Turns out the RCMP had closed the room for security reasons; the prime minister was on his way to dinner and they were not allowing civilians into the room. Being regulars on the Hill, and having been on their campaign plane, we were, as they say, "known to police." We had clearance and were welcome to stay.

It was an education to watch Stephen Harper and his team have a quiet dinner in an empty restaurant. For starters, that's who was at the table—Harper, his people and no one else. It was very low-key. I couldn't help but wonder where the premier of the Northwest Territories was. Where was the local mayor? Where was the MP? Harper was all about work, not about ingratiating himself to the locals or the local riding association.

Also telling was his interaction with the waitress. I watched him place his order. He was polite and courteous, asked a couple of questions about the food. But that was it. There was no small talk. I don't think it occurred to him that, seeing as he was the prime minister, he might want to ask her how her day was going or whether she was originally from Yellowknife. Even a comment about the weather might have gone a long way.

Does he not realize, I thought, *that this is a big moment for that waitress? So much so that she might be telling this story for the rest of her life?*

"Did I ever tell you that I once had a conversation with the prime minister of Canada?"

"*Really?* What did he say?"

"He said . . . 'I'll have the soup.'"

That's a hell of a story. We should get the movie rights.

But this was Stephen Harper.

Those close to him reported that, while he was never comfortable with people when out in the real world, behind closed doors he could be funny and even self-deprecating. I don't know if that's true—how would I? I'm not a member of the inner semicircle. But I do know that when he put his mind to it, he could come off quite charming.

I know because a scant eight months after he was first elected prime minister, Team Harper, in a moment of clarity, decided they should engage in a charm offensive.

Nobody was more surprised than me—because they decided to do it on *RMR*.

We had shot with Prime Minister Paul Martin twice at 24 Sussex Drive. So it made sense that when Harper was elected, we put in the same request. In fact, we put the request in more than once. The response was always the same—no, thank you.

The third time we were lucky.

The ask was pretty clever, I thought. I would come to Sussex, and we would have a very straightforward interview, but the gag would be that the prime minister would be outrageously pleasant and kill me with kindness. He would lavish me with hospitality. I didn't need to explain why this was amusing. Not a person in the country could picture Stephen Harper being nice to any media personality, let alone me.

Why they said yes, I have no idea. But they didn't have to say yes twice. We headed to Ottawa.

We wondered if this was an indication of a change in the Prime Minister's Office. Were they now comfortable enough in their position to entertain the notion that maybe everyone wasn't out to get them?

Short answer? No.

The night before the shoot, we were all in Ottawa. John was having a coffee with a friend and got a call from the Prime Minister's Office. It was very direct.

"David Chan is not coming to 24 Sussex Drive."

Chan was an Ottawa-based freelance photographer. He was a ubiquitous figure on Parliament Hill. We rarely hired a photographer, but when we were shooting with someone big—Rick Hanson, or to a lesser extent a prime minister—we would hire a photographer. David was the go-to guy in Ottawa.

John had sent David's name to the RCMP a few days prior. They required the names of anyone on the crew so they could run a security check. It was just a formality. John, Don and I had been cleared many times over, and David would have been cleared more than us.

"Is there a security concern?" John asked.

"No, but David Chan worked for Paul Martin, so you'll have to find someone else."

And then the call ended.

I guess the charm offensive hadn't quite kicked in yet.

It was true that Chan had worked as Paul Martin's photographer (for the five minutes that he was in office), but if anything, that only indicated he knew his way around both a camera and Sussex Drive. It had never occurred to us that they wouldn't want someone in the house because they thought that person was a Liberal. What was he going to do, make the photos blurry?

So John had the unfortunate task of calling Chan and telling him he was being un-hired. No freelance work for you, sir. Not in this town. Not anymore.

Ottawa is by nature a partisan town, but under Stephen Harper, or the people around him, it had become hyper-partisan. In Toryland there was no sin worse than consorting with the enemy.

And there were many enemies. Some of them, apparently, were photographers. Who knows—there could be Liberal barbers out there too. Careful where you get your hair cut!

Conservative staffers were told to avoid socializing with Liberal and NDP staffers. They were told what pubs they should avoid. I had a friend who worked for the Conservative Party, and often when I was in town we would meet up for a drink. When the Tories were in opposition, he and I would always meet at Zoe's, which is the bar in the Château Laurier. This was about as convenient as it could get: I stayed in the hotel, and he worked a stone's throw up the street. After the Tories formed government, he would always suggest that we meet at an Olive Garden seven blocks away from Parliament Hill. When I arrived, he'd be in the back, behind a plant. It felt like we were having an affair. And in some ways, we were. Because I was on the CBC, having a drink with me was akin to a hate crime.

But here I was, about to go on a date, not with my old chum, but with the boss.

EARLY THE NEXT MORNING we pulled through the imposing gates. Twenty-four Sussex had a distinctly different vibe now that the Harpers were in residence. Both inside and out. Approaching the building, it was clear that a family with children lived here. There was a basketball net in the driveway, kids' bikes by the front door.

And inside? Well, let's just say the person who greeted us at the door didn't refer to the prime minister as "Stephen," and there was nobody lying on the couch.

Harper always had a team of young, very dedicated staffers with him. This was not new. Prime ministers and cabinet ministers have always attracted staff that will look up to them as if they are a combination of Winston Churchill and Albert Einstein. But Harper's staff took this to a whole new level. Harper wasn't surrounded by eager young idealists so much as child soldiers who had pledged fidelity to their jungle lord. They were aggressive out of the gate.

There were many questions. "What exactly are you doing?" "What words are you going to be saying exactly?" "When can we see the script?"

The answers being "I don't know," "I don't know" and "There isn't one."

This didn't worry me. The prime minister had agreed to this shoot and that's all that mattered. And as far as giving them a script went? I may not be Linden MacIntyre, but I had some standards. I'd die before I did that.

The vibe from these staffers, right out of the gate, was that of barely camouflaged hostility. I knew what was going on. Politicians, for the most part, have thick skins. The same is true of the senior staffers and chiefs of staff. The young ones, the junior staffers, on the other hand, are very quick to take offence. If anything critical is said about their boss, they become personally wounded. The expression in Newfoundland is they are "quick to hurt." If their boss is the prime minister of a functioning democracy with a free press, they are in a constant state of distress. Easily triggered are the little ones.

I didn't know who these people were. I hadn't seen them on any of the campaign planes or buses I had been on. That said, they were standing in the prime minister's house, so they couldn't be ignored completely. My guess is they were well raised by mothers and fathers with impeccable connections to the Conservative

Party. But if their job was to welcome us and give us a hand, they missed the memo.

Unfortunately, none of the contacts I had at the PMO were there. At the time, there were, at all times, three omnipresent figures around the prime minister: Dimitri Soudas, Kory Teneycke and Ray Novak. I got on with all of them. I could have a straightforward conversation with any of them. They would tell you exactly what the lay of the land was, and I appreciated that. They were a funny bunch. There was a bit of a cult of personality happening around them, and they enjoyed it. One reporter told me Dimitri wanted the members of the press gallery to refer to them as "The Three Wise Men" but they were having none of it. The closest they might have got was "Mopey, Dopey and Lopey."

All three were incredibly loyal to Harper, Ray in particular. Ray had gone to work as a child intern at the National Citizens Coalition when Harper was its president. The NCC is a rightwing think tank, and it was there, over a mutual distaste for the social safety net, that their platonic love developed. They quickly became inseparable. Like Barney to his Fred, Ray was never far from Harper's side. He followed his leader everywhere. Including when Harper changed jobs. When Harper became leader of the official Opposition and moved into Stornoway, the official residence, Ray slept in a room over the garage. Ray was available 24/7, ready to dispense strategic advice or warm milk in a binky cup.

Not only would Ray stay with Harper during his tenure as prime minister, rising to the position of chief of staff, but he would follow Harper into private life. He is currently one of two associates at the private consulting firm Harper and Associates. As a practising Viking, Ray has made it clear that when the time comes, he wishes to be buried with the former prime minister in Harper's tomb.

But sadly, on this day at 24 Sussex, neither Ray nor any of the other wise men were on hand. Instead, we had a welcoming committee of suspicious and nervous staffers. From the minute our gear was brought into the house they began to second-guess each of our set-ups. We didn't see this coming.

Our understanding was that we had access to the entire downstairs of the residence. The staffers didn't like that idea. The first thing we did was to place two chairs in the middle of the room.

One of them stepped forward. "Actually, if you don't mind, can you not move any of the furniture? You'll have to put those back."

Don, John and I shared a look. We hadn't even begun to shoot. We had far more intrusive set-ups yet to be revealed.

John gently explained that we needed to move the chairs together in a classic interview set-up if we were going to have a classic interview.

Another one of them, appearing very concerned, looked at the light stands Don was assembling.

"Do we really need to have these stands in here?"

I politely informed them that, yes, if we were shooting in the living room, we would need some lights.

"Could you do it by the window?" he suggested. "It's brighter over there."

"You want us to move by the window for light?" I asked.

"Yes," he answered, looking very pleased with himself. He looked at his colleagues as if to say, "Well, I certainly took care of that."

"If we move there, our backs will be very close to the wall. You are okay with that?" I asked him.

"Yes, you'd be close to the wall. That's fine."

I had no choice but to take him to the woodshed.

"Okay. But you *do* understand that the most important part of framing an interview for television is creating a sense of depth behind the subject, so the greater distance we can put between the prime minister's back and the rear wall, the better. It makes for a much more lush and attractive background. He will look much better. If he's up against the wall, it will look cramped and flat."

For added measure, I said: "He may look like he's having his mug shot taken."

I moved on to the lights.

"You would rather we not use lights?"

"Well," he said, "it's very bright in here. I don't see why you need to put up lights."

"The lights make it look better."

"I just know the prime minister probably won't like to see lights in his living room."

"I'd suggest to you the prime minister will expect to see lights in his living room because this is a TV shoot. Also, the lights will make sure there are no creepy shadows under his eyes. My guess is he knows this."

He turned around and walked away, heaving an audible sigh as if to say "There is no dealing with these people!"

It is always amazing to me when someone has the confidence to offer strong opinions on subjects they literally know nothing about. "Hello, my name is Oliver. I have never read a single article about television lighting or framing, but I think what your camera operator is doing is all wrong. Sure, he may have shot World Cup downhill skiing and *The Nutcracker*, but I work for the prime minister of Canada. I'm also available to provide advice on how to do bypass surgeries if any doctors are asking."

Thankfully, Ray showed up before a mini war broke out. He arrived with the prime minister, who was seemingly in a good mood. He welcomed us to the house and said he needed to run upstairs and make a call. Before he left, he delivered some good news.

Because the conceit of the piece was my spending a lot of time at the house, we had asked if the Harper children might want to make a cameo. I'd assumed this was a long shot, but the prime minister had said he would leave that entirely up to them. Turns out they both wanted to do it. "Apparently, they watch your show," he said. "Obviously, behind my back."

Funny guy, I thought. *This is good.*

The prime minister then went upstairs, leaving John, Ray and me to walk through the shoot.

Once Ray was on the scene, everything changed. The staff who were moments ago in our faces about every little thing were now standing against a far wall, silent. They, like pets, were not allowed on the furniture.

Ray could not have been more open. Every gag I suggested, he said yes to. And he clearly spoke for the prime minister. In many ways they were two versions of the same person. He even readily agreed when I told him I wanted to take every cushion off every couch and build a fort in the living room. Ray got it. Mr. Don't Move Any Chairs pursed his lips like a nun being admonished by the mother superior.

Clearly, we were on a roll. We were being given the run of the place. And then we hit a roadblock. I told Ray I wanted to get a shot of me sitting at the piano with the prime minister. We would then cut to the two of us playing a duet of "Chopsticks." And then we would cut to the prime minister playing something classical for me—ideally, something in the public domain so I wouldn't have to pay royalties.

Ray said, "No, that won't work."

"There's a piano right there," I pointed out.

"Comes with the house. Rachel plays a bit."

"But the prime minister can play piano," I said.

"I don't know where you got that idea."

I started to make a suggestion: "Well, maybe if we just sat at the piano and began to—"

"There's not going to be any piano," he said.

I know a third rail when I see one, but this didn't make any sense to me. I wasn't suggesting he appear in blackface, an obvious career ender; I was suggesting he play "Music Box Dancer" while I looked on with a goofy smile. Yes, if need be, I would pay for "Music Box Dancer."

Regardless, you pick your battles.

A few minutes later the prime minister arrived and we walked him through the premise: I'm here to shoot an interview, and halfway through the interview the prime minister will start fawning over me and eventually convince me to spend the night as his guest. And with that, we were good to go.

It started out as a straight-up interview—shot in the living room, as Don envisioned. We covered Harper's time in office thus far.

And then I moved on to something that was being talked about on every newscast but about which the prime minister himself had not commented: his government's signature piece of environmental legislation.

"The Clean Air Act?" I said. "Are we really supposed to be impressed that you want to lower carbon emissions by the year 2050?"

At which point something completely unexpected happened. The staffers at the back of the room, up until this point, had been silent. So much so that I'd basically forgotten they were there. The little darlings had their backsides so tight against that wall that if they got any closer, their bums would have been embedded in asbestos.

As soon as I mentioned the 2050 target date in the Clean Air Act, one of them came alive. It was like he was hit with a bolt of electricity.

"*No!*" he shouted.

Both the PM and I looked up. I was startled. My guess is Harper was as surprised as I was.

The staffer stammered, "This is *not* supposed to be a real interview. There's *NOT* supposed to be any talk of the Clean Air Act. Nobody said there would be questions on that."

This was followed by an appropriate awkward silence. Had he got his inside voice confused with his outside voice? This was a stunning thing for a staffer to yell at anyone, let alone someone interviewing the prime minister. And never mind that the camera was rolling.

From the very beginning of *RMR*, we decided we were never out to "get" anyone. We would not be underhanded. We needed people to trust us. So we would never be accused of playing any dirty tricks. And we decided that if someone did something or said something in the heat of the moment, we would simply not use it.

And it happened on a few occasions. Sometimes someone would, in a misguided attempt to be funny, get carried away and say something out of character. I remember talking to a Liberal cabinet minister once about New Year's resolutions, and while attempting to be funny he said something that would not only get him thrown off a wharf in Cape Breton but probably thrown out of cabinet. We didn't put it on TV.

But this was a new one. This was the prime minister being asked a question about a government policy and some unelected young person yelling "*Noooo!*" as if they were trying to stop a child from running into traffic. This was the PMO supporting the narrative that they were controlling weirdos who were distrustful of the media.

Thing is, I have no doubt Harper himself had said he wouldn't be talking about the Clean Air Act. But this kid was clearly overstepping. He was freelancing. Either that or having a stroke.

I looked over at the PM and said, "Yeah—we won't put that on TV."

The prime minister smiled and said to the young man: "It's okay, I'm more than happy to answer any questions he has. On the Clean Air Act or anything."

I have no idea how long that poor fella ended up hanging from his ankles in the punishment room, but I never saw him again during the prime minister's tenure.

After a chat about the Clean Air Act, we moved on to some gags. The first one involved the prime minister feeding me. We set up in the kitchen so he could make me a sandwich.

While we were setting up, one of his support team began to brief the prime minister on how to make the sandwich. It was a surreal moment: "All you have to do, Prime Minister, is take two slices of bread, put butter on one, put it on the cutting board and then lay some ham on it. Then get some cheese . . ."

He nodded politely and said, "I can make a sandwich. I'll be fine."

I couldn't tell if we just got him on his best day ever or if his medications had been miraculously balanced, but for a man who didn't suffer fools gladly, he took being talked to like a dimwit by a staffer remarkably well.

We shot the scene and I have to say his comic timing while making the sandwich was good. But what was more impressive was his ability to act—and act naturally. Later on, after he convinced me to spend the night, we shot a scene where he tucked me in on the couch and read me a bedtime story from his government's much-lauded piece of legislation, the Federal Accountability Act. At one point he paused and said, "You know, sometimes when I can't sleep, I count ridings."

He delivered the line as if he were a slightly wistful, melancholy Leonardo DiCaprio. It was funny.

But what impressed me most was his agreeing to the final shot of the piece.

We shot the exterior of 24 Sussex as if it were early the next morning. We see the PM sending his kids off to school. He says goodbye to Rachel, tells her to have a good day, and then reaches out and shakes her hand. She shakes it back solemnly. He then says goodbye to his son Ben, passes him his lunch and shakes his hand. Ben responds in kind.

The camera then reveals I'm there. The prime minister passes me a lunch bag, says, "Goodbye, Rick," and then pulls me in for a big hug.

And he went deep. Big hug.

He was willing to be self-deprecating about the grief he received for shaking his son's hand while dropping him off to school. And maybe he was also owning it.

From a straight-up comedic point of view, the piece was good. It moved along at a nice clip, and it certainly was unexpected to see Harper have fun, let alone at his own expense. There were lots of jokes.

Conservatives loved it. It must have been a very odd feeling for them to watch their leader come out of his shell and appear downright human on the CBC. They must have felt like they had slipped into a parallel universe. There was also some mild rage from Liberals who felt I somehow betrayed their cause by allowing Stephen Harper to be funny. I told them I had tried my best to make Liberal leader Stéphane Dion appear amusing many times, but it couldn't be done. After all, it's a microphone I hold in my hand, not a magic wand.

Terry Mosher, the celebrated editorial cartoonist for the Montreal *Gazette*, marked the occasion by portraying me as a sell-out who would work for anyone. What an honour to be eviscerated in a Mosher cartoon. Naturally, I did what hundreds of Mosher's victims had done before me. I sent a cheque to a food bank in Montreal, and in return Terry sent me the original cartoon, suitable for framing.

I admit I have always been conflicted about the piece.

And I was for the longest time baffled about why they circled the wagons around the piano. Because while I didn't know much about Stephen Harper, I *knew* he played the piano.

The previous year, I'd received a random call from someone who said a friend of his was in St. John's on business and needed some information about the town. In particular, he wanted to know if there was a place in the downtown area where one could buy sheet music.

Like all Newfoundlanders when called on to provide local intel, I was happy to report that on Water Street there's a store called O'Brien's Music. "O'Brien's is legendary," I said. "It's been there forever. It was founded in 1939. The guy who scored the *Star Wars* movies used to shop there in the '50s when he was stationed at the US military base."

He cut me off before I could tell him it was also the go-to place to purchase an accordion, jaw harp or glockenspiel.

"The guy needs sheet music," he said. "He's travelling with Stephen Harper, and when there is a piano in his room, Harper likes to play Beatles music to relax."

"Man plays piano to relax" struck me as an entirely benign and not very interesting fact—little did I know I was now in possession of a closely guarded secret.

It was a very long time before it was explained to me just why.

Turns out, when Harper first made a run for the leadership of the Canadian Alliance party, his people analyzed every positive and negative about the man. Some of the positives were obvious— he loves hockey! My god, he's halfway to prime minister already.

But some of his negatives were serious liabilities. One of those, they'd determined, was his passion for the piano. According to the people around Harper, the piano was an elitist instrument. It was only played by rich people, and it was mostly played by women. And classical music on the piano was completely out. As a hobby, it was not acceptable.

As a result, if Harper were ever to talk about hobbies or interests, he would focus exclusively on hockey. He could say he liked *listening* to music, but he would never admit he played any, let alone on piano.

As far as his people were concerned, if he copped to playing Chopin in the evening or if he were seen tickling the ivories in a hotel lobby, he might as well announce that he had spent his twenties moonlighting as a gay liberal-arts professor.

The irony is, because of these societal views on the piano, Stephen Harper was for most of his public life deep in the closet. The love that dares not speak its name in his house was his affection for a Steinway.

When I told people about Harper's refusal to play piano on the show, they would look at me like I was a conspiracy theorist of the highest order. It was one thing to believe Stephen Harper had a hidden agenda, but to believe he was hiding his ability to play an instrument was a bridge too far.

After all, one could draw a direct line from Bill Clinton playing the saxophone on late-night TV to Bill Clinton moving into the White House. And when Bob Rae was running for premier of Ontario, he would stop at every piano he saw. Aides had to carry a crowbar to keep him on schedule. Hiding one's ability to play a musical instrument was too absurd to contemplate.

Three years would pass before Prime Minister Stephen Harper came out of the closet. He shocked the country by walking out onstage at the National Arts Centre during a gala performance by internationally acclaimed cellist Yo-Yo Ma.

This was an unexpected move. The prime minister's wife, Laureen Harper, was known to be a lover of classical music and theatre, but Harper famously avoided cultural events. When Mrs. Harper went to such things, she was almost always accompanied by cabinet minister John Baird.

On this occasion Harper not only appeared onstage, but crossed the stage, sat at the piano and played a duet with the living legend.

The place went mad. He received a standing ovation.

It's amazing what a tolerant country we are.

How was this possible? people wondered. How was it that so many profiles had been written about this man and none of them mentioned that he played piano?

If anything, it made Harper appear smarter and more interesting.

I would like to say that it was a great day for Canadian culture, but it did not turn out to be. His relationship with the arts would remain hostile.

But it was a great day for Stephen Harper the man. Because on that day he made the difficult and personal decision to come out and reveal his true self. And by doing so, he learned that the people who were the most important to him, those who loved him, his base, would accept him for who he was.

A piano-playing elitist.

Disturbing? Yes. A dealbreaker? No.

They decided to hate the sin, not the sinner. He survived the duet.

And in certain circles, it was never mentioned again.

11

Belinda Makes an Entrance

I had my first encounter with Belinda Stronach in mid-February of 2005. The show was brand new and so was she.

She was the newly elected member of Parliament for New-market, Ontario.

For an Opposition MP she was pretty darn famous. The year before she had run for the leadership of the newly minted Conservative Party of Canada. She might have lost to Stephen Harper, but she made a giant splash while doing it.

Everyone was surprised that, after losing, she kept her promise to run as an MP. Candidates for leadership always say they will run, win or lose, but they never do.

In our camp, we were even more surprised that she agreed to be on the show. Or, I should say, we were surprised that she got permission to be on the show. From the minute Stephen Harper became leader, it was very clear to us and to everyone in Ottawa that nothing could happen in that party without permission from the leader's office.

A controlling leader was not new in Ottawa, but this was something else. The level of control being demanded by Harper's office was pathological.

The reason was obvious. For close to a decade, Stephen Harper's party—the Conservatives, and the Canadian Alliance and Reform Party before that—had been knocked off message almost daily by some obscure rogue MP or candidate. They had people who appeared to wake up every morning wondering what offside opinion they could float into the universe that would make the conservative world unravel.

To an observer of politics like me, it was great fun to watch. For a conservative like Stephen Harper, it must have been excruciatingly painful. He was all about discipline. In fact, he liked discipline so much, I'd bet money it was the number one word in his Google search history.

At first, MPs weren't used to this level of control coming from the leader's office. But when push came to shove, they surrendered to Harper's will as fast as the French in the Second World War. The difference being, there was no resistance.

I once met a Conservative staffer who confided in me that very early in Harper's mandate, he was pulled into the Opposition leader's office and entrusted with a very special task. He was given a list of Conservative caucus members who had spoken to the media about random subjects over the previous few weeks. None of the interviews were problematic or controversial, but the new rule was simple: nobody talks to anyone, even local press, without permission from head office.

The first six MPs on the list had each done an interview where they were asked what jobs they held when they were students. It was all part of a story on a current "hire a student" campaign. Politicians love to be asked about their first job because it gives them an opportunity to wax nostalgic about how hard they worked waiting tables at the Calgary Stampede or spreading manure on an uncle's farm.

But as great as the press coverage was, the Opposition leader's office felt it was a slippery slope. If MPs think they can answer questions about mowing lawns when they were fifteen, next thing you know, they might want to discuss policy or promote Autism Awareness Week. This young man with the deep voice was told not just to remind the MPs they needed permission to do interviews, but to remind them in a way they would not forget. He was given permission to take them to the woodshed.

And so the nineteen-year-old staffer spent his first days on the job berating members of Parliament, some of whom were three times his age.

In light of this we were mildly surprised when we found out that Harper's office had given Belinda the green light to be on the show. What we didn't know, but which became abundantly clear to everyone over the next weeks and months, is that Belinda didn't ask Stephen Harper's permission for anything that wasn't directly related to her critic's portfolio.

This was not a woman used to being told what to do.

We wanted Belinda for the same reason everyone did. She had a huge amount of star power, something that is traditionally lacking in Canadian politics.

The other parties were clearly a bit jealous of what she was bringing to the Hill. The most glamorous MP the Liberals had at the time was a short guy who used to be a meteorologist on the Weather Network. What passed for glamour on the NDP benches was a woman who once famously busted up a bar fight at a union conference by breaking an ironworker's nose.

I was very much looking forward to meeting Belinda Stronach.

Her office in the East Block of Parliament Hill was like so many other MPs' offices, with one very large exception: the art. It was clear she wasn't decorating her walls with hand-me-downs from the Canada Council Art Bank. It's not every day you walk into a Conservative MP's office and there's an original Warhol portrait of Chairman Mao leaning against a wall, waiting for a home.

We were met in Belinda's office by a young male staffer. He was very handsome—in some ways straight out of Central Casting. But my first impression was coloured not by his looks but by the colour of his shirt. He was wearing a pink dress shirt with a brown and pink tie tied in a very large knot. The shoes were long and pointy. He was, as we say in the business, "fashion-forward."

Today, a pink shirt would not be noteworthy, but believe it or not, in those days I was a bit taken aback. Wearing a pink shirt in the office of a Conservative MP at that time was akin to wearing a sticker on your forehead that said, "Hello, my name is Mike and I am a homosexual."

That was his name by the way: Mike Liebrock. Nice fellow. Very down-to-earth. Welcomed us warmly and told us to make ourselves at home while he went to fetch Belinda. "She's just on a call," he said, moving towards the back office.

MPs are always on a call, even when they are sleeping on their couch or trying to figure out how to put an attachment on an email.

"She's looking forward to it," Mike said, before disappearing into the inner sanctum. "She has some surprises up her sleeve and some ideas."

Great. She had some surprises and ideas.

As luck would have it, I hate both.

Is there a man alive who likes a surprise? If such a man exists, I haven't met him.

And ideas? Ideas are not bad in theory, but after years of shoot-ing television I have learned that, when it comes to politicians, the ideas are almost invariably of the bad variety. Sure, they can be genuine and well-meaning, but they tend to be impractical and far too long or complicated.

"I have an idea," a cabinet minister might say. "I think it would be funny if, when you enter my office, I'm sitting at my desk with three large pizzas and I act surprised. I'll look up and say, 'What are you doing here, Rick? I thought the interview was tomorrow!'"

Then he will explain: "It's funny because last August I did an interview with a newspaper in Sudbury, and I said my favourite food is pizza! Can you believe that? Pizza!"

Usually there are two or three staffers nodding and laughing as if they are in the presence of Richard Pryor.

This is where my stickhandling skills come in.

If the idea was simple, which it rarely was, we would do what we called a "courtesy roll." We would just shoot the pizza gag, knowing full well it would never make it into the show. Unfortu-nately, the ideas were often too time-consuming for a courtesy roll. Then I would have to explain, diplomatically, why it was a bad idea.

"Well, it's certainly hysterically funny that you said your favou-rite food is pizza, but there's a slim chance that the thirty-five mil-lion people who didn't read the article in the Sudbury paper will know this about you. Also, eating three large pizzas alone may appear wasteful or extravagant or gluttonous, which may not be the best look for a cabinet minister. People who run food banks are notorious for their lack of sense of humour, you know. But what the hell—let's shoot it anyway. Your idea is funny!"

Then the staffers would huddle and confer among themselves until one would eventually say, "I don't think we have time for the pizza gag, Minister. You're going to be needed on that phone call with the president of France in a few hours, so we should really get going."

Mike disappeared behind a closed door and I was wondering what Belinda's ideas might be.

I heard Don mumble to himself, "Hmm, a Tory in pink. Imagine that."

"Times are changing, Don," I said. "It's a brave new world."

Eventually the Tory in Pink (that's how I thought of him now) returned with the one and only Belinda Stronach.

She made quite an entrance. The always elegant and well-put-together MP was wearing a hockey jersey made from jerseys from two different teams, cut in half and sewn together. And she had an armful of what I assumed were props.

I began to make small talk. "So great to meet you, really looking forward to this." But what I was really thinking was *What is she wearing? What are those props in her hand? And how do I stop this?*

The props were eventually revealed to be large Valentine cards that we could exchange on-camera. Like all Valentine cards, they had a verse or two or three written on the inside. I assumed the idea was that we would read these cards out loud to one another. I could handle people saying I suck up to politicians, but it was another thing to go on national TV and read love poetry to them.

The show *was* airing on February 14, and we had pitched a "Valentine's Day skating date on the Rideau Canal" as the premise of the shoot. Belinda or her people ran with it. The cards looked like someone had put a lot of work into them. Where did she find a calligrapher on such short notice? They were goofy, but not very funny. They seemed like, well, actual Valentine cards.

I had the distinct impression that some speech writer, or maybe even a comedian, had been hired to prep her on this shoot and this is what they'd come up with.

Turns out the jersey was non-negotiable. She was simply not going skating on the canal without it. I didn't care so much, but it meant we would have to devote precious moments on-camera to explaining what she was wearing. Otherwise, the audience would be distracted by the wardrobe choice. They would wonder, "Is this what they're wearing at Fashion Week in Paris?"

When I floated the idea that the Valentine cards and surprise gifts wouldn't really work, Mike gave me a look that said they wanted to use the cards. "I think they are cute," he said.

Luckily, at that moment Belinda ran to grab something in her office and I turned to him and said quietly, but firmly, "Look, trust me on this: they aren't funny, it will look contrived, she will look bad."

He stared at me for all of two seconds, said, "Got it," and went to find Belinda.

And we never saw the props and cards again. Good job, Mike. Out she came with a big smile and we headed to the canal.

The interview was going take place while we enjoyed everything the Rideau Canal had to offer in the winter. We would rent skates, do some doubles skating, enjoy some snacks and push each other around on giant sleds.

I LIKED BELINDA IMMEDIATELY. On our walk to the location, she did something that TV crews always appreciate: she offered to carry some gear. We travelled light by TV standards, but an extra hand was always appreciated. Once loaded down with cables and battery bags, both Belinda and Mike joined Don, John and me and strolled to the canal.

There were a few selfies on the way down. And Belinda was relaxed and charming with the tourists. She definitely had a bit of a movie-star vibe going on. Some of them were taken aback that we were together. I suppose we were an odd couple in their eyes. "We are dating now," Belinda deadpanned. "It's really quite something." And then she made a face as if she was complimenting me on something—not quite sure what, but the gaggle of lady tourists she confided in seemed titillated.

I have pretty good instincts about these things, and I can always tell after a few minutes how good someone is going to be on-camera. I knew Belinda was going to be great. And then the cameras came on.

I set up the premise: "Its Valentine's Day and I have a date with the It girl of the Canadian right, Belinda Stronach."

As I write that now, I'm kind of embarrassed about that introduction. I was guilty of doing exactly what so many journalists and columnists did during Belinda's career: write her off as an "It girl" and "heiress." No mention of her corporate career. Forgive me for my sins, but that is how I set it up, and then the interview started.

I welcomed her to the show and she gave me a great smile. Out of the gate I said, "There are always reports about how Belinda Stronach is such a great dresser and how she has extravagant tastes for designer clothes, yet we go on a date and you dress like a hobo."

This gave her the chance to push the local hockey teams from her riding. To explain she loved both and couldn't choose, so she had this unique jersey made. And it allowed her to drop the name of her riding about six times in ninety seconds. All politics is local, and I had to admit, the jersey was good politics for someone who someday would be looking to be re-elected.

And then we moved on, skated down the canal and began the interview.

"Why in God's name," I asked, "would someone leave the corporate life you enjoyed and go into politics, where you knew the best-case scenario was being a backbench Opposition MP?"

And to be clear, Belinda's corporate life wasn't like the average corporate life on Bay Street. She wasn't giving up access to a nice table at the fancy Keg in downtown Toronto. The Stronach family were the majority shareholders of Magna International. They had a fleet of airplanes at their disposal, there were ski lodges in Colorado, estates in Muskoka. In theory, once she became an MP, she could not avail herself of any of those things. And if she ever sat in government, she wouldn't be able to look at a private jet again, let alone ride on one.

Her answer to this question was lifted straight out of the obvious stock answer playbook, a copy of which is given to every individual who hopes to serve in municipal, provincial or federal politics in Canada. She said she left corporate life because she believed in public service.

I was having none of it. "Oh stop," I said. "Next thing you'll say is that you did it to give back."

She looked at me and said, "I did it to give back."

There was no sense of irony.

With that stock answer out of the way, I figured we would move on to the elephants in the room—and there were many.

And this is when the segment began to resemble a hostage video.

On same-sex marriage, she reiterated her absolute support. When asked if she felt at home in a political party where so many of her fellow members disagreed with her about gay marriage, she didn't say yes but she didn't say no. She just looked as if she was being waterboarded. She said she admired that "the leader" wanted a free vote on the issue.

It was then that I realized that the entire time I was with her, she never once said Stephen Harper's name. She would only refer to him as "the leader." Years before anyone had heard of Harry Potter, Belinda was ahead of the curve. Clearly, Stephen Harper was her Lord Voldemort. He who shall not be named.

When I pressed her on the "leader" running ads against gay marriage, she said simply, "Obviously, if I was leader, I would not have run those ads."

Well, this segment was short of laughs, but it was becoming very insightful. Rarely if ever does an MP publicly disagree with "the leader." When challenged about a policy they privately don't support, they dodge, duck and obfuscate instead. Belinda answered a direct question with a direct answer. Unheard of.

It began to dawn on me that Stephen Harper's office hadn't, in fact, given her permission to do this, because she clearly hadn't requested it.

When the camera was off, I asked her, "Did you run this interview past the leader's office?"

She responded, "It's a free country, Rick. I can talk to whoever I want, and I wanted to talk to you."

I said, "I don't think that's how it works up here."

She replied, "The last time I asked a man for permission, I was probably eighteen. I'm not about to start again, not as a woman and certainly not as a member of Parliament."

I couldn't help but think, *Where was that fire when you were running for leader? And for that matter, where was that fire five minutes ago when we were on-camera?*

When the cameras were rolling again, I started mining for

something that could be remotely passed off as fun and light. In the back of my mind, I wondered how long it would take for Mr Liebrock to sprint back to the office and get those giant novelty Valentine cards. He certainly looked athletic.

I brought up her leadership campaign. "I noticed," I said, "that you had Dr. Jeffrey Sachs as a special policy advisor."

"Yes," she said. "I'm a big admirer of his. I really enjoyed his last book. He was one of the first people I called and asked his advice on policy."

"He's American," I said. "Isn't that weird?"

She said, "You get the best advice you can, no matter what the source."

I said, "Well, I guess that's true. And if you're running for the leader of the Conservative Party, I suppose who better to advise you than a leading expert on brain abnormalities?"

I was relieved. That was a bit of a joke, at least. Except Belinda looked at me and said, "I think you're thinking of a different Dr. Sachs."

Oops.

"Am I?" I asked.

She said, "Jeffrey Sachs is the head of the Earth Institute at Columbia University and is the UN special envoy to Africa."

Well, who was the idiot now? Two guesses, and it wasn't Belinda. I *was* thinking of a different doctor. I was thinking of Dr. Oliver Sacks, whom Robin Williams played in the movie *Awakenings*. I had even read one of his books about bizarre brain phenomena—people who get hit in the head and wake up speaking Portuguese, that sort of thing.

"Right," I replied, before turning to Donny to say, "Cut!" One advantage of having your own show is that when you've revealed yourself as a total moron on-camera, you don't have to put it on TV.

We kept the rest of the interview light, but Belinda was overly cautious. When talking about being a Conservative she was excellent, but when talking about being in the Conservative Party as it was at that time, she sounded very much like someone who was trying to make a doomed marriage work.

In the end I knew we had what we called a double. Certainly not a triple and very far from a home run. But we had a piece, and that was all that mattered.

On our way back to the Hill, Belinda suggested I read Dr. Sachs's book about Africa. Still mortified about the mix-up, I said I would.

"I'll send one to your office," she said. "We have your address."

And then she added, "I'm hoping to go to Africa with him at some point and visit some aid projects. You should come."

I didn't think much of it. In fact, I thought "You should come with me to Africa" was a rich person's equivalent of saying, "We should get together sometime for lunch."

You say, "I'd love to," but you know it's never going to happen.

THE PIECE AIRED, AS planned, on Valentine's Day. There weren't a lot of laughs, but it certainly caused a stir in political circles. Her straightforward support for same-sex marriage did not go over well in the Conservative caucus, where people began to demand that she lose her portfolio as critic for international trade.

The thinking was: How can you in good conscience have a woman who ran an automobile parts company that operates in sixteen countries serve as a trade critic if she thinks some farmer named Gus in Alberta should be able to marry his boyfriend and raise gay cattle?

A few days after it aired, Dr. Jeffrey Sachs's book showed up at my office.

Personally, I never thought much about Belinda Stronach again—until the day three months later when I found myself sitting in a café in Yellowknife, having a cup of coffee. It was about eight in the morning and I was scrolling through headlines on my BlackBerry. All eyes were on Ottawa. There was much drama playing out. The Paul Martin Liberals were on the verge of tabling a budget and Stephen Harper was making it clear that, with the support of the NDP, he had enough muscle to defeat the government on a vote of non-confidence. This was a very big deal. It would trigger a federal election and effectively put a bullet in the Kelowna Accord, which was being hailed as the largest and most comprehensive support package for Indigenous peoples in the history of Canada.

I couldn't believe the NDP were going to back the Tories and kill Kelowna, but it very much looked like that was the case. It very much looked like the government was going to fall.

I was eyes-deep in my BlackBerry when I heard a very deep voice say my name. I looked up to see the most enormous Indigenous fellow I think I have ever encountered. I shook his hand, and I remember distinctly how very small my hand was in his. He looked down at me and said, "Why did Belinda Stronach cross the floor?"

I assumed this was the opening to a joke.

"I don't know," I said. "Why *did* Belinda Stronach cross the floor?"

Instead of a punchline, he said, "I don't know either. I thought you might."

And then my phone began to melt down.

Five minutes earlier, Belinda Stronach had ceased to be a Conservative backbencher. She was now a Liberal cabinet minister. There would be no vote of non-confidence. The Liberals were saved. Stephen Harper was outplayed and humiliated. Mongolian sandstorms were minor compared to the political shitstorm that was engulfing Parliament Hill.

I went to pay at the front of the café and there on the TV was Belinda, sitting next to Paul Martin. The press conference was playing out live for all the world to see. She looked fantastic and relaxed. I couldn't help but notice she looked more at ease next to Martin than she ever did next to "he who shall not be named."

Political observers love this stuff. We live for this stuff. My mind was boggled at the machinations that must have gone into this backroom deal.

God, I thought. *I would kill to get her alone someday for just ten minutes and ask her how exactly this came to be.*

But that, I knew, would never happen.

Two months later the telephone rang. It was Mike Liebrock. He was very much still with Belinda. In fact, he was named acting chief of staff within minutes of her crossing the floor. He was quick and to the point. "It's July, the House is not sitting, Belinda is planning a trip to Africa, it's just the two of us, and she wants to know if you would like to come along."

He added, "She isn't going as a cabinet minister, but as a private citizen."

And then: "We leave next week."

Mike told me Belinda wanted to see some development projects in Africa with her own eyes. She had read the books, she had a relationship with Dr. Sachs, and when she was running for the Conservative leadership she was committed to the notion that Canada should increase its foreign aid to Africa. But this was her, as a private citizen, heading out on a fact-finding mission.

"Okay," I said, "but why me?"

"She said you were interested in Dr. Sachs's work?"

Well, I did email her and thank her for the book, and I told her I'd read it and found it interesting. Which was partially true. I did read the book and it was interesting, but under oath I would have to admit that I skimmed some of the chapters. When it came to book writing, Sachs was a tad dry. The book was called *The End of Poverty: Economic Possibilities for Our Time*. It didn't have a lot of laughs in it.

Mike suggested that I give Belinda a call and gave me her number. I got her on the phone and right off the bat she promised me she had no agenda. She was going on the trip regardless, and when it became clear there was room for one more, she thought of me.

I told her there was no scenario where I would come back from Africa having turned into one of those people who never shut up about Africa. The world had enough white saviours parading around talking about Africa, as far as I was concerned.

She assured me that was fine. There were no strings attached.

I told her I would seriously think about it.

She said, "I'll have Mike send you a list of the shots you'll need to get."

"Off the top of your head, what countries would we visit?" I asked.

"No idea yet," she said. "Wherever Sachs goes, we will go."

I WAS OF TWO minds about going, but time was of the essence. So I spent the next couple of days being vaccinated for everything from yellow fever to typhoid. The list was long and the diseases were scary. I am not a vaccine-hesitant individual; I said yes to each shot on offer. And I got a prescription for anti-malarial pills. Of all the bad things that might befall you on a visit to Africa, malaria was surely one of the worst. The nurse at the travel clinic also advised me to buy a mosquito net. "If you bring anything, bring the net."

I told a doctor friend about what I was considering. She had travelled to aid projects before and had some idea of what I might end up doing. She prescribed me some "just in case" medications: a strong antibiotic, some eye drops and some Cipro in case of "infectious diarrhea." She read the look on my face. "It happens," she said. "You want to be prepared."

Also, she hooked me up with some completely insane painkillers. "In case you find yourself with a compound fracture and there are no doctors or clinics, and you need to fly home with a bone sticking out of your leg."

This was a bit much. "I'll be travelling with Belinda Stronach," I said. "I think it's going to be pretty swish."

Antibiotics? Painkillers? Yellow fever? Dengue fever? This was overwhelming. Normally when I'm going on holiday, my must-haves include sunblock, moisturizer and a sleazy Hollywood memoir.

"Oh," the doctor said. "Take this suture kit. If you need it, you'll figure out how to use it. It's just like sewing up a pillow."

In for a penny, in for a pound. I called Belinda and said I was in.

Two weeks later we left Canada.

12

The Palace Was a Low Point

It was July 2006.

I was very excited to get the itinerary. But I have to say I was also a little shocked. I didn't know Belinda that well, but I assumed she would, when possible, travel in style (this proved to be true) and at a leisurely pace (nothing could be farther from the truth). If I was going somewhere far, I liked to break up the initial travel. Not Belinda.

The first leg of our trip was two legs sewn together. We took the seven-and-a-half-hour flight from Toronto Pearson to London Heathrow. Then we had a few hours to kill at the airport before taking the eight-and-a-half-hour flight from Heathrow to Nairobi, Kenya.

Welcome to Africa. When I arrived, I was one discombobulated traveller.

Mike was, too. Meanwhile, getting off the plane, Belinda looked refreshed and rested, like she was emerging from a Four Seasons spa. Finding our way through customs and immigration, Mike

and I were walking into walls, and she looked like she was walking a runway.

Initially there was little culture shock. Nairobi, being the capital, is a modern metropolis. It has a glittering skyline and is
home to the stock exchange—and, I assume, the African corporate
headquarters of a pile of Fortune 500 companies.

The hotel was quite lovely, although as anyone who has experienced extreme jet lag will tell you, nothing matters at that point.
You just want a glass of water and bed.

At the time, the United Nations were championing a development model called the Millennium Villages Project. In a nutshell,
this meant that an area of extreme poverty would not only receive
aid in the traditional sense—for example, emergency food or shelter—they would also receive certain "inputs" that Sachs believed
would lead to long-term sustainability.

Sachs's argument was that a community experiencing extreme
poverty doesn't just need food, they need fertilizer, which will
allow them to grow food. They also need a place to store this
food. They need a truck as a means to get their food to market.

They do not just need an occasional fly-in visit from doctors
from an aid organization; they need a small permanent clinic
staffed by a nurse. They need bed nets to keep them healthy. They
need to be healthy to work and have a decent quality of life.

These inputs, he argued, would lead to a sustainable future. He
believed people needed not just aid but the ability to create an
economy. To riff on the Chinese proverb, he wasn't suggesting
that the UN teach a man to fish, he was suggesting they give the
man the means to fish.

Sounded good on paper, but Belinda wanted to see for herself.
That was the entire purpose of the trip. So, the next day we were

up early. Very early, so we could drive to a series of Millennium Villages already in operation and catch up with the Sachs team.

WE WERE HEADED TO an area called Sauri. It was a short drive outside of the capital—a scant six hours. Piece of cake. Not unlike waking up in Toronto at four in the morning and driving to Woodstock, New York, for a lunch meeting.

The Millennium Villages we visited were almost exactly as advertised. Each village had a small school and clinic; there were children playing; there was a well with clean water; there were— and this is the most important thing—fields of corn. Food was growing in fertilized ground, and surplus food was being stored and would later be brought to market.

The next week was a blur. There was no downtime. We covered a lot of territory. Five countries in under seven days.

It's almost impossible to describe the highs and lows of this trip or the extremes that we experienced. I want to be very careful about judging anything we saw or experienced by "Western standards." But I will report that upon checking into a small hotel in rural Ethiopia and being told, "There is no water tonight," Belinda didn't bat an eyelash. She slept on top of her bed, fully clothed, wrapped in her bed net. I had a suit bag, so I removed the contents, crawled inside and slept in there. Mike, out of chivalry, slept in Belinda's room on the floor by the door.

When you roll with the likes of Belinda Stronach, you are rolling in the big time.

The next day, after a long drive into the North, the reason for the trip became evidently clear. It was there that I witnessed poverty like I had never seen before. Dr. Sachs took us to an area where the population had literally nothing. This is where he wanted the next Millennium Villages to be built.

There was a desperation here that I knew existed theoretically, but which I had no real concept of. Women would walk up to four hours every day to reach small amounts of water that they used for cooking. Along the way they would have to collect firewood. Food was incredibly scarce. What crops there were seemed to be failing. There were no schools and there were hardly any children. Many of the men seemed quite sick. There was nothing here but suffering.

Sachs again talked of inputs. He talked about the difference that nitrogen would bring to the soil. The difference a single deep well would bring to the community. And they needed bed nets, he declared. The most important input of all was bed nets. The reason there were so few children in this area was that so many of them had died from malaria in the previous two years. "When the children die, there is no point in carrying on. These people need nets."

Not only did I feel helpless, but I felt intense shame at the contents of my briefcase: the little "in case" kit I had prepared for this week-long journey to the continent. I had more drugs and antibiotics in my bag than could be found for probably two hundred kilometres. If there was a nurse, if there was a clinic, I could have handed the drugs over. There was nothing.

I also had a thousand American dollars hidden in the wall of my backpack, "just in case." Even if I wanted to, there was nobody to give money to. There was no economy here. A protein bar would carry more value than a fifty-dollar bill. These people were completely on their own in devastating circumstances. This is why Sachs was so passionate about the villages.

———

NORTHERN ETHIOPIA HAS STAYED with me. The idea that Millennium Villages could be established there was a grand vision, but an important one.

After witnessing the extreme poverty in northern Ethiopia, I realized the villages that Sachs initially showed us were, in fact, paradise. The schools, the clinic and those fields of corn weren't rudimentary; they weren't rustic. They were game changers. They were oxygen.

It was on the walk back to our SUV, with our bottled water and air conditioning, that Belinda said, "I guess when we get home, we're going to have to find a way to buy a lot of bed nets."

"What's a bed net cost?" I remember asking.

She said, "Does it matter?"

THE REST OF THE journey involved so many experiences that I have a hard time processing even now.

We toured the port of Djibouti. One of the busiest container ports in the world. Modern in some areas, but in others you saw hundreds of men loading and unloading ships by hand. Scurrying up and down ladders. The air was so dry and hot it felt like being in a blast furnace. It was hard to imagine standing in this heat for an hour, let alone performing hard physical labour.

Belinda was travelling as a private citizen with no security—save occasionally for Mike, asleep by the door—but the RCMP presumably knew where the cabinet minister was at all times. It was in Djibouti that we were contacted and told we shouldn't spend the night there. The advice was to move on. We headed to Rwanda, where we stayed at the Hotel Rwanda, well known as the place where roughly a thousand foreign nationals and civilians holed up during the genocide. A movie of that name had been released not much earlier.

In popular culture it is often portrayed as a luxury hotel, and perhaps by Rwandan standards of the time it was. By Western standards it very much felt like a perfectly fine Holiday Inn you might find on the outskirts of Edmonton. It did have a small swimming pool. It wasn't lost on us that, having just witnessed some of the most extreme poverty on earth, we were checking into a hotel and saying, "See you by the pool in twenty minutes."

The world has seen many genocides, but the Rwandan genocide of 1994 is history's most recent. Over a period of a hundred days, from April 7 to July 15, civil war reigned outside the walls of this hotel. The Hutu majority slaughtered the Tutsi minority indiscriminately and in the streets. Over five hundred thousand people were murdered. That many, or more, were left seriously wounded.

And here we were, just eleven years later, bobbing around in the pool that hotel guests had to drink from to stay alive while taking shelter from a horrific conflict.

It felt very recent because it was. To put it in context, at the peak of the Rwandan genocide, *Seinfeld* was the number one TV show in America and Céline Dion was at the top of the charts with *The Colour of My Love*. That seems like yesterday by today's standards. On that day in the pool, it seemed like five minutes ago.

The next day, we toured the Kigali Genocide Memorial, which is not just a permanent exhibition that tells the story of the genocide, but is also the final resting place of a quarter of a million Tutsi people. The horrors are well illustrated by the display of thousands of preserved human skulls with machete wounds.

That's a day trip that will never leave you.

The next day we travelled on to Uganda and saw more Millennium Villages. Smiling children, schools, the whole nine yards.

To my eyes now, the villages were the greatest places on earth.

And, of course, we saw areas in desperate need of aid. In desperate need of Sachs's vision. In the last country we visited, Uganda, we had perhaps the strangest experience of them all.

It was here, in the capital city of Kampala, that Dr. Sachs was scheduled to meet with President Yoweri Museveni. Museveni had discovered that a Canadian delegation that included a cabinet minister was travelling with Sachs and insisted we come along. He was extending his hospitality.

And so it was, on the last day of our trip to Africa, that Belinda, Mike and I found ourselves standing in the lobby of our hotel, waiting to be picked up by a presidential motorcade. If memory serves me correctly, we were to be picked up at 6 p.m. for a one-hour meeting, after which the three of us were going to find some food.

The motorcade didn't show. But we waited. And waited some more. We didn't even want to attend, and now it looked like we were being stood up. Or were we? It was impossible to tell.

I didn't care. If it weren't for Belinda, I would have gone back to my room or out for a stroll. I'm pretty sure she would have left as well, but she has a cooler head than I do, and she was a minister of the Crown. "Canadian TV dork skips meeting with Ugandan president" was hardly going to cause any diplomatic ripples, but with her, who knew.

When the motorcade did show up, three hours late, it was exactly as you might think. At the risk of sounding culturally insensitive, knowing what I did about Uganda and Museveni, I couldn't help but wonder whether we were on our way to an over-the-top evening we would never forget or were soon to be never seen again.

The ride to the palace was surreal. I had never been in a motorcade before, and certainly not one screaming through the streets of Kampala. *Is Scorsese directing this?* I wondered.

We arrived at the palace and my first takeaway was gold. Lots of gold.

I find gold gaudy at the best of times. Seeing gratuitous gold in vast quantities just hours after seeing unspeakable poverty is very unsettling. I remember suggesting we steal a few candle holders and put them in Belinda's purse. We could open a Millennium Village with that.

At the palace we were directed to a waiting room where Sachs and his group were also waiting. And together we waited. And waited some more.

At some point someone entered and explained that Museveni is very much "the late owl."

And then the thirst kicked in. Actual thirst. But there was no water and no washrooms we could see. This had to be intentional. Under Museveni, Uganda received vast amounts of financial aid every year from the United Nations—and so, indirectly, from countries like Canada. He clearly wanted to show his gratitude by making Mr. United Nations and Ms. Canadian Government wait in a room for hours without water.

Finally, Belinda stood up and knocked on a door, and when a man answered, she said politely, "My colleagues and I are leaving. I have a meeting. We will need a car to take us back to the hotel, or we can walk."

"Oh, but President Museveni would like to see you now!"

God, how I wish he had said something else.

We were directed to a lavish dining room and introduced to the man himself. I assume it was a dining room. There was nothing to dine on. I wasn't expecting dinner, but at this point I would have killed for a box of raisins.

On this day, the dining hall was doubling as a lecture hall. Sachs and Museveni were supposed to discuss aid. Museveni had other plans. He wanted to lecture Sachs on a myriad of subjects, very few of which were relevant. Try as he might, Sachs could barely get a word in edgewise. Museveni held forth like Castro on coke.

The room was scorching hot. Other parts of the palace were air-conditioned. Museveni didn't seem to mind. We, on the other hand, were fading fast. Mike looked unwell. About an hour into the lecture, I finally thought, *This is insane.* I stood up and walked out the door I came in. Not to leave, but to look for water. As I walked out, Museveni looked at me with what I would have to suggest was complete contempt. I sensed he did not like me.

Outside, I found "a guy" and asked for water. He brought me one glass. I walked it back in and laid it in front of Mike and took my seat. Again, there were daggers. I thought, *Dude, I didn't go outside and take a leak on your floor. I got my buddy some water. Relax.*

The lecture continued. The upshot, as far as I could tell, was that he didn't care about poverty very much at all. His favourite subjects seemed to be how great he was and what a genius he was. If you needed proof, look no farther than the gold hat he owns.

At this point, Museveni had been president of Uganda since 1986. I am sad to say that as of this writing, he is still president. Politics has been good to him. He is estimated to be worth over sixty million dollars, he has a legacy that includes the use of child soldiers, and he continues to champion legislation that would see gay men imprisoned for life for being, well, gay. Was he aware, I wonder, that he had in his dining room that night two big homos and a politician who had made same-sex marriage a cornerstone of her political career?

Also, to this day, he still doesn't care about his people starving.

In hindsight I wish I *had* taken a leak on the floor. Would have been time better spent.

It's unfortunate that our last evening in Africa was spent in his company. We had met so many wonderful people at the villages. So many great locals everywhere we went. To be in his company was a low point.

Somehow, we got up the next morning and started travelling, and again muscled straight on through to Toronto Pearson. When we landed, I don't know if I was ever so tired and confused in my life. The last week had left me—left all of us—with a lot to digest and a lot to unpack.

And when we were saying goodbye to one another at the airport, Belinda said, "About those bed nets?"

I told her, "Remember when I said I would go on this trip? I said I would not come back from Africa having turned into one of those people who never stops talking about Africa."

"Agreed," said Belinda. "Think about it and give me a call."

FOUR MONTHS LATER, THIS release went out:

MONTREAL, 9 November 2006—"1 Net. 10 Bucks. Save Lives. Spreadthenet.org." It's a mantra that Belinda Stronach and satirist Rick Mercer want everyone to understand, repeat and do something about over the next two years. The member of Parliament for Newmarket–Aurora joined one of Canada's funniest comedians, Rick Mercer, and world-leading economist and global anti-poverty advocate Dr. Jeffrey Sachs to launch Spread the Net.

It's an innovative partnership with UNICEF Canada with the goal of purchasing 500,000 insecticide-treated bed nets at the cost of $10 each over the next two years. . .

"The problems of disease and poverty in Africa can seem overwhelming," said Rick Mercer. "Spread the Net brings it all down to a straightforward human level. Canadians don't agree on much, but we can all support a war on mosquitoes. . . It's the ultimate Canadian solution."

And just like that, I was in. I became that guy.

13

Spreading the Net

Spread the Net was something I did on the side. I never talked about it on the TV show. And for very good reason. *RMR* was a comedy show. Malaria is not an amusing subject. Malaria kills more children on the continent of Africa than all childhood diseases combined.

People in my line of work like to say there are no rules in comedy. That's not true. There is one very important rule: never talk about children dying of a terrible disease in the middle of your show.

Makes sense. I couldn't imagine making a joke about a cabinet minister's penchant for expensive orange juice and then trying to come up with an elegant way to remind Canadians that infants in Nigeria were dying, before throwing to a road piece about polar bears in Churchill, Manitoba. And so I never even considered talking about Spread the Net on TV.

And then disaster struck.

Not a disaster by the true definition of the term. I'm not talking

I would like to say my participation in a firefighters calendar helped raise a fortune for charity but there is no evidence of that. I will say out of all the participants I had the shortest month.

Me, still standing upright and with a smile on my face, shortly before being tasered.

On a fact-finding mission to Africa with then-MP Belinda Stronach. She didn't ask Stephen Harper's permission to appear on the show. This was not a woman used to being told what to do.

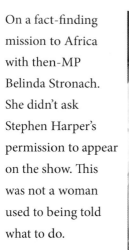

In a Millennium Village in Uganda. Compared to what Belinda and I had seen earlier on our trip this was one of the greatest places on earth.

The Spread the Net Student Challenge led to some of the most personally rewarding television I have ever been involved in. Students from all parts of Canada stepped up to the plate year after year and raised astounding amounts of money for anti-malaria bed nets in Africa.

Jann Arden became a regular guest on a TV show that didn't have regular guests. I couldn't stop myself. I loved to hear her scream, and the audiences did too.

Parliament Hill never gets tired for me. Changing the flag on the Peace Tower might not be on everyone's bucket list, but it had been on mine for quite a while.

As the *Ottawa Citizen* put it, "A few weeks ago, there was no such thing as a 'vote mob.' But an idea hiding in a deep, dark corridor of comedian Rick Mercer's brain has, quite by accident, unleashed this holy terror onto unsuspecting Canadians." I don't know if that's true or not but I was happy to take the blame.

Fishing with Bob Rae. You'll just have to imagine what came next. If you
saw it on the show, it's probably seared into your memory.

The Right Stuff: The brave men of the Rossland bobsled team celebrate surviving the race.

about an airplane crashing into a Scottish village, but rather a disaster by TV production standards.

One night after we shot our dry run, after jettisoning some desk material that just wasn't working, we realized we were light. By "light," I mean we didn't have enough material to fill the entire show. We were two minutes light, to be exact.

In TV terms, two minutes is an eternity. This was the disaster. Never mind that we were contractually obligated to come up with exactly twenty-one minutes of material ever week. Anything less would be a technical breach of contract. The CBC would have no choice but to put on another commercial for the walk-in bathtub.

Coming up light was unheard of—Gerald had a savant's ability to line up the show in his head. Week after week the show would come in almost exactly on time. He kept track of all the timings like Rain Man. Come in heavy and it's a piece of cake. You can always find a place to cut a minute, or even two. But come in light and you are hooped. Luckily, we had a backup plan. Occasionally, when we came up light, we would announce a silly contest.

I liked running contests on the show. We had run a few at this point. We'd staged one asking Canadians to send in video and pictures of "Canada's best shed." We had one where we asked for pics and video of "Canada's best toboggan run."

I had huge hopes for the toboggan run contest. I had visions of us cutting together lots of footage of kids from all over Canada, racing down snowy hills, hitting jumps and having spectacular wipeouts. It would be fast, fun and über-Canadian, and as a bonus the content would be free. The only problem was that very few people sent in toboggan video. The contest was a dud.

This was a real disappointment. Some of my favourite moments on TV shows I'd been involved with contained a certain amount of audience participation. On 22 *Minutes* I launched a petition demanding that Canadian Alliance leader Stockwell Day change his name to Doris, and 1.2 million people signed the thing. It was wildly popular, and it drove Stock insane, so it was a win-win.

Using the same website, we had thousands of Canadians send messages to Canadian peacekeepers serving in Bosnia over the holidays. It was wildly popular and made people cry at Christmas.

So far, we hadn't come up with the right way to engage our *RMR* audience in the same way. And here was another opportunity to try, because we had two minutes to fill at the end of the show. The perfect amount of time to announce a contest.

Problem was, we didn't have one. In a perfect world we would have had a competition all written up and standing by for just this kind of situation. Unfortunately, we weren't that clever. But on the upside, we did have a full half-hour to come up with a contest, create some rules and get it all in the teleprompter.

I was trying to come up with the most Canadian contest imaginable: best butter tart recipe, best camping disaster video, best impersonation of John Diefenbaker. You know, something to really excite the kids.

It was Gerald who said, "What about Spread the Net?"

"What about it?" I said.

"Challenge students to buy your nets."

Gerald always has a way of keeping me guessing. I was shocked he was suggesting this. There is nothing he hates more than a TV show suddenly trying to act important. And when I first told him that Belinda and I were planning to start this charity, he was supportive, but said, "If you ever start sounding like a Kielburger, I'll have to murder you." Gerald liked nation building. He liked funny. He liked speaking truth to power. He liked good satire. He hated when people got self-important.

So I set about trying to figure out how we could have a contest that would make sense for the show and at the same time, hopefully, lead to a few bed nets being purchased. Piece of cake. After all, we had an easy fifteen minutes at this point to write it up and get it into the teleprompter. The audience was filing into the studio upstairs.

"Okay," I said, "we will keep it very simple. We will challenge students to raise money to buy nets and we will give them a hat or a mug. First, second and third place to the students who buy the most nets?"

"*Schools*," said Gerald. "Whichever school buys the most nets is the winner."

"That's a lot of hats," I said. "The hats might cost us more than the nets."

"No hats," he said. "You will go there. You'll be the prize."

"They might prefer the hats," I said.

"No—the prize is, their school gets to be on TV. You would have killed to be on TV when you were in high school. We need more young people on the show anyway. It always works. You like them, they like you."

So we would be saving children's lives and we would be getting content for TV. That's show business in a nutshell right there. Philanthropy for philanthropy's sake; content, and ratings, for god's sake.

I banged out the basic contest rules, emailed them to our script co-ordinator and went upstairs with an entire minute to spare. And an hour later, right at the end of the episode, I turned to camera three, and before saying goodnight, I said the following:

"And this week we are launching a brand new contest: the *Mercer Report* Spread the Net Campus Challenge. We are challenging high schools and universities all across Canada to raise money for Spread the Net. To purchase anti-malaria bed nets for distribution in Africa."

Then, without delving deep into the horrors of the disease, I instead pointed viewers to the Spread the Net website, which took care of all that. I said, "In February of this year I will visit the winning school. We will show Canada why you have the best school in the country."

And then the tag: "Ten bucks buys a net and saves a life."

I signed off and headed into the weekend.

Two minutes of TV, just like that. And if we managed to get a few hundred nets in the bargain, that would be the gravy.

From the minute the show aired there was a phenomenal response to the contest. Far more than I anticipated. That night we got over fifty emails from students in schools around the country, wanting more information on the contest or committing their school or university to the challenge.

I was on the road for the first few days of the week, and when I returned to the office in time for Wednesday's read-through, everyone was buzzing about the contest. I was pumped.

The first guy I saw as I came through the door was our production co-ordinator, Baron Evans. I said to him, "Can you believe the feedback for the Spread the Net Challenge? We might end up with seventy-five schools."

"It's unbelievable," Baron said, "but I have to tell you, you've never done anything on the show that has upset people like this. Some people are very angry."

This was not what I expected. And immediately I felt like my head was going to pop off. Who, I wondered, would get upset over something like this?

I asked Baron, "What kind of person would be upset about high school students and university students raising money for bed nets? Who are they?"

"Children," said Baron. "Most of them are children, grades one through six."

Turns out, elementary students were disappointed that they weren't eligible to join the contest.

"That is so bizarre," I said.

"Why aren't they eligible?" asked Baron.

"Well," I said, "malaria is serious stuff. It kills children. Small children. I don't know if it's appropriate to talk about that in elementary schools. It's more suitable for young adults. Also, I made up the rules in fifteen minutes and never gave it much thought."

· Well, it turns out it didn't matter what I thought. Over the next few days, more and more schools signed up. On the form we sent them to register, they had to check a box to indicate whether they were a post-secondary institution or a high school.

Many of the high schools had names like Immaculate Conception Elementary or Upper Canada Lower School. Clearly, these schools were lying.

I found out that kids had already learned about malaria in school, knew exactly how deadly it was for children, and when they heard they could save a life by raising ten dollars, they wanted in.

Not for the first time, I caught myself saying, "What is wrong with kids today?" What kind of world are we living in when entire schools full of kids were entering contests that they weren't eligible to win? It's like they were doing it for altruistic reasons or something.

And from that moment on, the momentum never stopped. Every week, more and more schools were getting in touch with us. Spread the Net clubs were popping up in schools in every province and territory.

We were hearing stories of inventive fundraisers. There were media reports all over Canada about schools attempting to buy the most nets. The relief organization UNICEF was suddenly being inundated by businesses and community groups who wanted to fundraise to purchase nets.

Unlike my idea for Canada's best toboggan run, this was a contest that captured the imagination of young people everywhere. The response was well beyond anything I could have imagined. As we headed to the finish line, 250 schools were participating in the Spread the Net Challenge. Together they raised over three hundred thousand dollars. Even I could do the math: students in Canada took it upon themselves to save thirty thousand lives.

Again—what is it with kids today?

And the school that won? Dalhousie University in Halifax, Nova Scotia. They raised over seventeen thousand dollars.

AS PROMISED, IN THE middle of February 2008 I went to Dalhousie to crown them the winner and to show the country how great their school is.

It was not a hard job.

And the easiest job of all was to highlight the organizers as incredible citizens.

The organizers were three young people: Hilary Taylor, Keith Torrie and Victoria Jones. Hilary had seen me talking about the challenge on George Stroumboulopoulos's show, called two

friends and that was it. Despite a full academic load and the pressing social obligations of the young, these three students threw
themselves headfirst into a fundraising campaign and managed
to get the entire campus on board.

First up, they put their money where their mouths were. They
used their own funds to invest in a line of T-shirts made by a
local company emblazoned with a Spread the Net Dalhousie
logo. They sold them on campus and made thousands. For the
record, no student loan money was used to finance this start-up.
That would have been wrong.

Then they cleverly encouraged the various professional soci-
eties on campus to compete against one another. Pitting the
engineering school against the law school proved to be particularly profitable. They approached the student union, and the president, a soft-spoken young man by the name of Mike Tipping,
jumped on board and committed the resources of student government to the campaign.

Mike was a great interview. He was incredibly passionate and
rightly proud of his school. I was taken with his quiet resolve, and
he struck me as the kind of leader we needed more of in this
country. I predicted then and there that one day we would see
him sitting in the House of Commons or a provincial legislature.
He became my guide as I explored the campus and created a profile of the school for the show.

It being a university, I learned a few things.

The professor who ran the beer-making program informed
me that brewing was a multi-billion-dollar industry in Canada. It
was bigger than dairy! In that department, I also met a young
man who was working towards his PhD in beer. I didn't even
know such a thing existed. I had an uncle with a PhD in rum and
Coke, but it was an honorary doctorate.

And the great thing about the kid who was getting his PhD in beer? He had recently become engaged to a young woman who was doing her master's in lager. I assume they are married by now and producing a brewd of brews together.

The engineers at Dalhousie showed me how quicksand worked. They put me in a barrel of the stuff and I began to sink. It eventually encased my legs and hardened. I felt like I was inside of a blood pressure machine. I was worried my weak bones would be crushed on national TV. My, how they laughed as they explained the science behind the torture.

The young people at the law school were incredibly well spoken. It's no surprise the Dalhousie law department is so highly respected. The two smartest lawyers I've known in my life—famed criminal defence attorney Larry Cohen and the Honourable Frances Knickle, Justice of the Court of Appeal of Newfoundland and Labrador, are both graduates of Dalhousie Law.

But on this day, they were proudest of another celebrated alumnus. They pulled out a yearbook and showed us a photo of law student Peter MacKay, the former leader of the Progressive Conservative Party of Canada and current justice critic for the Conservatives. Peter always had to fight the perception that he was a frat-boy jock. These future lawyers put that to rest by showing us various pictures of Peter in the yearbook. The most prominent showed the future attorney general of Canada sitting in a chair with a tube in his mouth that was attached to a large funnel. Three young men with ginormous heads were pouring numerous beers into the funnel, which would of course be shotgunned at enormous speed and pressure down the soon-to-be Honourable Member's throat.

To be fair, the caption indicated he was sucking on the beer bong for a good cause—namely, he was fighting for the right to party.

They provided me with copies of the photo in all formats. Digital and analog.

As I moved around the campus interviewing students, it seemed that everyone was aware of the Spread the Net campaign. And they had all taken in a bake sale or bought a T-shirt or put a few bucks in a bucket. They were, to a person, amazing. And this wasn't just about being on TV. Students even then didn't care about TV the way I did at that age.

They cared about doing their part. It was about checking their privilege.

I couldn't remember when I found a shoot so satisfying. It just felt great. And they had an energy that can only be found in the young. My only surprise was that I felt a slight feeling of regret.

I never went to college or university. I never considered it. And my ill-spent youth guaranteed I wouldn't have been able to attend even if I did have an interest in it. Seeing these young people, all so accomplished and confident and so eager to be at school, really drove home what I had missed and what I was too stupid to figure out.

I'm a very lucky man. I have few regrets, but that is one of them. Stay in school, kids. It's an experience that should not be missed. And when you're there, make sure on occasion you partake in something far bigger than you. You won't regret it.

As I left Dalhousie, I knew this wasn't the end of the Spread the Net Challenge. I knew it would become baked into the DNA of the *Mercer Report*.

I could see it getting bigger in many ways.

And it certainly did.

In fact, looking back, the only thing I was wrong about on that first shoot was my impression of the president of the student union, Mike Tipping.

I thought for sure he would end up being a Canadian politician. I was off the mark.

He is currently a state senator in the great state of Maine.

Turns out that, although he was going to school in Nova Scotia, he was a citizen of the place next door.

WITH THE SUCCESS OF the Spread the Net program, the best thing happened. My fears that only the largest and most affluent schools would win were completely unfounded. Year after year, a dark horse would emerge. Some school that, on paper, didn't look like it stood a chance would take the prize.

Make that one of the *four* prizes. Eventually, we were visiting four schools a year—three winning schools and one that received honourable mention. And every time, we were thrilled to find out it was all about the students. Certainly, some teachers championed and challenged their students, but the winning schools were always powered by motivated kids who got it into their heads that they could beat the entire country in raising money for bed nets.

And then, on occasion, there were the kids who wanted to hijack the contest for their own political gains. How fantastic is that? As a political junkie, nothing could make be prouder.

I'm speaking most of all about the students at PCVS, a.k.a. Peterborough Collegiate and Vocational School in Ontario. Disruptors of the highest order.

In 2012, forty-seven schools across Canada took part in the Spread the Net Challenge. Together, they raised over a quarter of a million dollars. But one school stood out above all others. PCVS, with just seven hundred students, and which had never entered the challenge before, raised a whopping fifty-three thousand dollars. One-fifth of the grand total came from one modestly sized school.

So, of course, off we went to Peterborough to discover the secret of their success and find out what their motivation was.

I knew there was something special about this place the minute we pulled up. For starters, it didn't look like any school I had seen. It was a stately stone building in the heart of downtown. It looked like a private school from the movies or a large Manhattan public library. It was clearly a heritage building. It was welcoming. The kind of building that made you think, *I'd like to work in there.*

The building and school were established in 1827. And as I said in my introduction to the piece, "Prime Minister Lester B. Pearson went to this school, and with a fundraising spirit like this, they are clearly just hitting their stride."

After I shot the introduction, Don said, "Beautiful." He wasn't referring to me, but the building. He pointed out that in all our years of shooting introduction pieces in front of high schools in Canada, he always struggled to make them look remotely interesting or welcoming. "They all look like prisons," he said. "This building is beautiful."

It certainly was. On the outside, it had character for days. And on the inside, there were characters for miles.

First, we met the organizers of the challenge. I was eager to learn all the usual things: Why Spread the Net? How had they raised the money? But my Spidey senses were tingling and there was an elephant in the room. There was a very exciting not-so-hidden agenda.

When we pulled up to the school there were Spread the Net banners in the windows and hanging from the marble pillars. It was very elegant. But you would have had to be blind not to notice, as you drove through downtown Peterborough, some other extremely prominent signs. It seemed like in the window of every business and every home was a sign that said, "Save Our School," "SOS" or "Save PCVS."

It turns out that this school was slated to be permanently closed at the end of the academic year. And the kids were having none of it. We had wandered into a highly orchestrated campaign, run entirely by students, to fight the Government of Ontario and save their school.

Be still, my beating heart. This was a hotbed of activism.

Out of the gate, I had questions.

First of all, "Why?"

I went to a pretty good high school; it was considered one of the better ones in the city of St. John's. I owed a lot to that school; it was there I found the drama club. The school did well academically, the sports program was pretty good, the gym was big, and there were several large soccer fields and playing surfaces nearby that proved popular every spring when they became covered in a carpet of psilocybin mushrooms. In other words, it had something for everyone.

My point is, if there had been a poll among students, I'm pretty sure the results would have been overwhelmingly positive. That said, had the government of the day announced they were closing the school, had they announced they were going to blow it up or burn it to the ground, I think the news would have been met with a collective shrug. There probably would have been some high-fives.

And for kids in grade twelve? Their final year? Why would they care if the school was being closed? They already had one foot out the door.

Things were very different in Peterborough.

In September of 2012, when the students there were just settling in for a new academic year, a memo went out that the
school was being closed. There was no warning. There was no
real justification, there was no option to appeal. For the folks in
Peterborough this was a literal bombshell—students were devas-
tated, alumni were outraged, parents were afraid.

I decided my mission was to determine why these students,
this community, were so passionate about this old stone building
on a busy city street. After all, it was only a school. The country
has thousands of them.

Turns out the mission was not that difficult. Just walking up
the stone steps, you felt history under your feet—in the stone and
in your bones. The erosion of Canadian granite doesn't happen
overnight. And yet you could see in each of the stairs the gentle
concave of dimples and divots caused by tens of thousands of
feet over the last 185 years.

Did Lester B. Pearson take these stairs two at a time? Did he
sit on them and debate politics with his fellow students? A friend
of mine, the comedian Seán Cullen, was on the PCVS website
as a notable alumnus. Did he discover his first audiences on
these steps?

Inside the giant front doors, you were greeted with an equally
imposing, very wide corridor. High ceilings were but a joke. And
the art? The place was dripping with student-created art. This
was not an official arts school; this was a regular school and a
vocational school. But the arts clearly played a big role.

We met the organizers of the challenge, who were over-the-
moon proud of themselves, and rightly so. And they revealed their
nefarious plan immediately. From the moment the school closure
was announced, the students mobilized and raised money for a
legal challenge. They learned how to lobby, how to get noticed.

In the local community they had practically unanimous support. For a very long time, businesses in downtown Peterborough had been powered in part by these students. They backed them all the way.

The students knew they needed attention. And when they heard about the Spread the Net Challenge, they came up with a simple plan: raise way more money than anyone else in Canada, get Rick to come to the school, and get the message out—save our school.

They presented the plan at a general assembly and the entire student population bought in.

With our cameras rolling, we headed to the auditorium. There was going to be a rally, the presentation of a giant cheque and a special presentation. They hid me away backstage to wait until I was introduced by the president of the student council.

I have done this many times before. Usually when you're backstage at a high school waiting to be introduced, there is a classic vibe. There is a principal at the microphone, rules are being discussed, some guy is being told to "stop doing that." Attendees are being reminded, "If you want to be treated like young adults, you should act like young adults."

This was different. It sounded like we were at a rock concert. And when I peeked out through a curtain, I saw that we *were* at a rock concert. There was a full rock band onstage, made up of students, and they were taking the roof off the place. It was a good band.

Before long I was introduced, I walked out onstage—and wow. The performer in me almost fell over. This was a beautiful auditorium—a proper one, very rare in today's world—with raked seating for 550 students, plus a large balcony for another 300. Across that balcony hung a huge hand-painted banner saying, "PCVS Saves Lives." Every single student wore a "Save Our School" T-shirt.

I spoke to the students and congratulated them; they presented me with a cheque, and then put me in the front row and gave us a show. The rock band played again. The kids from the school musical came on and did a number that was killer. Then there were dancers, there were singers, it just kept going. I noticed that students were running the sound board, the lights, hosting the entire event. The teachers were off to the side, enjoying the spectacle.

It was pretty easy to see why they loved this school.

From there we ran around the building, visiting various classrooms and making a music video. This one featured students lip-synching to my favourite Canadian rock anthem, "Raise a Little Hell"—the RMR theme song that never was.

Never has the song been used so appropriately.

Again and again our minds were blown in each class we visited. The science lab was fantastic—Bunsen burners were on bust and the teacher had students doing visually exciting experiments involving lots of flames. The shop class area was top-notch. There was a dance studio. This was a vocational school, and nobody graduated without knowing how to change their tires, change their oil and use a drill and a mitre box.

Don was over the moon with the natural light streaming into every classroom and laboratory. "Natural light! In a school!" he said. "Who knew?"

At recess we were presented with another cheque from the Gay-Straight Alliance. The entire school cheered them on. There was not one unkind heckle, only cheers. I generally don't cry when I'm at work, but I couldn't help but think of Jamie Hubley, the gay teenager from Ottawa who took his own life after being bullied. How different things might have been if this had been his school, if this was the kind of support he experienced every day.

I found out that PCVS had a twenty-four-hour anti-bullying hotline. If a student felt unsafe at any time, their call would be forwarded to a teacher-volunteer on duty who'd been trained in the field. Any hour of the day or night, they could call. Nobody had called in three years.

What was this place?

Continuing work on our rock video, I went to the office and asked if I could make an announcement requesting that any students with instruments line up in the main hallway.

The principal smirked and said, "That's pretty much all of them."

Instead, I asked for anyone with a guitar to come to the main hallway.

Twenty minutes later Don was running up and down the hallway shooting two lines of seventy students playing all manner of guitars. And they were *playing*!

We had our video in record time and were very happy with every student we spoke with.

We met a student who donated her entire paycheque to Spread the Net. I had never heard of such a thing.

"Where do you work?" I asked.

"Red Lobster," she said.

"How much was your paycheque?"

"Two hundred and twenty," she said.

She donated two hundred and twenty dollars to Spread the Net! Then I found out that seven other students had done the same thing, donating their paycheques. I asked one young woman why and she said, "I saw the presentation on malaria in Africa, I had my paycheque in my purse, I thought, *I was going to spend this money on clothes, I have clothes, I'm giving it to them.*"

Yet again I found myself wondering, "What is wrong with kids today?"

And in case you think it was only the students who were exemplary, I learned that when word got around about those seven students donating their paycheques, the teachers at the school matched the sum out of their own pockets.

We heard about bake sales, bottle drives, car washes and talent shows. They did not leave a single stone unturned. There were many early mornings and many late nights.

And then it was time for the student council. I wanted with every fibre of my being to let the student politicians talk about saving their school.

I spoke to two students, Collin Chepeka and Kristen Bruce. They told me that they had held dual fundraisers all year, raising money to fund the Save Our School campaign and for Spread the Net. Together, the two campaigns had raised over a hundred thousand dollars.

The Save Our School money was needed for all their signs and T-shirts. And they chartered buses and drove five hundred students to Queen's Park in Toronto, where they rallied to save their school.

They needed me, they said, to try to force the government's hand. They needed me to draw attention to the school closure and to get the premier's attention.

And then I asked the stupid question.

"Why do you need me?" I said. "What did the premier say when you went to Queen's Park?"

"He won't meet with us," they said. "He wouldn't address the students at the rally and he wouldn't have a private meeting with representatives from council."

"What did the minister of education say?"

"He hasn't returned our calls."

I should emphasize that the premier of Ontario at the time, Dalton McGuinty, liked to call himself the "Education Premier."

I don't know what his minister of education was called at the time, but I could make a few suggestions.

This revelation from the students broke my heart. And honestly, it shattered a lot of my belief in our system. Because these students were about as passionate as any young citizens you are ever going to meet. They were whip-smart and very organized. And they were fighting for the greater good. Many of the students were in grade twelve and were preparing applications to university, but they were still fighting. Not for themselves—they would be graduating in a few months—but for their little brothers and sisters. They were fighting for the kids they didn't know, who were in the system behind them. They were fighting for their community.

I know that governments must make unpopular decisions sometimes. And I know that not every decision gets overturned because five hundred people stand on a lawn and peacefully protest. But when a premier refuses to meet with young people like this, he's lost the plot. It's time to go.

And honestly, I don't understand how any politician worth their salt wouldn't walk over broken glass to meet these kids. Even if they couldn't give them what they wanted, this was literally a cohort of future leaders and political activists.

You want to get on their good side.

But instead, they ignored them. I guess they didn't care that these future Lester B. Pearsons would forever know that the Liberal Party of Ontario was not the place for them.

I loved these students. They had me at "We will never stop fighting, the stakes are too high"—and boy, were they right. This was a school worth saving.

In the end, I'm embarrassed to say I was as naive as they were.

I was so pleased with the episode we shot at PCVS. Anyone

could see what a special place it was. And I guess I was under the misguided assumption that the power of the segment, and a rant I wrote about the experience there, would compel the premier or the minister of education to at least meet with these students.

I even allowed myself the fantasy of believing that the segment might change the government's mind.

No such luck. There was no meeting. Ever.

It was a tough lesson for those students. In writing this book, I decided to get on social media and track some of them down. They are all in their late twenties now. They are all, as expected, thriving. They have careers, some have young families, and many are still in Peterborough.

They are all active in their communities. They are the citizens we want.

They all have fond memories of the fight to save their school. To a person, they say it unleashed an activist spirit in them that has never entirely gone away.

Out of curiosity, I asked a few of them if they identified as Liberals, or ever supported the party. I know it's very rude to ask someone how they vote, but I really wanted to know.

Not one of them, even the ones I suspected of being Liberals, would cop to it. That was a bridge too far.

They should have been given the courtesy of a meeting.

Good job, Liberals. You reap what you sow.

THE SPREAD THE NET Challenge would remain part of the *Mercer Report* for eleven years.

From a production point of view, putting the winning show together was a nightmare. We couldn't control who was going to win, so we never knew where we were going until the last minute.

For John and Tom, this involved some serious sorcery. It's hard to plan when you have no idea where you are going. And of course, as luck would have it, we would often end up with winning schools that were at opposite ends of the country.

But once we arrived at a location, the shoots themselves were always epic. The kids who organized the fundraisers were always fantastic. They were usually school leaders, and they were always impressive on-camera. Confident, well-spoken and committed to a cause. And the rallies we held were just too much fun. Getting everyone in school into one room was an excellent way to thank the entire student body and get as many faces on-camera as we possibly could. And it was a great opportunity to get kids to dance.

The Spread the Net shoots always ended with a music video featuring kids singing along to a classic Canadian rock tune. At the rallies, I'd invite students to come forward and dance in front of the entire school. When I was in school, nobody would have done that, but times have changed. We had kids doing traditional Punjabi dancing, Irish and Scottish dancing, ballet, hip hop, the whole gamut. And so many kids, without any training, just let their freak flag fly.

Don, who likes to shoot dance more than anything, would be drenched but smiling.

We shot an astounding amount of footage on these Spread the Net shoots. The camera never stopped rolling. Which meant Al MacLean, our master editor, would have to work harder on these montages than anything else all year. He never complained because after they were screened, there would never be a dry eye in the house.

But it wasn't the hardest work in the world because, never mind the smiling faces and youthful exuberance, there was always an over-the-top compelling story to tell. For example, in 2017, kids in Fort MacMurray, Alberta, raised over ten thousand dollars. That alone is a great story, but this was also the school year that saw those same kids evacuated from their homes because of wildfires.

Many of these students lost everything in the fires, hundreds of students were displaced, all of them were traumatized, and yet they decided to step up and raise money for Spread the Net. They wanted to make sure kids on the other side of the world slept safely at night.

If you can't make that into a good TV segment, you should go into another line of work.

The Spread the Net Challenge wasn't just good TV, it was restoring-your-faith-in-humanity TV. When I returned from a Spread the Net shoot, I was always walking on air. The future of the country never seemed as bright as it did after I spent time with the students.

And always we were witness to incredible generosity on the part of some students who didn't want to be on-camera. Students who went above and beyond, who made great personal sacrifices for a cause they believed in. And who, in the true spirit of charity, didn't want any attention or credit. I would have preferred it if they'd wished to be on TV, but I got it.

Over the years we featured students from all over Canada. Spread the Net tapped into a river of generosity that flows through the entire country. Young people helping young people they will never meet or know.

Over the life of the challenge, students raised over two million dollars. Imagine that. Two hundred thousand bed nets were purchased. I've seen these nets in use and I know they work. A lot of lives were saved.

And every bit of the heavy lifting was done by students. Students who were acknowledging how privileged we are to be Canadian. Students who were at the forefront of a global movement. A war on mosquitoes.

It was a happy pill for the soul. And probably our greatest work.

14

Jann Arden Is the Answer

J ann Arden saved my life. Not literally, but pretty darn close.
Ironic, really, because I have a bit of a reputation for putting
her life in danger.

When the *Mercer Report* crew went out on the road, we were
always working without a backup plan. Not because we didn't
believe in them but because it wasn't practical. There was no
time, there were no resources.

The fact that we pulled this off month after month, year after
year was pretty much all down to Tom. He would produce the
segments from his desk. All the nitty-gritty production details
would be worked out over the phone long before we hit the
ground. But because there was no face-to-face contact, because
there was no location scout, there was always an element of the
unknown. We had to put our faith in the people we were doing
business with. Unfortunately, on occasion some of these people
wishfully exaggerated or went full pathological liar on us.

There's nothing quite like driving to a town in the dead of winter, expecting to shoot a segment with hundreds of people on a beautiful Northern Ontario lake that has been groomed with five outdoor hockey rinks, only to find a small pond with a dodgy surface and exactly one street hockey net. The star attraction, a famous ex-hockey player, is not there as promised, but in his place is a man claiming to be a distant relative, who seems to have had his ear removed—and somewhat recently. "We can do anything you want," he said, "although I can't go within two hundred metres of the school or the community centre."

Days like that really kept us on our toes.

And it was on such a day that the show was changed forever.

It was a crisp November afternoon in 2004 and we landed in Calgary only to receive word from Tom that the next day's shoot was cancelled. Somewhere between the time we took off in Toronto and landed in Calgary, Tom had determined the segment was simply was not as advertised and needed to be brought to the woodshed and shot. I can't remember what the details were; they don't matter. All that mattered was that we had to figure out something else to shoot and figure it out fast.

We'd had some luck in the past with high-profile members of Parliament giving us tours of their ridings. We reached out to the office of Jason Kenney, a senior minister in Harper's government, and were informed he was not in the city. I don't know why I bothered. During most of his political career he famously avoided Alberta. He would pop in on occasion, but that was it. During elections he spent his time not knocking on doors in his riding, but in the party's war room in Ottawa.

By the way, let that term sink in: "the war room." All major political parties during an election period call the room they strategize in "the war room." They are all children pretending to be Churchill. But I digress.

We contemplated my touring Calgary on my own, but that would make no sense. I'm not from there. I had no voice of authority. Who, we wondered, would be the best person to show Canada a good time in the city that cowboys founded and oil made tall?

The answer was both obvious and a long shot.

Jann Arden.

She had it all. She was a famous singer-songwriter. Her songs "Insensitive" and "Could I Be Your Girl" were international hits. She had a mittful of Junos. She would be perfect. The only problem was, I had never met the woman, I had no relationship with her and I was a little worried that the writer of the saddest songs in the history of Canada might not be a great fit for me. Anything earnest made me feel awkward. What if she wanted to discuss *feelings* or something? But I was in no position to do anything but go for it. This being Canada, I managed to track down a contact number and put in the call.

I texted her: "Hello Jann Arden, this is Rick Mercer. I have a question. Could we talk?"

She responded within minutes.

"Lose my number, Mercer." Not the first time she would send me this message.

The phone rang. I answered.

"Hi, this is Jann."

God, that was fast. I barely had time to prepare my pitch, so I just started blathering.

"Hi Jann, big fan of yours. Listen—we want to do a segment for the show in Calgary. We want someone to show the rest of the country why Calgary is such a great city to live in—a personal tour, as it were. I can't think of anyone better than you. Would you be interested?"

The crowd from Alberta are like the crowd from Newfoundland: they can't shut up about their province and they will never miss an opportunity to brag about it or show it off. Jann is no exception to this rule. And she agreed to be my guide to Calgary.

Unfortunately, that was followed up with talk of logistics.

"I'll do it, Rick, but I don't know if I have any time. And I need to run it past my manager. I'm leaving on a tour tomorrow night. When I get back, I have a day to do laundry and then I have a gig in Europe. After that it's Nashville. But there's a week or two in Alberta before I'm in the studio in BC. We can do it then. That's, like, a month and a half out."

"Oh," I said. "I was hoping we could shoot this tomorrow."

"Jesus," said Jann, "give a gal some warning."

There was silence.

"Are you asking me on a date?"

"Yes," I said. "That's what I'm calling it: 'My Date with Jann.'"

"Okay," she said. "I'll come to your hotel at 10 a.m. tomorrow, but I've got to be done by six."

And just like that, I had a date.

"And I don't know what you've heard about me, but I'm not putting out," she added.

"Okay, 10 a.m. it is," I said. "Tom in my office is working the phones. He's going to find some locations and we'll put our heads together and I'll email you some details tonight."

"Oh, don't worry about that," she said. "I'll figure all that out."

"Um, okay," I said. This was a bit odd. I like a plan. This didn't sound like "a plan." This sounded like making it up on the spot. I hate making things up on the spot.

"Do you have makeup?" she asked.

"No, there's just three of us, but I think we could find a makeup artist for the day if you want."

"No," she said, "I'll take care of it."

"Okay, then, I'll see you tomorrow morning." And we hung up.

I told Don and John that we were shooting the next day with Jann Arden, I had no idea what we were doing, and she was bringing her own makeup artist.

"Her songs are so sad," said Don. "I bet she's shy."

And then there was nothing we could do except find dinner and accept that we were at the mercy of a person none of us had ever met.

"Well," said Johnny, "we shall see what tomorrow will bring."

What it brought, the next morning, in the parking lot of our hotel, was a whirling dervish.

Jann Arden arrived in my life exactly as she had threatened, at 10 a.m. She pulled into the parking lot and jumped out of the car and said, "Okay, Mercer, who the hell cancelled on you?"

"It was nothing like that," I said.

"Oh, you just hopped on a plane and came here without a plan. Come on, let's get this date started."

As far as us being on a "date," she was, as we say in the business, completely committed to the bit.

My God, I thought, *the woman is a method actor.*

Also, I couldn't help but notice that not only did she not have an assistant of any kind with her, but there was also no makeup artist, and she was not wearing any makeup at all. Until this point in my life I had never met a professional entertainer of the female persuasion who would appear on TV without makeup.

"Okay," I said, "let's do this thing."

We set up the introduction. Standing on the streets of Calgary, with its iconic tower in the background, I said, "You know, when

I think of Calgary, I think of three things: that great big tower behind me, the Calgary Flames and Jann Arden. And look at this, I've got two out of three right here." And with that, Jann walked into frame and said, "Welcome to Calgary, Rick. This is my town."

"Thanks for having me," I responded. "We are going on a date."

"Yes, we are," said Jann. "And I'm so excited because I haven't been on a date since 1989, and the good news is," she said, looking straight into the camera with a big smile, "I'm not on my period."

I saw Don's eyebrow go up.

So much for being shy.

Wow. I did not see that coming. *Can we even have her say that on this show at eight o'clock?* I wondered. Well, it didn't matter because Jann was headed for her SUV. "You drive with me, Mercer," she said. "Let's get this date started."

Standing next to the SUV, she briefed us: "I was thinking we could go to the zoo first and feed some animals. They have elephants. Maybe go to Canada's Olympic Park, where they had the Winter Olympics. See what we can do up there. And we can wrap it up with dinner at my restaurant."

This did not make me feel better. The reality is, and I know this to be true based on hundreds of segments I have taped on the road, you can't just waltz into a zoo or a facility like Canada's Olympic Park and start shooting. These things must be negotiated far in advance. And it *is* a negotiation. Organizations are very concerned about how their facilities will look on TV. And they all have existing policies in place for dealing with TV shoots. There are always hoops that need jumping through.

I had visions of us standing outside the zoo with a security guard telling us we had to move across the street and away from the public entrance.

But we had no choice, so off to the zoo we headed. I exchanged dubious looks with John and hopped in the passenger seat next to Jann.

"Follow me, boys," she shouted and put it in drive.

This was just not the way things were done.

Turns out, of course, I was right. You can't just waltz up to a place like the Calgary Zoo and start shooting a TV show. The notion is absurd. But there is a caveat. You can't waltz up to a place like that and start shooting a TV show—unless you are in Calgary and you are with Jann Arden.

In Alberta, Jann is like a noble gas. She can get through any door.

We literally walked up to the front of the zoo, Jann said hello, and within minutes the king of the zoo was there, offering us whatever we wanted in the kingdom. They were happy to see me, but they were *thrilled* to see her.

They didn't just grant us access to the viewing areas of the zoo. We went backstage. I love backstage, and so does the audience. And where better to start a date than ankle-deep in hippo poo, feeding a pair of half-tonne water mammals?

As we approached, one of the hippos, unimpressed, turned around, revealing two ginormous buttocks. "That, out of all the animals," said Jann, "most closely resembles my ass."

When I was told by the zookeeper to take the water hose and shoot water directly into the hippo's mouth, Jann said, "This reminds me of eating dinner with Ralph Klein." And then she added, "Except in Ralph's case, it's beer."

This was the woman who wrote "Good Mother"? Jann was on fire.

And then we were off to the African Safari Pavilion, where we were met in a giant room by two elephants.

I had never been close to an elephant before, and I was some-what alarmed. I was thinking of those YouTube videos where you see an elephant go on a rampage and step on the trainer's head. But if I was scared, Jann was more so. And it was in the not-so-attractive light of the elephant enclosure that I saw in Jann's eyes something I found irresistible: true fear. She was terrified, but she was going for it. I remember thinking I liked everything about this woman.

Any worries that Kamala the elephant would step on my head were quickly erased. Instead, she used her trunk to either kiss me all over my face or smell me—I'm not sure what she was doing, but it was extremely intimate. And this exploration continued south of the border. Jann and I were the ones supposed to be on the date, but so far I had gotten to second base with an elephant. Technically, I suppose that made us a thruple.

But there was no time to explore that arrangement because we were suddenly back in Jann's car and driving to Canada's Olympic Park.

Once again, Jann's presence opened every door. Before we knew it, we were not only getting a tour of the facility, but we were also told that we could use it. If I signed a waiver, they said, we could take a luge toboggan for a spin. I knew this would be good TV, but I also knew what would make even better TV: Jann doing the luge first. Which I arranged and sprung on her.

When I gave her the good news, once again I could see the fear in her face. And I didn't blame her. This was outside her comfort zone. This is a woman whose natural habitat is sitting by a fire, strumming a six-string and trying to find yet another word that rhymes with *pain*. Now she was staring at an Olympic luge track. And let's face it, the luge is one of the most absurd and danger-ous winter sports of all. When you're standing next to the track, it seems completely ridiculous. Who was it who said, "I wish I had a long tunnel of ice that ran down the side of a mountain. If

I did, I could get a toboggan that's built for a four-year-old, lie on it backwards and face up, with my hands crossed on my chest as if I were in a coffin, and then ride down the mountain at eighty kilometres an hour."

Honestly, when we were looking down the track, I didn't think she would go through with it. And that was before we were given helmets and the briefest of briefings.

Apparently, the most important thing to remember in luge or skeleton is to be very careful about where you put your thumbs. In the event of a crash, keep your hands by your side. If you try to brace yourself for any fall with your hands, the runners on the sled could go over your hands and sever your thumbs.

We were told of a legendary Scandinavian skeleton coach who was recognizable both for his long blond hair and the fact that he only had four digits on each hand. No matter how well Team Norway performed on the hill, they never got a thumbs-up. The most they could hope for was a clap.

The warning fresh in our minds, we went to the track, with Jann yelling, "You know it's going to be a bad date when you're required to wear a helmet!"

"And you have to sign a release form," I said. "There's a couple of waivers."

She signed on the dotted line. And then, halfway through our first date, she was flat on her back, wearing a helmet.

I wished her godspeed and then, ignoring her protestations, I pushed her with all my might. Feet first, she disappeared down the chute like a shot out of hell. As the screams of terror echoed off the mountains that hosted Calgary's triumphant Winter Games, I knew I was in love.

And I knew the country would soon fall in love with Jann Arden all over again.

They had known her for years as a beautiful singer-songwriter who wrote heart-breaking songs about loss and love. But she was about to be reborn as a saucy, extremely funny, reluctant stunt woman and romantic love interest of a short, gay Newfoundlander with a large head.

When she emerged safely, thumbs intact, I followed her down the hill.

The truth is, by then I knew I would follow her anywhere.

Our date came to an end at the Arden Diner, the downtown restaurant owned by Jann and her brother. I was incredibly happy with how the date had gone. I was thrilled that we could promote the diner. The day had been a home run. I could say "we" pulled off the impossible, but there was no "we." It was all Jann. It was her personality, her presence and her generosity of spirit and time that saved the day. That and the immense goodwill the people in Alberta feel for this talented troublemaker.

Before the piece aired, before we looked at an inch of footage, I knew that our show, which had never had regular guest stars, now had a regular guest star. I couldn't get enough of Jann, and, I suspected, neither would the country.

She wrapped up the evening by suggesting I "try the meat loaf."

I thanked her for the date and predicted there would be many more to come.

"I don't think so," Jann said. "Lose my number."

OF COURSE, I DIDN'T lose Jann's number. The audience wouldn't allow it. Nor would they put up with Jann not returning my calls.

Immediately after the segment aired, people began to ask the same question: "When is Jann going to be on again?"

This made no sense. Our show was different every week. When I jumped out of a plane with Rick Hillier, people didn't say, "When are you jumping out of a plane with that general again?" Nobody said, "Will that funny oyster fisherman from PEI return?"

But with Jann it was different. People demanded it.

OURS WAS A SHOTGUN MARRIAGE. And oddly enough, some people actually thought we were married, or engaged, or secretly dating. Someone once sent me a link to a piece of "fan fiction" that featured a short story in which Jann and I were having a torrid affair while working on a cattle ranch. It was sort of a middle-aged, heterosexual *Brokeback Mountain*. I don't know what was more far-fetched: the two of us herding cattle or the notion of us "getting lost in each other's eyes while the moonlight kissed their lips."

I was happy to have Jann return to the show many times. And truth be known, she was such a great guest that if she hadn't been so busy with her own career, she would have been on the show even more.

But no. Between the songwriting trips to Nashville, the recording sessions, the touring, the writing of books, the acting gigs and the time spent on her secret bacon farm, she is quite frankly very busy.

But I kept a very close eye on her schedule, and with the help of her incredible tour manager, Chris Brunton, we managed to keep the relationship alive.

And it blossomed into a real friendship.

It turns out we have a lot in common. I am not an adrenalin junkie, and neither is she. Left to my own devices, I would not have done many of the things I did over the years. I never grew up with dreams of being in a demolition derby or being submerged in a sinking Toyota. But it was my job. So I did those things. And yes, while there were times I was afraid, I was never 100 percent legitimately terrified.

On *RMR*, Jann was often terrified.

How she coped, I have no idea. She is like those mothers you read about who out of nowhere exhibit superhuman strength because their babies are in danger. "Nursing mother lifts Toyota," "Mother of three body-slams grizzly," that kind of thing. Jann's like that. When the green light on the camera comes on, she can do things she never would have thought possible.

It's why, despite her paralyzing fear of heights, she managed to put on a harness and fling herself down a mountainous zip line. It's why she was able to put on a harness and tackle a vertical climbing wall. It's why I managed to talk her into putting on a harness so she could dangle off the edge of the CN Tower. After years of hanging out with me (literally), is it any wonder that she's been known to fall over in Canadian Tire when she accidentally finds herself in the aisle with the safety harnesses? Harnesses and personal injury waivers are a serious trigger for her now.

I'd say she's brave, but she's not. At least not when it comes to those things. And I am eternally grateful for her. And honestly, knowing her as well as I do, I would have bet serious money that she would take a pass on the CN Tower. But no, she pulled it off. And she kept coming back.

I learned a lot about her over the years. I learned she doesn't like snakes draped around her person and is not keen about large insects in her hair. I learned that she will sing in the car, and that is a good thing. I learned—the hard way, on a paintball course—that she's a very good shot. I learned at a donkey sanctuary that while Jann loves people, she loves animals more.

And behind the scenes, I learned that she is one of the most generous people I have had the privilege of knowing. Certainly, she has always been generous with her time with me, but it goes past that. The horses saved, the money she has raised, the numbers are staggering. I once said to her on the phone, "Jann, this group of kids in Newfoundland have won a spot at a rock camp showcase in Madrid. They are fundraising. They need to raise ten thousand more dollars if they are going to make the trip."

Before I could finish talking, she said, "Okay, I'll give them five grand, you do the same, and it's done, easy."

I answered, "I was going to suggest we sign a picture for them for their auction."

Thanks to Jann, they made the trip. She changed the lives of group of teenage rock and rollers she didn't know.

Just like she changed mine by agreeing one day on very short notice to show me around Calgary.

15

Bear with Me

Nation building, in my lifetime, seems to have gone out of fashion. The men and women who find themselves in positions of leadership in Canada see the role of government as maintaining the status quo.

Canadians of my vintage do not know what it's like to see a prime minister articulate a vision on a par with the creation of the St. Lawrence Seaway, the Trans-Canada Highway or a railway to connect the country from sea to sea. Nation building over the past fifty years has consisted of announcing yet another study into the feasibility of high-speed rail. The result of that study will be that it's totally feasible, but nobody has the political will, the desire or the energy to follow through.

Governing used to involve bold visions, some that would bring glory but others that would ensure the opposite. Some visions were simply ahead of their time.

If I could go back and kiss any leader from the past on the lips, those at the front of the queue would be every premier and prime minister who used their powers to create a park. And yes, that even includes Brian Mulroney, who was the driving force behind many protected spaces, including the incredibly significant Bruce Peninsula National Park in Ontario. Significant because it is a literal paradise for our feathered friends. Smack dab in the middle of this continent's most important migrating path, it is the natural habitat for hundreds of species of birds, including the golden eagle and the great blue heron. Also Margaret Atwood.

It's one thing to have a vision around parks in these allegedly enlightened times. But imagine public reaction in the late nineteenth century, when that generation's version of hippies and tree huggers started making noise about the impact of logging and resource extraction on the environment. Today, environmentalists are written off as kooks in the *National Post*. Imagine what was said of these people in the 1890s—they must have been portrayed as completely unhinged. And yet, somehow the political will was found. The political capital was expended and in 1893, under a premier named Oliver Mowat, it was declared that 7,600 square kilometres of prime Ontario wilderness would be saved for the rest of time.

Yes, they declared, we may be hewers of wood and drawers of water, but some of that wood and some of that water needs to be protected. Protected from its greatest destructive force. That would be us.

That is what you called vision.

And that is why, smack dab in the middle of the province, where Southern Ontario meets Northern Ontario, there lies Algonquin Park. So old it's not just a park, it's a national historic site. Seven thousand, six hundred square kilometres of rugged beauty that will never be damaged, developed or paved to satisfy our basest desires. The current premier of Ontario, Doug Ford, may go to sleep at night dreaming of building a monorail and a Ferris wheel within its boundaries, but it will never happen.

Good job, Ontario.

Having not grown up in Ontario, I never visited Algonquin as a young person. It wasn't on my radar. As a provincial entity, it's not part of the national park system that we glossed over in school, so I don't know if I even heard the name. But once I moved to Ontario, that changed. You don't have to spend much time in the province before you hear the word *Algonquin*, and it's always spoken in reverential terms. And often by the people of Toronto.

Toronto is a great city. Like so many before me, I moved there for work. I could start typing the reasons I love this city now and I'd still be at it this time tomorrow. But I will say this: one of the drawbacks to life in Toronto is that it is very hard to escape. It's possible. But for the most part, if you want to get out, it means taking your life in your hands and travelling on Highway 400.

Ontario is Canada's largest and most populated province, Toronto the country's largest city, so it is only fitting that Toronto has a modern highway that functions as a racetrack filled with millions of cars that act as if they're fleeing for their lives. Before you hop on the 400 and go for a spin, it's a good idea to get your affairs in order.

If you do find yourself driving on the 400, a good rule of thumb is that you should leave a full two inches of space between you and the car in front. Also know that there are two speeds on that strip of asphalt: too fast and stopped. It occasionally becomes a parking lot that doesn't move. By occasionally, I mean often.

Many of the vehicles on the 400 are headed for Ontario's fabled Muskoka region. This is classic Ontario cottage country. Famous the world over, it was once a playground for regular working folks from the big city. They would head north in the summers or on weekends to enjoy modest cottages on beautiful lakes. Teachers, nurses, electricians and plumbers would go there and create beautiful memories at family cottages or roadside rentals. Those days are gone. The area is now home to some of the most expensive lakefront real estate on the planet. On beautiful Lake Rosseau, for example, you're far more likely to get run over by some rich guys in a pontoon boat than run into a middle-class family enjoying the water.

But not too far away, accessible to everyone—not just the wealthy or well-connected—is Algonquin Park. And it holds a mythical place in the hearts and minds of millions. This is where generations of Ontarians learned to camp, canoe and canoodle.

Our system of parks, which dot the entire country, whether you use them or not, are theoretically perfect. If you have the desire and the cash, you can spend a fortune on camping or hiking. But the flip side is that you can also spend very little. And at the end of the day, the quality of Gore-Tex or the brand name on the tent won't make a difference to the quality of the sunset or the dip in the pond.

When I was growing up there was no money for vacations. Save for one road trip to PEI, there was no travel involving hotels or rented accommodations. There were, however, countless nights spent in tents and sleeping bags that had been passed down from some ancient civilization. To this day I can close my eyes and smell the thick, bare foam mattress that lived in the back of the station wagon for summers on end. It's not a pleasant smell, but they are beautiful memories. And is there anything more perfect than a boil-up on a beach? Which is what Newfoundlanders call lighting a fire, boiling water and having a cup of tea. The cost? Tea bags.

———

My introduction to Algonquin was, I admit, better than most. I didn't roll into the park in a school bus packed with campers or drive through the gates while bouncing around unbuckled in the back of a station wagon with my brother. Although those are great options.

No, thanks to the miracle of network television, I pulled up to the headquarters of the Ontario Ministry of Natural Resources and hopped aboard a shiny yellow helicopter.

But before I did this, I had some work to do. I looked into Don's camera and recorded my introduction: "Welcome to Algonquin Park in beautiful Northern Ontario. This is the place that inspired the Group of Seven. They loved to come here and paint its rugged beauty. That is, when they weren't running away from the over two thousand black bears that make this park home. How do we know how many bears there are? Well, every winter someone has to track them down while they are hibernating in their caves, and then crawl inside those caves and tag the mother bears and any babies they may find. And this week, that person is me!"

How did we get here? is right.

The helicopter ride over Algonquin was beyond spectacular. We flew low over the tree canopy, along riverbeds, over lakes and past marshes. It goes on forever. We saw moose galore. Moose and their calves seemed to own the place.

And there were wolves. Most people know that when you're walking in the woods in Canada, wolves are rarely far away. You can spend a long time listening to them howl at the moon and never be lucky enough to see one. From the helicopter, we saw packs of wolves roaming with impunity.

And as a slight reminder that we weren't flying over the Garden of Eden, we saw a recently felled moose, its body in the middle of a clearing. You could see the path the desperate animal had taken as it fled its predators. And now it lay there, lifeless, surrounded by so many wolf prints it looked as if a mosh pit had dispersed, leaving a half-eaten carcass in its wake.

And then we landed.

We had a date with Dr. Martyn Obbard, resident bear biologist with the Ontario Ministry of Natural Resources. He was straight out of Central Casting. A bespectacled, bearded professor in his natural habitat, surrounded by eager students just beginning their careers.

Before this trip, I admit I didn't know very much about bears. I didn't grow up in Labrador or Churchill, Manitoba, where kids have been known to go trick-or-treating with armed guards on the lookout for polar bears. And I was, like so many, guilty of lumping all bears together under the banner of beautiful creatures who are very bad news.

There are a lot of myths about bears.

In parts of Alberta, home to grizzlies, they once distributed pamphlets at lookouts along the highway that said, "If you are approached by a bear, do not lie down and pretend you are sleeping." Do grizzlies "approach" people? When I hear that someone has been "approached," I think of an employee at the Foot Locker walking up to a lady and offering to find a sensible tennis shoe in her size.

The tragedy is, for these pamphlets to have ever existed, someone must have done just that. Imagine the eyewitness account. Must have been horrifying. "Well, I was parked at the lookout, enjoying the scenery, and there was a fella parked next to me doing the same thing. Except he was standing outside of his car. Well, the darndest thing is a grizzly showed up. And instead of getting back in his car the man laid his binoculars on the roof, closed his door, lay down and started snoring. Damn bear started chomping at his feet and worked up to his earbuds. All that was left was a fanny pack and a Tilley hat."

But today was all about black bears. And with the camera rolling Dr. Obbard laid out the day and dispelled some myths. First I learned that black bears, or least the females, were not hibernating. So far that day I had recorded a twenty-second introduction to the piece and I was already guilty of disseminating false information.

They do not hibernate because they have babies, and the babies need to be breast-fed. So, basically, the moms quasi-hibernate. They look like they are dead to the world and zoned out, but somehow they know what the babies are up to and on occasion have to stop them from wandering away and getting into trouble. I think most mothers can relate.

The doctor then told me my job on that day was to do exactly as I was told. That always works out.

He told me that many bears in the park had electronic collars fitted with batteries that lasted for a year. The collars didn't give an exact location, but narrowed it down to within a few hundred feet. Today our job would be to go find a young, tagged bear in her den. The question was whether she was alone or with cubs. We were to find the den, pop in and say hello to the mother and then take her babies away, weigh them and maybe administer some ear drops.

I don't know much about the animal kingdom, but I know the few basic rules, the big one being: never get between a mother and her cubs. My guess is pulling a baby off a bear's teat and plopping them up on a meat scale would also qualify.

With those instructions out of the way, we were off, snowshoeing through the middle of Algonquin Park. And instead of looking out for bears, we were looking *for* them.

I've never understood snowshoeing. I understand the mechanics, that snowshoes are used to stop you from sinking into the snow, but what I don't understand is why anyone would volunteer to do it. Sure, if you're a von Trapp fleeing the Nazis through the Alps, strap on a pair. But I've never grasped why anyone would use them for pleasure. That changed in Algonquin.

We needed the shoes because we were walking in deep snow and we had a job to do. Turns out the bears don't like to build their dens next to groomed walking trails. They go deep into the wilderness, where no human is likely to find them. For these bears, the blinds are drawn, the phone is off, the Do Not Disturb sign is on the doorknob.

It was on this trek, deeper and deeper into Algonquin, that something completely unexpected happened. I won't say I had a spiritual experience, because I have yet to enjoy a visit from our saviour, but it was close. In fact, even before I laid eyes on a bear, I'd had about as perfect a day as anyone could.

Algonquin, with its silence, its beauty, its ruggedness and raw nature, grabbed me whole and held me tight. Why call it a park? Call it a cathedral. I imagined a time, hundreds—or thousands—of years in the future, when civilization as we know it is wiped out and gone. The victim, no doubt, of a self-inflicted fatality. Earth is visited by an alien race. The aliens will look around and see evidence that we were once here. They will see ruined cities and massive industrial development. They will look at our once-functioning infrastructure with some amusement.

What will they think of us? Nobody knows. But the evidence of a civilized society will not be the abandoned charging stations or billboards advertising Viagra. The evidence that we were civilized will be our parks.

"They weren't completely stupid," they will say in their telepathic click language. "They had the wherewithal to protect Algonquin Park. I wish we'd thought of that on our planet."

And they will gaze at Algonquin and be in awe. And it will look pretty much the same as it does today.

So, yes, it's safe to say on this day I fell in love with Algonquin and my mind was drifting.

I was brought back to earth by Dr. Obbard, who tapped me on the shoulder and said, "We are very close."

Right. I remembered our task: find a bear and remove her cubs.

"Remind me," I said, "why nobody has a gun."

"Black bears are not aggressive," he said.

"They are never aggressive?" I asked.

"Well, sometimes they can be. They will want to protect their cubs."

"So," I said, "they are not aggressive, unless they are aggressive?"

"Exactly," said the doctor.

"And if they become aggressive?" I asked.

"You have the shovel," he said. "If the bear looks like she's about to attack or move on us in any way, you block the opening of the den with the shovel."

I looked down at the shovel he had given me. It was at best a thirty-five-dollar aluminum Canadian Tire special. I wondered if I would die in this cathedral.

There are worse places to go, I thought. But it wasn't the location of my death I was opposed to as much as the part about being torn limb from limb.

The professor indicated that I should follow him. Together we approached a large fallen tree. At the base of the tree the roots had been ripped out of the earth, creating a natural canopy of protection. This was the den. It was covered in snow except for a small opening no larger than a loaf of bread. We gently and quietly approached the opening and peered inside.

There, eyes wide open, was a mother bear.

We were face to face.

I locked eyes with a bear.

"Don't worry," I said, "we won't hurt you."

(I don't know if I said the words out loud.)

"Hurt my babies and I will hurt you," she answered.

She didn't say that out loud exactly, but she did manage to get the message across with a look.

Dr. Obbard told me to stand by with my shovel. I felt woefully unprepared in the event of attack. This was truly absurd.

This must be what the Canadian Rangers feel like, I thought. They are Canada's first line of defence against Russian aggression in the North. For over 70 years we issued them complimentary sweatshirts and .303 British calibre Lee Enfield rifles. With that, they were expected to beat back the Ruskies.

While Dr. Obbard prepared a dose of happy juice, I stood on guard for thee, for he and for the students who watched from afar. If that bear came charging out of that den, I'd charm her by asking, "Can I shovel your driveway for five bucks, miss?"

Ignoring my suggestion that he double up the dose, Dr. Obbard lay on his stomach, crawled towards the opening and gently placed his stick inside the den. He looked like a pool shark doing a one-handed trick shot with his cue. He pulled back and jabbed forward. A slight groan emanated from the den. Nobody breathed. Nobody moved.

Eventually the good doctor withdrew the poking stick, stood up and came to my side.

"Now," he said, "your job is to determine that she's under. You must crawl inside. Just your chest and arms, reach out, and pull on her ear. Give it a good, strong yank. Tell me if she makes any noise or moves at all."

There are times when the phrase "Have you completely taken leave of your senses?" seems like an understatement. Pull on her ear? It sounded like the worst idea ever.

But in the interest of science, and a good segment, I went in.

The first thing that went into the hole was my head. What struck me immediately was the smell. I had assumed a bear den would be foul. Imagine all those months of farting and burping in a small, enclosed space.

I was completely wrong. Bears smell much nicer than humans. They smell pine-cone fresh. Their breath—I know this now because my mouth and nose were inches from hers—is divine.

I mumbled, "Forgive me," reached out towards this majestic creature and yanked her ear like I was starting a lawn mower.

Nothing. She was in la-la land.

My next job, if you could call it that, was to reach inside and pull out the babies. One by one I pulled out three tiny bear cubs that, because their eyes were not yet open, were estimated to be just six weeks old.

Once out of the den they had to be kept warm. While the first of them was weighed and measured, the doctor told me to take the remaining two cubs and place them inside my jacket. Once there, each headed for an armpit. The snuggled in and went to sleep.

If you ever get the chance to stand in the pristine wilderness of Algonquin Park while two baby bears doze under your arms, you should not hesitate. I highly recommend it.

When the time came to pull them out from under my coat and go for the weigh-in, they did not like it. Remember what it was like to be dragged out of bed as a teen? That's how these babies felt. They wanted no part of it. They wanted to sleep for the rest of the winter right where they were. As far as I was concerned, they were welcome to. One of them howled and cried like there was no tomorrow. I named him Danny Williams, after the not-so-shy premier of Newfoundland and Labrador.

They were weighed. Their craniums were measured. They were given a drop of some sort. I am so proud to live in a country where baby bears have universal health care. If these bears were in Yellowstone, they would have to mortgage that den twice over for this kind of attention.

And then we went and got Mama. Together, the doctor and I pulled her out. We removed her collar and replaced it with a newer, sleeker model, one that could store way more songs. We weighed and measured her. She was insanely healthy.

A healthy bear and her healthy babies in a healthy park.

And then the doctor and I returned her to the den. One tries to be gentle and respectful in these situations, but it was not unlike getting one of your first semi-conscious roommates out of the backyard and upstairs into bed. One hundred and forty-five kilograms of dead weight. No help at all.

Eventually she was in place. Then came the hard part: returning the cubs. These adorable, cuddly, puppy-like things that were literally trying to suckle on my chest when they were under my shirt had to go home. I crawled back in the den with the mother, and Dr. Obbard passed them forward one by one. I placed each of them against Mama's chest, where they quickly went back to feeding. As I was extraditing myself from the cave, her eyes opened. We stared at each other once again. I felt like she was saying, "I know all three are back, we are good. It's time for you to go now."

And I slowly backed out.

We laid some branches over the opening, put the shovel to good use and covered the branches with snow, leaving mother and babies content and dozing.

They would stay that way until the spring, when Mom and three very active, eyes-wide-open cubs would begin to explore their home—oblivious to the fact that, unlike many other bears in North America, theirs was the greatest home on earth. They were safe and sound in a park established 125 years earlier by Canadians with vision.

16

Flag Day

W hat happens on the road, stays on the road.

It's a cliché, but it's not entirely true.

Especially if your job, like ours, was to make TV. We didn't keep things quiet, we literally broadcast them.

But when you are on the road, there is always an element of the unknown. Situations will arise that you never saw coming. And occasionally something will happen that is so far beyond the realm of the possible that you would not even have allowed yourself to imagine it.

It is also true that with the road comes temptation, and sometimes it can get the better of you. It happened to me during a shoot on Parliament Hill, when, completely unexpected, I had an intimate encounter with one of the most famous men in the Conservative movement.

I didn't ask for it to happen, but the opportunity came along and I went for it. Sometimes you must follow your heart. Or at least do it for the story.

The Hill has always been one of my all-time favourite places. Not because of the people who sit in Parliament. Those I can take or leave. My affinity for the place is all about the bricks and the mortar—not the pricks and the mortals.

The first time I laid eyes on the buildings, they took my breath away. They are the most iconic structures in Canada. And they live up to the hype.

I'm not alone in my appreciation for the place. Before the current renovation began, 150,000 Canadians a year signed up and took the tour. And why not? It's well worth the price of admission, which is free. The tours are gone now while important restoration is being done. But on any given day you can walk to the Hill and stare.

Over the last thirty years, I don't think I have ever visited Ottawa and not taken a stroll around the buildings for a gawk. If you find yourself in the nation's capital on a fine, brisk day, I recommend you walk across the Alexandria Bridge over the Ottawa River to Quebec. From there, you will get the greatest view: the back of the buildings, even more magnificent that the front, and they jut out dramatically over the river's escarpment. Also, from this angle you see the beauty that is the Parliamentary Library.

I feel about these buildings the way some people feel about sunsets. The way Justin Trudeau feels about mirrors. I can gaze at them all day.

I have been lucky to spend a fair bit of time in them over the years. Our access has always been phenomenal. I've spent time in the prime ministers' offices, I've wandered the corridors unsupervised, I've explored the secret passageway tucked away in the Opposition leader's office. I've sat in numerous offices with random MPs. I've dined in the Parliamentary dining room and the plebeians' cafeteria. I have sat on the lap of a paralyzed MP and ridden him down the hall like he was public transit—his idea. Made possible because he was in possession of both an electric wheelchair and a fine sense of humour. Also, security was legitimately baffled as to what rule was being broken.

But what I always love about any institution is backstage. Bringing our audience behind the scenes has always been a big part of the show. But Parliament Hill is a bit like the theatre. It is not a collection of show-business professionals, but it is close. People in showbiz don't like it when people peek behind the curtains. "Don't show 'em how it's done," goes the adage. On the Hill, transparency is a conceit that does not extend to the boiler room, the catwalks, the tunnels or the roof. And it does not extend to the Peace Tower.

On Parliament Hill, when it comes to access, one person is king: the Speaker of the House. If you are on good terms with the Speaker's office, miraculous things can happen. They control the place with impunity. Mind you, it is a benevolent dictatorship. On the Hill, permission from the prime minister is helpful. A thumbs-up from the Speaker is gold.

The Speaker controls everything you see. Everything, that is, in the front of house. But in the back? That's a different story. Backstage is the domain of an institution that is more powerful than the Illuminati and more mysterious than Opus Dei.

I speak of the Department of Public Works.

They are not elected, and for the most part they are not seen. They are part of the civil service that keeps government functioning. They do what needs to be done on Parliament Hill to ensure the lights are turned on and the heat remains consistent. They have the keys to every room and every closet. If you want to study the entrails, this is the society with which you must ingratiate yourself.

And in October, 2009 Tom Stanley did just that.

He not only talked to the head of Public Works, he convinced them it would be a good idea to let me have the run of the place.

To say that this excited me would be an understatement. It was one thing to have a parliamentary press pass. But to have that magic ring of keys that hangs from the belt of the Department of Public Works was a whole other level. We had made the trip to Parliament Hill many times over the years, but this time would be different.

I remember expressing my mad excitement to Michal on the flight to Ottawa.

One of the reasons I loved travelling with Mike is that he's such a passionate guy. He's easily excited. His excitement always reminded everyone on the crew how cool our job was. How lucky we were on any given day. But this trip to Parliament Hill made me feel like Mike. This time, *I* was the kid in the candy store.

I told him that for me to wander around those buildings was like him being given the chance to wander the set of the original *Star Wars*.

To cross the floor of the House of Commons and sit in the Speaker's chair? It was the same as Mike being given the keys to the *Millennium Falcon* and being told he could take Chewbacca's seat and play with the buttons. And getting to hold in my hands the golden mace that has been used to open every sitting of Parliament for 151 years? That's like being allowed to caress Luke Skywalker's lightsaber.

This, for me, was going to be the full geek experience.

NORMALLY WHEN SHOOTING ON the Hill, we would start at the press gallery office to get temporary credentials, and then it would be off to an MP's office.

Not today. Today I was meeting with someone far more impressive: Brian Cook. The manager of operations for Parliament Hill.

What a title. Imagine if you were sixteen years old and someone you knew was named "manager of operations" of the local movie theatre. You would never have to pay to see a film again.

Meeting Brian was like that, only better. Finally, here was a guy who could get me exactly where I wanted to go.

We met, not in a secret location, which was a tad disappointing, but out in the open and standing next to the Centennial Flame. The buildings under his care towered over our shoulders.

I told him exactly where I wanted to go. I wanted to go directly to the top. Not to the prime minister's office, but to the top of the tower. Up high, past the observation deck. I knew that cameras were not allowed there and neither was the public. It's not designed for civilians, it's not practical, it's not safe. The only people who had access to that area were the flag master, who changed the flag every day, and one of Canada's few musicians with a full-time job: the woman who played the carillon bells.

He agreed to take me up, but there was a catch.

It wasn't just audiences that liked to see me suffer. Sometimes the guests did, too.

Brian told me I had to earn my way to the tower. You get to the top by starting at the bottom. And, he said, at the bottom, "There is a prominent Canadian in need of attention."

Not knowing what I was getting into, I readily agreed. Which is how I found myself standing on a stepladder, pressure washer in hand, cleaning prodigious amounts of pigeon poo from the forehead of John Diefenbaker, his giant lips a mere foot away from mine.

It doesn't get much more intimate than that.

There are nineteen statues on Parliament Hill, and Diefenbaker was not just a favourite with tourists, but clearly the birds as well. Legend has it the ones from Quebec make special flights over the river just to spend time on his head.

As I sprayed a stubborn spot on his upper lip, he gazed into my eyes as if to say, "You missed a spot, commie."

And sure enough, upon closer inspection I saw that a seagull had left a deposit on his clavicle. A gull no doubt unhappy that the man who destroyed the Avro Arrow fighter jet program had a statue in his honour. Gulls are like that: diehard fans of cutting-edge aviation.

I accepted that for me to get to the top (of the tower), I had to start at the bottom. But I had no idea there would be so many political legends badly in need of a wash. I didn't care. I was willing to do what was required of me. With poo water spraying me from head to toe, I risked avian flu and pink eye in my quest to go skyward.

Eventually Brian pulled me off statue duty. He had worked with enough men over the years to see that I had the upper-body strength of a small child and the stamina of a geriatric. He didn't want me on any more ladders. He had visions of me braining myself on Laurier's boot or Sir John A.'s tumbler of whiskey.

He brought me back to the Centennial Flame. It was safely on the ground, but also in need of cleaning. It had to be scrubbed, and it had to be emptied of nickels, dimes, quarters and loonies. None of which, it turns out, goes to the dude doing the scrubbing, but to charity.

The flame is a huge draw on the Hill, and a relatively new addition. It arrived in 1967 and has been lit on and off since then. Not unlike Mike Duffy.

For this task, Public Works gifted me a pair of standard-issue size ten rubber boots, one of which didn't have a sizable hole.

The coins that are thrown into the fountain get everywhere—
I think the expression is they "gum up the works." Getting the
coins out of the hard-to-reach areas is awkward and hard on the
shoulders. I complained to Brian, saying, "It seems ridiculous
that this must be done by hand. Isn't there some easier way? Isn't
there a tool?"

"Rick," he said, "*you* are the tool."

I've been called worse.

I won't lie, it was an exhausting morning. After squeezing as
much physical labour out of me as possible, Public Works pulled
me from the job site. They declared me a liability.

"Come on," he said. "Let's go to the tower."

"Excellent," I said.

"Well, I'd say you earned it but . . ."

Being lousy at my job got me promoted. Not the first time that's
happened on the Hill. Although this was long before Mélanie
Joly turned the practice into an art form.

Nobody has ever said, "Which way to the Peace Tower?" It
cannot be missed. With its four-faced clock and its massive, com-
manding flag, it is the centrepiece of our Parliament Buildings.

But it is so much more than that.

It is not just a good-looking front porch to Parliament, or a
place from which to let our freak flag fly. It is not just a famous
architectural feature, and it's more than just symmetry and
design. The tower was built as a memorial to those Canadians
who were lost in the First World War. It houses, on its third floor,
the Memorial Chamber, the permanent home for Canada's seven
Books of Remembrance, listing the names of all the Canadians
who gave their lives in service to their country.

To this day, every morning at eleven the pages of these books
are turned. This ensures that every name, at least once a year, is

prominently displayed to visitors. So many of these names are no longer spoken, their stories no longer told. How many Canadians have vague recollections of hearing of a distant uncle, whose name escapes them, who was lost during the Great War? The tower stands so that those names will never be forgotten.

Memorials to those lost at war exist the world over. But unlike many other countries, when we named our monument, we didn't use the word *war* at all. We called our tower "Peace."

The Peace Tower.

And really, how cool is that?

Visitors to the Centre Block can experience much of the tower. They can visit the Memorial Chamber, and many do. There is always a steady flow of people: political junkies, *Architectural Digest*-ers and those who clearly have some connection to the names appearing in that day's book. I'd wandered through this space many times before, but never with a camera rolling. It's a solemn place, and immediately upon entering you can feel that. You feel it in your bones and in the stones beneath your feet, all collected from the battlefields of Europe—Ypres, the Somme, Vimy Ridge and Verdun.

You carry on up the tower, mercifully in an elevator. It takes you to an observation deck that allows you to look through the four clocks on the tower. For anyone who has spent a lifetime looking at the Peace Tower on TV, in textbooks and on the twenty-dollar bill, it's like you've been granted the ability to look through someone else's eyes—or at the very least, through a famous clock's face.

And this is where, on this day, Brian and I left the civilians behind and approached a small door. The magic ring of keys did its job. He turned a key in a ninety-five-year-old lock. Hinges creaked, a door opened, and we stepped through a portal to the past.

We were backstage.

From the day these buildings opened, every inch of the Hill used by members of Parliament has been lit, buffed, polished and improved. But up here, where the workers walked and climbed? If there had been a single improvement or change in the last nine decades, I couldn't see it.

For 108 feet we continued upwards, climbing stairs and ladders, none of which would meet any building code currently found on earth. A very cool climb towards a very big job.

Changing the flag on the Peace Tower might not be on everyone's bucket list, but it had been on mine for quite a while. And honestly, I was a bit nervous. Any time I was tasked with a job on the *Mercer Report*, I would try my hardest. Sadly, as I have learned many times, your best is sometimes just not good enough.

I say the following not because I lack self-esteem or confidence, but because it is simply a fact: I could screw up a two-house paper route. It's been a blessing and a curse. It has served me well. People don't mind watching someone fail, especially at something they think they might be able to pull off. And I don't care if I am exposed as inadequate or lacking. That's all part of the gig. But usually, the stakes are not high. The worst thing that can happen is that TV Boy is humiliated in front of a million people.

But this was different. My job on this day was to change the flag on the Peace Tower. Not just any tower; the most important tower we have. This was not your run-of-the-mill flagpole. This was Canada's flagpole. The symbolism and the protocol surrounding this flag and this pole could fill the world's longest and driest doctoral thesis.

Flags in general are a serious business. They have been around from the moment people started carrying swords and clubbing each other on principle. Our flag, of course, was born not out of bloodshed or invasion but out of a parliamentary committee. Still, it's serious stuff.

For the curious, the Government of Canada's website includes the rules and conventions surrounding the display of all Canadian flags. There's not a lot of wiggle room.

But here is the salient point about this particular flag: every single weekday it is changed. And this has been the tradition since February 15, 1965, the first day the Maple Leaf was hoisted above the Hill.

The nation's flag is never supposed to touch the ground or the floor. On Parliament Hill this rule is sacrosanct. I didn't want to think about what would befall me or the country if I let the flag touch the ground. All I knew was that it would be bad. At the time, there was no known case of it happening. Since then, there has been one: it happened in the early hours of July 13, 2017. Three hours later Justin Trudeau came up with the bright idea to appoint Julie Payette as governor general.

And never mind the floor business. The most important part of displaying this flag, or any flag the world over, is this: it must be right side up. It is universally understood around the world that if you fly a flag upside down, you are indicating that you are in extreme distress or danger.

Getting the flag facing the right side up is easier said than done. The flags that fly above the Peace Tower are huge. They are not your standard backyard flagpole special. Because the flag is so high in the air, it measures seven and a half feet by fifteen (2.3 m by 4.6 m). You can't just shake it out and look at it before it goes on the pole. You must make sure the toggles on the flag's edge are in the right place before it even comes out of its special flag purse.

Can you imagine if I got my flag toggles mixed up and flew the thing upside down? If I sent a message to the world that Canada had crashed against the rocks and was beyond repair? I don't think I could live that down. Canadians would not consider it fair comment. And worst of all, I'm pretty sure Brian would be fired.

The pressure was on.

Brian gave me my final instructions. I thanked him for his confidence in me. And I was sincere. It was pretty good of him to trust that I wouldn't intentionally make a mockery of this national voodoo ceremony. Truly, I did not want to screw this up. This was their house, and I was the guest. Also, it was not lost on me that directly below me, those pages were about to be turned. For the sake of the lads who were getting their day in the sun, let it be a day without a national incident.

Brian brought me to a ladder. He placed two "purses" around my neck. One held the day's new flag. The other was empty. Into the empty one I would place the flag that was currently flying up above.

Together we went up the final ladder until we came to a small room. I can best describe it as a tree house or a hidey-hole. It was very plain on the inside. Decidedly not ornate. The designers knew that dignitaries would never spend a minute here. Its walls were white. And what was so fantastic was that they were covered with signatures of people who were lucky enough to make the trek and hang out in this perch. Luckily, I always carry a Sharpie.

Brian reached up and pulled the handle on a hatch. It opened and the wind howled. He told me it was time for me to go, wished me godspeed and advised me to hold on for dear life.

Looking up at the hole in the roof, I could see the flag on the top of the pole. The base of the flagpole, which is embedded in the roofline of the tower, is 92.2 metres off the ground. The pole itself is 10.7 metres tall.

When standing on the roof at the base of the flagpole, you are 302 feet off the ground. And you are alone. At just four square feet (0.4 m²), there is only room for one. The front seat of a Smart car has more room. And this is where I found myself: all alone, just a man with two purses staring up at a flag.

Taking the flag down was relatively easy, but there was still protocol involved. Most importantly, the flag had to come down at a slow and steady pace. You cannot stop and take a break just because your arms are tired. If you do that while the flag is half-way down, it will look like someone important has died.

I managed to get the sucker down without causing any death rumours, and mercifully the whole thing fit into my empty purse without incident. It never touched the ground. I lowered it down to Brian.

And now it was showtime. I looked up at the naked flagpole. It's funny, but I don't think I had ever seen the pole not in use before. I certainly couldn't remember it. As instructed, I opened my purse and connected the toggles to the rope, praying that the flag had been inserted properly.

Brian told me that in all the years he'd been there, the flag was flown upside down once. An investigation determined that the incident was caused by human error—not on the account of the person who flew the flag, but the one who packed the purse. So, this was no different than getting ready to jump from a plane, where I was at the mercy of the person who packed my chute.

Toggles connected, I did as instructed and pulled the flag out of the purse completely and threw it into the wind. I pulled on the rope like I was trying to start a dead lawn mower.

Up it went. Slow and steady.

If a flag has ever unfurled as perfectly as that flag, on that day, I am unaware of it.

It was glorious, and it was right side up. The sun was shining, the flag was flapping. Job done, I reached into my pocket for my digital camera and took pictures for posterity from an angle that very few have enjoyed.

From down below, Brian shouted, "Take a few minutes!" and closed the latch.

Nice of him. I might have been embarrassed to ask.

I get the appeal of standing on the summit of Mount Everest, but I have never had the passion or the discipline to conquer mountains. But I do understand, especially now, the feeling of standing on the top of the world. Sure, there were plenty of places higher, but I would argue none grander or more impressive. And I doubt I've ever laid eyes on a better view.

From there I could see up and down the Ottawa River. I could see across to the Gatineau Hills in Quebec. I could see the entire Ottawa skyline. I could look down on the roof of the East, West and Centre Blocks that make up the Parliament Buildings. I could see the tourists walking the lawns and taking pictures of the flag. The prime minister's motorcade was driving on the Hill. The little green buses were ferrying parliamentarians from building to building.

I could see birds circling the tower, riding the wind. I watched one very impressive creature drift down across the property and land with finesse on the head of John Diefenbaker. He had business to do.

The bird, not Dief.

"For god's sakes," I shouted, "Shoo! I just cleaned that!"

The hatch opened and Brian stuck his head out.

"Time to go," he said. "The job of the Department of Public Works is never done."

I looked at the defiled head of Dief the Chief and had no choice but to agree.

17

Rise of the Vote Mobs

I never got the "not voting" thing.

If you don't vote, I'm not judging. I'm not here to vote-shame everyone. But I was an adult before I realized that a lot of people don't vote.

I'd always assumed that everyone voted because my parents always voted. During an election campaign, they discussed their options. Politics was allowed at our dinner table.

Based on these discussions, I learned very early that when it comes to choosing a candidate, it's best to keep one's expectations low. As a child, it seemed to me that elections boiled down to picking the least bad option. As an adult, I know that observation was correct. Some things change. That hasn't.

I often tagged along when my parents voted. I found it very exciting. The little curtain, the pencil, the ballot. Granted, this was before cable TV and video games.

My guess is that my parents, during their sixty-plus years of marriage, have cancelled each other's votes out more often than not. But still they have always gone through the exercise. As have I.

I may be a little hard-core. In 1997, I was working in Nova Scotia but still a resident of Newfoundland. I flew home for the day just to vote in a referendum. It cost me three hundred bucks to mark an X to end the denominational school system in Newfoundland. Worth the cash.

But that's an extreme example. Every other time I've voted, it's been relatively effortless and free. And now, with the advent of advance polls and mail-in ballots, there really is no excuse for not partaking.

But I get it: for a lot of people, voting is conceptual. It's like talking about your feelings with your spouse. You know you should do it, and you know people who claim they do it, but it's a pain in the ass and it's easy to avoid. And really, what difference does it make? Then you blink, twelve years have gone by, you're getting divorced and Idi Amin is your mayor.

I HAVE MET PEOPLE who don't believe in voting, and I've met people who have made a conscientious decision not to do so.

The Jehovah's Witnesses don't vote because it's against their religion. They believe Satan controls all democracies, including your local town council, your condo board and the entire House of Commons. They may be on to something. I'd hate to have to debate them on that one.

And I know a former chief political correspondent at CBC News who once casually mentioned to me that, despite covering politics for over twenty years, he had never voted in a federal election. He said he was afraid that doing so would impact the way he reported on politics. He said, "I never wanted a team to root for."

I thought that was patently absurd, but at least he had put some thought into his reasons for staying on the couch.

Knowing the casual disregard so many people show for the actual act, I couldn't help but become intrigued when I heard that a couple of teenagers in Edmonton had shown up on a municipal election day and tried to vote.

Talk about hard-core. A *municipal* election?

They were turned away because they were sixteen.

Being typical slacker teenagers, they found a lawyer and sued the municipality to try to get the age limit overturned. They lost, appealed, lost again, and went all the way to the Supreme Court. Where they lost.

I admit I had never given much thought to the notion of sixteen-year-olds voting until I heard about these kids. And I liked it.

They had their day in court, but not much attention was paid to the story. My guess is, in newsrooms across the country, the view was that sixteen-year-olds wanting to vote was like ball-room dancers wanting to able to compete in the Olympics. The issue was met with indifference.

So I ranted.

My rant that week was all about them. And I made the point that "if stupid people can vote, if criminals can vote, why not sixteen-year-olds?" My argument was that if "we allow sixteen-year-olds to vote, they may find they like it. They may do it again, next chance they get. They may get addicted to democracy. And that would be good for all of us." I said, "It's called getting them while they are young. If the cigarette companies and the beer companies have that figured out, why can't the Government of Canada?"

Well, honestly, people went ballistic. The original court case didn't get much attention, but the rant did. Many people didn't like the notion of anyone legitimizing the cause, even if it was just some guy running around in an alley talking to himself.

I had no idea that, in the eyes of many, our democracy was so weak and fragile it would be destroyed if sixteen-year-olds were allowed near the ballot box.

A common refrain was "their brains aren't fully formed." I thought this was a strange thread to pull on. And what of the brains of our members of Parliament? Have you ever seen a backbench? I've known seals who were better critical thinkers.

People were also very concerned that teachers would somehow indoctrinate students and influence their vote. Someone emailed me to tell me that if sixteen-year-olds could vote, education-related issues would dominate provincial elections. I admit I had not considered that horrifying possibility.

Regardless, I decided to stick to my guns, and I became one of those people in the establishment who advocated for the voting age to be lowered. It was a fun issue; it got people going, but I also knew it was never going to be a ballot-box issue. There was no political will anywhere in the land to act on it. None of the political parties supported lowering the age, despite the fact that all three major political parties in Canada allowed sixteen-year-olds to join their party with full voting privileges when it came to choosing the executive and the candidate to represent their riding.

I didn't revisit the subject of voting directly for another three years. In October 2008 Canada once again found itself in a federal election, and the subject of voting was theoretically in the air.

For people who pay attention to the dark art of campaign strategy, one thing about the campaign was new. Taking a page out of successful presidential campaigns south of the border, all the parties were micro-targeting voting blocs in ways that had never been done before. I had someone who worked for one of the campaigns explain the entire process to me. It was fascinating stuff for a geek. However, when I asked him how they targeted youth, he looked at me like I was asking him how he was targeting space creatures.

"We don't," he said. "Waste of time."

I won't tell you which of the three major parties he worked with, but the truth is it could have been any of them.

So I ranted.

So here we are, the final stretch before the big vote. And all the political parties are busy courting every special-interest group in the country, no matter how small. If you've got one leg, two kids and you work on a farm? The parties all have a pitch for you. Unless of course you happen to be a student, in which case you are completely off the radar.

Not a peep on the subject from any of our leaders. Education was not even mentioned in the debate.

I'm not saying any politician would ever come out and say they don't care about the student vote. When they are pushed, they can all talk about education reform and crushing debt until the cows come home. But then, at the ten-minute mark, they will stop and lean in as if telling you a secret and they say, "You know, it's a real shame, but students in this country just don't vote." Which is code for "We don't care about students. We never have, we never will." . . .

There are a million students in this country, if you showed up to vote, believe me, elections in this country would never be the same again. Education would never be left off the agenda.

I ended with some simple instructions on how to vote. Which you might think is basic, but Elections Canada were running ads that year on how to vote that made it seem like it involved quantum physics. And they were pushing a confusing messaging about being "registered to vote." I reminded students that they didn't need to be registered. "Men died on beaches so you could vote," I said. "All you need to do so is a piece of official mail and your student ID."

And then, as an afterthought, "Your real ID, that is. Not your fake one."

The response to my rant? Well, you need only look at what happened one week later, when the election was held. Voter turnout among young people continued its downward spiral and plummeted to 37.4 percent. The political leaders in Canada were right: young people don't vote. Stephen Harper's Conservatives were re-elected with a minority government.

AS HISTORY HAS SHOWN, Harper's second term was marked by daily doses of joy and prosperity. During those four years, the air smelled of apple blossoms and the sun shone every day.

However, all good things come to an end, even minority governments, and once again in 2011 we were headed to the polls. Stephen Harper's rationale? Canada needed a "strong, stable majority government."

Also, he liked to remind us that "danger is lapping at our shores." Whether the danger was sharks, inflation, the green movement or youth, he never elaborated.

And once again I attempted to goad students into voting.

I figured if the desire for good government wasn't enough to motivate them, maybe spite would.

I ranted.

So here we have it, we are heading into an election—or, as Stephen Harper calls it, a dangerous and unnecessary exercise. Because as we all know, Canada is one of the world's greatest democracies, and the greatest threat to that democracy is that we get to vote.

But vote we will, so that means if you live in a retirement home, prepare to be targeted. Because these days, it's all about targeting the vote. All the major parties have well-publicized plans to target the ethnic vote, the women's vote, the blue-collar vote, the corporate vote. If there were more than five paraplegic lesbian Inuit women in Labrador, they would be a target.

Everyone is targeted except for one group: the youth vote. There are more than three million young, eligible voters in this country and as far as any of the political parties are concerned, you might as well all be dead. In fact, in some elections—in Quebec, for example—the dead have a higher voter turnout.

It is the conventional wisdom of all political parties that young people will not vote. And the parties? They like it that way. It's why your tuition keeps going up.

So please, if you are between the age of eighteen and twenty-five and you want to scare the hell out of the people that run this country, this time around do the unexpected: take twenty minutes out of your day and do what young people all over the world are dying to do.

Vote!

Three days after the rant aired, I heard the term "vote mob" for the very first time.

It was when I got a cold call from a reporter for the Canadian Press.

This wasn't entirely out of the ordinary. I have few skills, and one of them is that I can blather on at great length on many subjects whether I know what I am talking about or not. And I was one of those people the press would occasionally call on for a remotely colourful comment on a quiet election day.

I thought the reporter might want a comment on Michael Ignatieff's inability to talk to people without sounding like a poncey university lecturer. But no. She wanted to know what I thought of the "vote mob" at the University of Guelph. I pleaded ignorance because I was, as is often the case, ignorant.

"How can you say you don't know about the vote mob?" she said. "It was your idea."

Being in a conversation with a reporter, on the record, and being asked about something to do with a "mob" that you may be responsible for is not ideal.

I responded, "I can't hear you. I have a bad signal. Bloody Rogers . . ." And then I hung up.

When in doubt, blame Rogers or Bell.

Within seconds of hanging up from the reporter, I googled "vote mob" and "Guelph," and all was revealed. A video called "Vote Mob—University of Guelph" was trending on YouTube. It was already a day old. When I hit play, the first thing that came up in big, bold letters was the statement "Rick Mercer encouraged young people to vote—Rick, this one is for you." And that is how I saw my first vote mob.

It was a music video, sort of. There was music. And it was cut very well. The video featured hundreds of kids at the University of Guelph, holding signs and saying loud and clear that in the coming election, they would be voting. They were dancing and singing and waving Canadian flags. There was nothing partisan in the message. There were no Liberal, Conservative or NDP signs. The message was simple: we are voting.

It turns out the vote mob was the brainchild of two brilliant young women from Guelph, Gracen Johnson and Yvonne Su. They were whip-smart, involved and passionate. And when it came to the issue of young people being taken for granted during elections, they were very pissed off. So they were getting their message out with this really cool, upbeat video. They were targeting a demographic that was being ignored by the major parties.

The number of views continued to ramp up; suddenly, the video was being shared on Facebook pages across the country and Twitter was on fire with the hash tag #votemob.

And then a wonderful thing happened: it began to spread. It was viral before viral was a thing.

Gracen and Yvonne holed up in one of their bedrooms, and instead of studying for their finals they began to plan Guelph's second vote mob. But that became nearly impossible because so many students across the country began to reach out to them for advice.

Within days the University of Victoria, then McMaster and Memorial University in Newfoundland and Labrador all posted vote mobs. By the end of the week there were forty-five vote mobs online, from every province and territory. Every newscast in the country was featuring local vote mobs, which begat more vote mobs.

Suddenly, the political parties were being asked what they were doing to reach out to young voters and encourage young people to vote. Their answers were uniformly pathetic. None of them knew what had hit them. All of them were somewhat embarrassed that they hadn't thought of targeting the youth.

John Baird, spokesperson for the Conservative Party, handled it particularly badly. Baird is an accomplished politician, and rarely did he make things worse during a campaign. But when he was asked about the vote mobs, he said he found "the entire thing disconcerting."

Note to Mr. Baird: Never sneer at students. It's a bad look.

Michael Taube, Stephen Harper's former speech writer, was apoplectic that students across the country were assembling and threatening to vote. In a special column for the *Ottawa Citizen*, he wrote: "A few weeks ago, there was no such thing as a 'vote mob.' But an idea hiding in a deep, dark corridor of comedian Rick Mercer's brain has, quite by accident, unleashed this holy terror onto unsuspecting Canadians.

"Do you really think that any of the major leaders care that some 18-to-25-year-olds who wouldn't ordinarily vote have suddenly been convinced by a comedian's rant on TV?"

It was very odd to see such a highly placed Conservative, and one so close to the prime minister, become so unhinged in print. He ended by saying, "If vote mobs are ever considered to be a viable method of increasing political participation, I would much rather keep the numbers as low as they are."

As voting day got closer, another problem presented itself to the organizers of the Guelph mobs. Because the school year was ending, students who wanted to vote were leaving university and heading back to their home ridings. As a result, thousands of students all over the country were in flux, stuck between the ridings they lived in to attend school and the ridings their parents lived in. Many students were leaving for summer jobs in areas where they weren't qualified to vote.

The simple solution, the organizers believed, was to hold advance ballots on campus. The argument being that there are advance polls in senior citizens' homes all over Canada, so why not on campus?

Elections Canada set one up on campus in Guelph, and it was a huge hit. Workers were nearly overwhelmed by the number of students that showed up. Hundreds of them lined up.

When news of the huge turnout made it to the various political campaigns—and one in particular—panic hit. The communications director for the local Conservative Party candidate, a young man by the name of Michael Sona, raced to campus and ran up and down the line, declaring loudly that the Elections Canada polling station was illegal. He then attempted, according to numerous eyewitnesses, to do something unheard of in Canada: take the ballot box.

It took a gaggle of large athletes to convince Sona that he would not be confiscating their votes. Sona left and the voting continued.

For Sona, it was a good day at the office. Not only did his willingness to disrupt a polling station land him on the front pages of newspapers all across the country, but it caught the attention of the people running the Conservative campaign. That boy has moxie! Sona was offered work as a staffer in the office of the parliamentary secretary to the minister of national defence.

Sadly, his career came to an end when he was sent to jail for nine months after being found guilty of running a call centre whose objective was to stop people who identified as Liberal or NDP from voting. It was, of course, in Guelph.

I attended only one vote mob during the election. It turned out to be the nation's largest, and it took place in London, Ontario. Thousands of people, not just university students, showed up to wave flags, announce they were voting and encourage others to follow suit. The video is filled with the infectious joy of disaffected youth. It remains one of my favourite YouTube videos to this day.

That election was a game changer in Canadian politics. When the dust settled, Stephen Harper was not only still the prime minister, but he had achieved a majority government. The NDP, for the first time in history, had taken second place and would form the official Opposition. This was a historic victory for the party of Jack Layton. As for the Liberals, the party that likes to consider itself the "natural governing party of Canada?" They too made history, of a different sort. They were suddenly sucking hind teat and were in third place. Their worst result by far, ever.

But the biggest change of them all? The bright light? The silver lining? Voter turnout among young people, which had been on a precarious downward trend since 1975, was up for the first time in well over 35 years. That was a victory for everyone.

I THINK THE VOTE mobs were the most exciting thing that happened during that election. I loved every single one of them. And I was beyond chuffed when I got the credit. But the vote mobs started in Guelph with Gracen Johnson and Yvonne Su.

My rant about young people voting aired just two days before that first vote mob. Clearly, they had the thing mostly organized by then.

When I suggested to Yvonne and Gracen that they were planning to do them all along, they would only say they appreciated the rant.

My guess? They had no idea how the initial mob would go, and so they slapped my name at the top of the video. That way, if the whole thing went sideways, they could duck.

Well, I was glad to get the credit, and even prouder to take the blame.

But more than anything, I look forward to voting for Gracen and Yvonne someday, and if I'm not eligible, I'll show up and knock on some doors.

18

Let's Go Fish

Had I gone down another career path and pursued my first love, lower-end real estate sales, I doubt I ever would have gone in pursuit of a fish. A life without a line in the water would have been fine by me.

However, in my quest to figure out what it means to be Canadian, I had no choice but to go full "old man and the sea" on more than one occasion.

Fishing is a revered pastime in this country from coast to coast to coast. It makes sense. Over 20 percent of the world's fresh surface water is located within our borders. We are surrounded on three sides by oceans. What else is a person supposed to do?

Fishing is one of the things that connects us. It is a passion for millions of people, from all walks of life—not one of whom is me.

The Chinese say that if you give a man a fish, you feed him for a day; teach a man to fish and you feed him for a lifetime. Like China itself, it sounds good on paper, but it's not exactly practical. I don't know if the Chinese have a term for a man of my skill set, but Canadians do: "a dead loss." As in "Mercer can't fish. The boy is a dead loss."

Fishing requires many things, but most of all it requires patience. It's a funny thing, patience. I don't believe it can be taught. I think you come out of the womb with or without it. It's like an eye for design or an affinity for coriander. It's the luck of the draw.

I adore coriander, I love architecture, but patience eludes me.

When I am on hold with Air Canada and hear the recorded voice thank me for my patience, I want to commit murder. Telling me to be patient is a not a microaggression. It's macro.

My brother is the same. Impatient in all aspects of his life, save one: when he is in a boat.

For him, it's not a boat. It's a mood stabilizer.

When we were kids, my brother spent countless hours on the pond behind our house, fishing for rainbow trout. In those days the pond was 100 percent surrounded by trees. There was not a roofline or dock visible from the water. It was only 350 feet from our house, down a trail through the woods, but when you were on the water you might as well have been in the middle of a protected wilderness area.

He used a fly rod. Catching the rainbow on a fly was tricky business. But it was also silent. And for him, it was never a numbers game. He caught and released. He always returned happy, but empty-handed.

Silence was guaranteed on Jones Pond, but you weren't always alone. Every evening you were pretty much guaranteed to see Gordon Glenn. He was a lineman with Newfoundland Light and Power, and he lived across the street from us. He spent his days crawling up telephone poles, restoring power during windstorms and ice storms. In the evenings, weather permitting, he put in a solid shift alone in his canoe, casting a fly rod.

For Mr. Glenn, fishing in that small pond appeared to be an artistic endeavour.

I return to that pond regularly, walking Tiger, my mother's yappy chihuahua who happens to be afraid of ducks. It's different now. Mr. Glenn is no longer with us, and progress has ruined the view. Houses line the shore on the opposite side of the water. Trees have been removed to make way for lawns and aluminum baby barns.

For me, it's at best an irritant. For my brother, it's a knife to his heart. His favourite place in the world, his sanctuary as an adolescent, spoiled. He avoids it.

I do envy the people who love fishing. It's so simple and it brings them such joy. And it's not just a rural game. Throw a dart at the map of Canada and regardless of whether it lands on a big city or the tiniest town, you're likely to hit someone with a rod or a reel.

Walk the seawall on the edge of Vancouver, a city with close to three million people, and you will see Chinese men fishing with bamboo rods. In Calgary, Alberta, in the '80s, Ralph Klein was known to sneak out of the mayor's office on his lunch hour, remove his pants and wade into the chilly Bow River and have a few flicks. And no doubt, standing there in his underwear, legs numb, he experienced peace. The cold water cooling the usual electrical fire in his head.

I imagine you would learn a lot about a politician watching him or her fish. At least that was the thinking behind what was originally going to be one of our most ambitious shoots.

IN 2006 THE LIBERAL PARTY was looking for yet another leader. Paul Martin was out and a leadership convention had been scheduled. It appeared for the most part to be a fight between Michael Ignatieff and Bob Rae. Rounding out the race, in third place, was Stéphane Dion.

Ignatieff was what was passed for a star candidate in those days. He was a widely respected academic, author of many books, a star lecturer at Harvard and holder of many honorary degrees. He was—and everyone agreed on this—afflicted with a very large brain.

Bob Rae was no stranger to Canadian politics, and perhaps that was his problem. He was quite famously the NDP premier of Ontario for one term. After which he had an epiphany and joined the Liberals.

Stéphane Dion was a former cabinet minister under Jean Chrétien and Paul Martin. He was respected as a decent, hard-working and effective member of Parliament. He was also generally considered to be a terrible communicator in English. Surely to god that would disqualify him.

For some reason I got it into my head to invite them all on a fishing trip. I imagined it would be incredibly insightful for the nation to see these learned individuals discussing the future of Canada against a backdrop of changing leaves. Who knew what might happen with these men alone in the woods. It was downright cinematic. Ignatieff and Rae playing the part of the competitive brothers in *A River Runs Through It*, while Dion would be Ned Beatty in *Deliverance*.

Immediately my idea was shot down from on high.

Gerald pointed out, rightly so, that we did not have the resources to shoot a piece with three people. We didn't even have that many microphones. And it would be impossible to cover properly with one camera. Also, how big would the boat have to be?

He was right. Three guests were at least one too many. The choice was obvious. I decided not to invite Stéphane Dion. For obvious reasons: he was not a good interview in English, he had no sense of humour and his chances of winning the leadership were minimal at best.

The invite went out to Ignatieff and Rae. Now, this was a very interesting competition. They had been, for most of their lives, best of friends. Ignatieff famously helped Bob when he was fighting depression as a young man. At a time when people understood very little about that condition, Ignatieff was there for him. They both had impressive careers and they were each supportive of the other. But now politics and ambition had come between them. They were now decidedly not close.

How exciting was that? It was downright Shakespearean. It would make a great piece. The only question out of the gate was which one would drown the other.

Unfortunately, no sooner had the invite gone out than we hit a snag.

Ignatieff wanted to see samples of my work. Not surprising. He had spent the last twenty years living outside of Canada. He famously stated that he returned to Canada regularly to receive honorary degrees.

I knew someone in the Ignatieff camp, and he confessed that the real concern wasn't with who I was, but with what I might say. Ignatieff was somewhat sensitive to the fact that he had lived outside of Canada for so long and was worried I might pull on that thread. His camp was worried I might give him a pop quiz on Canada and ask him some tough questions, like "What's a 'double double'?" or "Who's your favourite Canadian recording artist: Steve Fonyo or Terry Fox?"

Ignatieff said no. He was going to run a classic front-runner campaign and hide.

That left Bob Rae, who, one supposes, had nothing to lose. I considered dropping the whole thing, but by then the trip had been planned.

And it was an amazing plan.

Mike Liebrock, who had become a great friend after we travelled to Africa, grew up in Sudbury. He was friends of the Wallace family. They were in construction. Through Mike I had met a couple of the kids in the family. The head of the family was Jamie Wallace, who was not only a prominent business person but also a big Tory. It's safe to say he was in the room when Mike Harris decided to run for the leadership of the Ontario Conservatives, and he was in the room the night he was elected premier.

The Wallaces might have been Tories, but they were first and foremost boosters of Northern Ontario. Through Mike I reached out to the family because I knew they were avid outdoorsmen, and more importantly, I knew they had a Beaver. Not the animal, but the plane. A beautiful vintage float plane. A dream prop and a dream ride.

When they heard I was going to shoot a fishing segment and was thinking about Northern Ontario, the family went into full-blown Sudbury hospitality mode. Mr. Wallace offered me the use of the plane, the boats, the rods and the reels. He even offered to personally make us sandwiches for our lunch. He promised stunning scenery and plenty of fish. And he didn't even blink when he was told my guest would be none other than Bob Rae. If he was put off by the notion of Fidel Castro eating at his table, he certainly didn't let on.

We met Bob very early on a Saturday morning at Pearson International Airport. We were on the first flight to Sudbury. I didn't know Bob that well, but well enough that it was a relaxed meeting. John, Don and I sat around and had a coffee with the candidate. What was odd, for us anyway, was that he was entirely alone. There was no minder. I had never seen anyone running for any position of any consequence who operated completely solo. There was nobody to run interference, nobody to make up excuses on the candidate's behalf.

I think we all remember that cup of coffee for the same reason. I asked a simple question: "Bob, why would you want to be prime minister of Canada, anyway?" This is about as soft a ball as one could throw. I expected a pat, made-for-the-camera answer.

No such luck. Not on that morning.

Bob's answer was completely unhinged. He didn't sound like he was running for the leadership of the Liberal Party; he sounded like a conspiracy theorist. He spoke of the United States of America being on the verge of a financial collapse the like of which had not been experienced since the Great Depression. He talked about literally millions of mortgages in the United States going underwater, potentially leading to the collapse of America's entire banking system. He warned that this carnage would spread north to Canada and trigger a mighty recession in this country as well. He said the government was completely unprepared for what was coming. Nobody was prepared, he said. Not in Canada, not in the USA. And nobody seemed to see it coming.

When he disappeared for a bathroom break, I broke the ice with the lads.

"Well, he sounds a bit crazy, doesn't he?" I said.

"Just a little bit," said Don.

"Nobody is getting elected with talk like that," said John.

It was funny because it was true. We all agreed. We were heading north with a nut.

I knew that, like all conspiracy theorists, Rae believed what he was saying. But what I found so astounding is why he would be running in this race if he thought economic catastrophe was imminent.

Bob's career as premier was famously destroyed by a recession in Ontario. He was the man on deck when the economy faltered. He bore the brunt and took the blame. The NDP never recovered, and neither had he. Why, I wondered, if he truly believed North America was on the verge of a financial collapse, would he want to be the prime minister when it happened.? Why captain the *Titanic* if you know its hull will crumble like a cracker the minute it encounters ice?

There were only two possible answers. He was either a complete masochist who enjoyed pain, suffering and humiliation or he was a legitimately concerned leader. The only hint he offered was the one comment he made after he described our bleak future.

He said, "I know what needs to be done."

We were seated separately on the flight to Sudbury, so there were no more chats about collapse, economic or otherwise.

I watched from a seat behind Bob as he regaled a civilian with war stories about politics.

When we arrived in Sudbury the hospitality shown to us at the Wallace home was spectacular. And as promised we were greeted with an incredible spread. Mr. Wallace opened his home and had arranged everything. All that was left was the fishing.

After we were fortified with sandwiches and coffee, Bob and I headed down to the wharf of this waterfront home.

And there we found our Beaver.

"Have you been in a Beaver before, Bob?"

"Yes, Rick, I have. Many, many times." He said this with not a hint of embarrassment.

He then went directly into politician mode. "A great plane, a sturdy plane, a workhorse. It opened the North. It opened up all of Canada. And did you know it was manufactured in Toronto?"

I did not.

And with the little history lesson out of the way, we hopped aboard. Bob in the front, me in the back.

"The Beaver could be configured in many ways," said Bob. "This one has four seats."

"Ironic," I said. "The same number of seats the Liberals have west of Ontario."

Good politicians are comfortable talking to anyone. And with Bob in the front seat you'd swear he had been flying this plane with this pilot his entire life. They became instant fast friends immediately after takeoff. So much so that when Bob said, "Can I take the stick?" the pilot said, "All yours."

Bob took the stick. He banked left, he banked right.

"Oh my god," I offered. "Bob Rae is flying this plane."

And he literally was. I saw Don's eyebrow lift. Which is about as much as you will ever get out of Don when he is rolling. Don's eyebrow often alerted me to danger.

Bob levelled the plane and said, "I'm not going right, I'm not going left, I'm taking it right down the middle." And with that we flew on towards Georgian Bay.

We landed in Killarney Provincial Park, a wilderness reserve whose beauty is, for the most part, accessible only by very long canoe trips and marathon hikes along backcountry trails. It exists because it was saved by artists, including the Group of Seven, who personally lobbied to protect it from the logging industry.

It is pristine. It is remote. In other words, you would have to be a complete idiot to not catch a fish in these lakes. Either that or you would have to be us. I don't know what's worse.

An aluminum boat and motor were at our disposal. A second boat was there for Don to use as a camera platform. Best fishing location ever.

Bob might have flown the plane, but I was driving the boat. As we headed out on the lake, Bob questioned whether I knew what I was doing. I was very proud of myself in this regard. This was one of those rare times where I did know what I was doing.

"Of course I know what I'm doing, Bob," I said. "I'm a Newfoundlander. We are all about boats. I've operated many boats, but in the salt water. That's a whole other animal. Have you ever been on the salt water, Bob? I've been on the nose and the tail of the Grand Banks—not in an outboard, but in a factory freezer trawler. I've been off the Flemish Cap as well."

Bob looked at me and deadpanned, "And what are you running for again?"

It was great chat, and we fished all along the way. When I asked why he wanted to be prime minister, he wisely chose not to go down the conspiracy theory road. He talked of beating Stephen Harper. He spoke of the failure of Harper's government, which was driven by a right-wing ideology. He spoke of a bright future for Canada, not a dystopian one.

He was smart and funny, there was no doubt about it. And the scenery was truly spectacular. We were blessed with fantastic weather and light. We had all the makings of a classic *RMR* shoot except for one glaring element: after a few hours neither of us had got a bite, let alone landed a fish.

This was incomprehensible. And it was a serious problem. I wanted this segment to resemble a fishing show. And the secret to a fishing show segment is that they *always* catch a fish.

Without a fish, there would be no ending. If we went to air without a fish it would be a disaster for the show and for Bob.

I could read the Facebook comments now.

Mooseknuckle69 writes: "Bob Rae wants to be prime minister and he can't even catch a fish in Killarney? What a loser."

HarperFan1 writes, "Mercer sucks and can't fish."

Michael-Ignatieff writes, "In what province is Sudbury?"

When we returned to shore, Bob admitted he was a little worried about how it was going to look.

"Some days," he said philosophically, "the fish just don't bite. But try telling people that."

"Bob," I said, "we need to do something to change the channel. We need to make this piece sing. We need to make it something everyone is talking about. We need people to forget about the fish."

He said, "What?"

I said, "Bob, we need to both get naked and jump in this lake."

He looked at me and said, "I am running for the leadership of the Liberal Party of Canada. Why in God's name would I take my clothes off on TV and jump in a lake?"

I said, "Bob, if you take your clothes off, I promise you: you will beat Michael Ignatieff."

Two seconds later he was buck naked. "Okay," he said, "let's do this thing."

Bob Rae may claim to be a centrist, but believe me, he leans slightly to the left.

And then we did what hundreds of thousands of Canadians have done before us. We jumped stark naked into a freezing-cold spring-fed Canadian lake.

And I believe we spooked the fish.

The day after the segment aired, it was all anyone was talking about. Bob Rae had jumped in a lake, naked, on TV!

By day's end there were a million views on YouTube. It was the most commented-on piece we ever posted on Facebook. Thousands of comments, mostly good, some bad. But not one comment said, "I can't believe they didn't catch a fish."

And that is how you change a channel.

It became a defining moment of Bob Rae's long and illustrious career as a politician and now diplomat. Skinny-dipping will be mentioned in his obituary. An obituary that will probably also mention that he did not, as I predicted, beat Michael Ignatieff. And in an odd twist, Ignatieff did not beat Stéphane Dion. None of these three men would ever become prime minister of Canada.

The only prediction from that trip that turned out to be correct was Bob's.

One year after his party chose not to elect him leader, the US financial markets were rocked by what we now call the subprime mortgage crisis. Millions of homes were lost. It led to the collapse of some of America's largest banks and an economic crisis on a colossal scale not seen since the Great Depression. Canada was thrown into a recession.

And everyone said the same thing: nobody saw it coming.

19

End of the Road

In television, things usually come to an end with a quick phone call or email saying you have been cancelled. Either that, or you show up for work and your security pass doesn't work and your belongings are sitting on the floor in the lobby in a banker's box.

Gerald and I avoided that fate by deciding to wrap things up on our own. I don't regret the decision—we had an epic run—but it was a giant change in my life. It's fair to say that overnight my life changed dramatically.

I won't belabour this point. I'm hardly the first middle-aged guy to find himself out of work. And I was lucky. I wasn't downsized or fired for tweeting something on a Friday that would have been totally acceptable the previous Monday.

We all tend to define ourselves by our work. And I admit I went through a period where I wondered: If I am not a guy who makes TV full-time, who am I?

Gerald helped me on this journey of reflection by referring to me as a "former TV personality."

I knew that when I left, I would miss the people I worked with. That was to be expected. What I didn't anticipate was losing access to my town. Because I realized, in hindsight, that I had stopped looking at Canada as my country. I looked at it as my home-town. Canada is so bloody big and for me, for a very long time it felt small.

I lived in a neighbourhood called Toronto, but I was constantly exploring other neighbourhoods as well. I loved the west end of town and went there often. Winnipeg, Calgary, Edmonton, Vancouver? I'd visit all of them five or six times a year. The east end of town? PEI, Nova Scotia, Newfoundland? Seemed like I was always in one of those places. I never made it to the north end as often as I would have liked, but a few times a year I'd pop up to Iqaluit to see what a twenty-dollar tomato tastes like.

What a gift to see your country as your town.

I was a regular at restaurants that were thousands of kilome-tres from my house. Michal, John, Don and I were on a friendly basis with people who worked at Air Canada counters in every single province, in pretty much every single airport. And if any of us had an old friend anywhere in the country, all we had to do was wait a month and we could see them in person for a coffee.

When the show stopped, that all stopped. Normal people don't fly to two different provinces every single week, hang out and laugh for two days and then head home.

Normal was a big adjustment. Suddenly, if I was headed west, I was on the Bloor line, not an airline.

If a major news story was happening in any other province, if there was an election in Alberta, I would follow along by watch-ing the news like everyone else. I knew I wouldn't be asking a cab driver in Edmonton for his hot take any time soon.

It never crossed my mind that when I walked away from the

show, I was walking away from my regular dose of the prairie sky, the Rocky Mountains and the Bay of Fundy.

And then the pandemic happened.

And for all of us, the ability to travel to anywhere, under any circumstance, came to an end.

I was one of the lucky ones. Very lucky. I had a place to hide. That being a small house in the east end of town, on the Atlantic Ocean. Otherwise known as my home province of Newfoundland and Labrador. The house, located in Chapel's Cove, had a shed and two wood stoves. It was basically designed for the apocalypse. It was perfect. I was very grateful and I thank God every day I wasn't in a small box in the sky in Toronto. And I didn't complain that for a very long time what passed for adventure was no longer a flight to the Northwest Territories or a date with the drummer from Rush, it was a walk up the road to say hello to the donkey.

It became part of our pandemic routine. Go look at the donkey.

And it was on the road, on the way to the donkey, that Gerald and I met Isabelle Wade.

We knew her to see her long before we spoke. She was often out walking, and when we drove past, we would wave, as would she. But one morning, on our walk, we found ourselves to be on the same route at the same time as Isabelle. The small talk was fantastic. I found her to be incredibly interesting. Gerald would always say that he pitied any stranger I bumped into, because now that I was no longer on TV, I had a tendency to interview people rather than just chat with them.

Isabelle was a great interview.

She grew up just a stone's throw from our place. A cute little traditional biscuit-box house with a perfectly preserved root cellar. People were always taking pictures of that cellar.

When I asked her how many grew up in the house, she said, "Fifteen children, plus Mom and Dad and Uncle Frank as well."

I thought I had it rough growing up as one of four kids with one bathroom

As far as a source of local intelligence went, it didn't get much better than Isabelle. She was a font of information. And over the next few weeks and months, I got it all. What families lived where, who owned that barn. Was there really a lobster cannery on the beach at one point?

Bumping into Isabelle became a regular occurrence. She was certainly a welcome pandemic distraction. She told a great story.

But she did more than that.

I don't know why she started walking the eight-kilometre route she walked every day. I didn't ask. Maybe it was for health reasons. That's why most of us drag ourselves out for a stroll. Maybe she found a walk important to her mental health. I know I felt that way.

But it was obvious from the day I met her, she wasn't just out for a walk. There was a higher purpose to what she was up to. Because while she walked she picked up garbage. Non-stop. Every cigarette butt, every scrap of paper, every Tim Hortons cup. It all went in a bag she carried. And she often made a detour across the beach below my house, an eagle eye peeled for a juice box, beer bottle or cap.

Chapel's Cove has always had a reputation as being neat as a pin. Now I knew why.

I appreciated on these walks that she would occasionally ask me about various places I'd been, people I'd talked to on the show. About jumping out of planes, about being in submarines. I was happy to talk about these things; I was starting to spend afternoons in the shed, writing about those years for this book.

And more than once I found myself in that shed thinking about that ridiculous hidden agenda that I saddled myself with at the outset of the show. To figure out what it means to be Canadian.

Clearly, I didn't have a lot of luck with that assignment.

If I was being honest, I think I probably stopped asking the question a decade ago. I became resigned to the fact there was no simple answer. We are too big, too divided, too unwieldy for a pat answer to a big question. But during all the years of the show, I held out some faint hope that somewhere on my travels I would meet that one person who would give me something close to an answer. Some modern-day Canadian Yoda would just drop in my lap and reveal all. Perhaps an Inuit hunter or a Ukrainian dancer.

It's not that far-fetched. For fifteen years, every time I turned around, I was talking to great Canadians. I rubbed shoulders with plenty of big brains. I spent time with people from all walks of life, from all parts of the country. Over the years I had talked to soldiers, athletes, hunters, writers, activists, comedians . . . the list goes on and on. It felt to me that the number of people who had occupations I knew nothing about was smaller than the list of occupations I had explored on TV.

What does it mean to be Canadian? Someone had to have a clue. My god, I had spoken to every member of Rush and every member of the Tragically Hip. And never mind every living prime minister—I spoke with our Women's World Cup champions in soccer.

But still, not one simple answer to the big question.

Just thinking about it made my head hurt. I interviewed thousands of people but the truth is, none of them really had much in common with one another. That's Canada in a nutshell.

What's a basketball coach in Labrador have in common with a sport fisherman in BC? What does the woman who plays the carillon bells in the Peace Tower have in common with the folks who work at the Edmonton waste management centre? Thousands of people, no common denominator.

Until one day in Chapel's Cove. It was a dull, rainy day. The kind of day where you just want to stay indoors. I looked down on the beach and saw Isabelle cleaning up after some people who had clearly had a grand time at a bonfire the night before.

I think we were all told as children that we should leave the place in better shape than we found it. Isabelle had interpreted the adage literally. She doesn't do it for glory; she does it because it needs to be done. And in all weather. She does not, as we say in Newfoundland, make a holy show of herself.

One day while walking, I told her that one of my favourite writers, David Sedaris, had developed the habit of picking up garbage on his daily walks in the English countryside. After years of this practice the local council decided to thank him by naming a garbage truck in his honour. He was quite chuffed. When I told Isabelle this story she looked completely mortified. She looked down at the garbage bag she carried, and she looked for a moment like she was going to dump the entire works out on the road, run home and never walk the streets again. She wasn't in this for the truck.

I like that about her. It really is quite impressive.

And while I was watching her pick up around the fire pit, I had an epiphany. Or what might pass for one in the rain at that early hour in the morning.

I did like her very much. And I liked every single person I met in my fifteen years on TV for the very same reason.

I saw the common denominator.

They were all a bit like Isabelle.

Whatever it is that they were doing, whatever it is that brought me to them or them to me, they were trying to make the place better than how they found it. Every athlete, professional or amateur, Olympian or Paralympian. They were committed to playing. But they were also committed to growing their game, making their sport more accessible.

The teachers I met during the Spread the Net visits. They had full-time jobs that involved teaching math, science and geography. But they also showed up on Saturday morning and taught, by example, that a bottle drive to buy bed nets is a worthy way to spend your free time.

Every community celebration I attended was driven by volunteers.

Every person I interviewed about their passion, about that thing that brought them great personal satisfaction or joy. They all wanted the same thing for others.

And don't think I was ever in a room where, if I had swung my microphone, I wouldn't have hit someone giving their time and energy to something bigger than them; they mightn't have seemed like they had anything in common, but they were all in their own way trying to leave the place in better shape than they found it.

It would be very easy to avoid the question of what it means to be Canadian by simply declaring as fact that Canada is the greatest nation on earth. To nip that foolish "what it means" talk in the bud by just saying we are number one.

Thankfully, we live in a place where such a statement seems somewhat un-Canadian. After all, why do we need to be the greatest? Why do we need to be better than Denmark or Australia? Or anyone, for that matter? Why can't we just strive to be great, or agree to settle on good?

Not that long ago, there was nothing controversial about either.

But we live in interesting times. We live in a time where we are encouraged not just to glorify all the wonderful things that we have accomplished, but also to reflect on the things we have done that are regrettable.

Yes, we are the nation that gave the world insulin, the zipper and the Bloody Caesar. And that should be celebrated. But we are also a nation that supported residential schools. And we can't continue to pretend that never happened.

I don't think anyone is under the illusion that we are perfect. Or that we are the greatest place on earth. But it is our home. In exactly the same way that Chapel's Cove is Isabelle's.

Her current home is not that far from the one she grew up in. It's her corner of the world. There's not much she doesn't know about the place. She has the big picture.

If you asked her if Chapel's Cove is perfect, I'm sure she would say no. She's not wearing blinders. She knows all too well it's a place where some people—not all people, but some—roll down a window and let fly with a Tim Hortons cup.

Does she complain about those people? I'm sure she does. If she sees someone throw a wrapper out the window, would she confront them? I would bet lots that the answer is yes. Will they ever do it again? I would suggest not.

But I also know she is clearly one of those people who sees something wrong and then quietly goes about fixing it. Or sees a way to improve on the past and goes about doing it. And this country is filled with those people.

Some people wake up and decide the way to fix things is to run for prime minister, premier, mayor or member of the condo board. Some people can't abide those positions and they head to a community centre. Some people have no interest in leaving their house, but they will still go through their closets and pass on clothes they no longer need.

And some people go for a walk across the beach in the rain and clean up after strangers.

Canadians have very few common denominators. I like that. Makes for an interesting country. If it were any other way, I doubt I would have gotten fifteen years out of the place. If we were a monoculture, I would have been bored and so would the viewers.

When it comes to Canada, I have more questions about this place now than when I set out on the road fifteen years ago. And I'm embarrassed that I was ever so naive as to think I would answer the question "What does it mean to be a Canadian?"

It was pure hubris. A decidedly un-Canadian trait.

I'll just have to take solace in the fact that, after years of pondering, the closest I can come to an answer is this: I may not know what it means to be a Canadian, but I do know I have never wanted to be anything else.

Acknowledgements

This book is about my time on the road with the *Mercer Report*. But the stories in these pages represent just a very small fraction of the adventures I was lucky enough to take part in. Over the course of fifteen years, I met hundreds of Canadians from all walks of life who were incredibly generous with their time and energy. People trusted us and invited us into their worlds week after week. To everyone the *RMR* crew met on the road, to everyone who helped us out behind the scenes or in front of the camera, I can't thank you enough. The best job in the world was made possible because of you.

It was my name in the title, but the *Mercer Report* was far from a one-man show. It takes a village, and executive producer Gerald Lunz assembled an amazing team both on the road and at head office. It was this crackerjack team that made the show possible week after week. It was the A team. And what a privilege it was to work with you. Thank you to everyone whose name ever appeared on a call sheet or a production list.

Thanks as well to writer and comedian Greg Eckler, who read an early draft of this book. His feedback is always a great help. Thanks and appreciation to the late Tim Steeves who not only served as a writer for the entire run of the *Mercer Report* but who also read early chapters of this book. Tim passed away in October 2022 from pancreatic cancer and right up to the end of his life he was writing comedy, giving me notes and helping me with my stand-up. The world is a much less funny place now.

Tom Stanley did heroic producing on *RMR*, always finding the right stories and the right people to talk to. Boy were we lucky to find you.

I met production manager Marilyn Richardson on my first day on a real movie set and we worked together for the next three decades. Thank you for running such a great ship. Gerald and I relied on you more than you know. Al Maclean and Miles Davren are the greatest video editors I have ever worked with and were mission critical. Thank you to Director Henry Sawer-Foner, who was so instrumental in the look and feel of the show. Thanks to Alan MacGillivray and Nan Brown for keeping us afloat. And I would never have gotten through a week without Kelly McNeil, Bob Graham, Meliase Patterson, Jill Aslin, David McCaughna, Nik Sexton, Matt Tsoni, Jon Sturge, Claire Wing, Baron Evans, Kevin Drysdale and Scott Stephenson.

I have to say I like this book business and owe great thanks to my literary agent Suzanne DePoe. I want to thank the folks at Penguin Random House Canada for having me, especially Kristin Cochrane, CEO; Scott Sellers, Associate Publisher; Amy Black, Publisher, Doubleday Canada; Terri Nimmo, Creative Design Director; Kaitlin Smith, Associate Director, Publicity and Marketing; and Kate Panek, Assistant Production Manager. Thanks also to freelance copy editor Lloyd Davis and freelance proof-reader Shaun Oakey.

The editor of this book is Tim Rostron. He is a great wit and a huge talent. I could not have done this book or any of the others without his guidance.

Picture credits

The *RMR* crew (page ix): photo by Michal Grajewski.

Rossland, BC: photo by Michal Grajewski.

The Train of Death: photos by Michal Grajewski.

Bee beard: photos by Michal Grajewski.

Rick with Sophie Grégoire and Justin Trudeau: photo by John Marshall.

With Paul Martin: photo by John Marshall.

With Jean Chrétien: photo © Rick Mercer.

With Stephen Harper: photo © Rick Mercer.

With Geddy Lee: photo © Rick Mercer.

With Alex Lifeson: photo by Michal Grajewski.

With Neil Peart: photo © Rick Mercer.

With Barenaked Ladies and Bruce Cockburn: photo by John Marshall.

With Sarah McLachlan: photo by John Marshall.

In Algonquin Park: photos by Michal Grajewski.

Firefighters calendar: photo by Michal Grajewski.

About to be tasered: photo © Rick Mercer.

In Africa: photos by Michael Liebrock.

Spread the Net: photos by Michal Grajewski.

With Jann Arden: photos © Rick Mercer.

Rick on Parliament Hill: photo by Michal Grajewski.

Flag: photo © Rick Mercer.

Vote mobs: photos by Michal Grajewski.

With Bob Rae: photo by John Marshall.

Rossland bobsled team: photo by Michal Grajewski.

RICK MERCER co-created and performed on CBC's *This Hour Has 22 Minutes*, created and starred in *Made in Canada*, and created and starred in *Talking to Americans*, the most-watched comedy special in Canadian television history. He went on to host the hugely successful *Rick Mercer Report* for 15 seasons. Rick was appointed an Officer of the Order of Canada in 2014 for his work with charitable causes and "his ability to inspire and challenge Canadians through humour." In 2019, he received a Governor General's Performing Arts Lifetime Artistic Achievement Award. His 2021 memoir, *Talking to Canadians*, won the Stephen Leacock Memorial Medal for Humour. He is from Middle Cove, Newfoundland and Labrador. In 2023 he received the Order of Newfoundland and Labrador, the province's highest honour.